SCOTLAND
AND
SCANDINAVIA

University of Aberdeen
THE MACKIE MONOGRAPHS

I

SCOTLAND AND SCANDINAVIA

800-1800

Edited by
GRANT G SIMPSON
Department of History
University of Aberdeen

JOHN DONALD PUBLISHERS LTD
EDINBURGH

ISBN 0 85976 220 3

Phototypeset by Beecee Typesetting Services
Printed and bound in Great Britain by Billings & Sons Ltd., Worcester

Introduction

The contributions in this volume are based (with one exception, noted below) on papers delivered at the First Mackie Symposium for historical study of Scotland's overseas links, held at the University of Aberdeen in September, 1987. The Symposium, and this publication, have been greatly assisted by generous provision of funds to the University under the will of the late Dr James R M Mackie of Glenmillan. An Aberdeen man, who graduated M.B., Ch.B., at the University in 1932, he spent the major part of his professional career as a consultant psychiatrist in the Leeds and Bradford area. After his retirement in 1971 he moved to Lumphanan in Aberdeenshire; and died in 1982. His strong interests in Scottish history, and his desire to promote study of it, have made it entirely appropriate that these funds from his estate should serve to support work of this nature; and the University has expressed its gratitude to his Trustees for their gifts.

Scots and non-Scots alike can agree that there is value in the area of study to which the Mackie Symposia and the Mackie Monographs are to be devoted: Scotland's contacts with other lands and Scotland's history set in a wide international context. The topic as a whole has had more than a century of investigation devoted to it. But both research and publication have proceeded in a rather patchy fashion, both as regards intensity of study and the flow of its results into print. To illustrate the situation, comments on a few selected works may be helpful; but no comprehensive survey seems necessary here. An early study, very full but occasionally inaccurate, was Francisque Michel, *Les Ecossais en France, Les Français en Ecosse* (2 vols, London and Edinburgh, 1862). The attempt at a general work by J Hill Burton in *The Scot Abroad* (Edinburgh, 1881) is uneven and rather 'over-literary' in presentation. In the first decade of the present century a remarkable German scholar, Thomas A Fischer, who had settled in Scotland, produced three pioneering books: *The Scots in Germany* (Edinburgh, 1902), *The Scots in Eastern and Western Prussia* (Edinburgh, 1903), and *The Scots in Sweden* (Edinburgh, 1907); and some of his general comments are approvingly quoted in John Simpson's contribution below (pp. 119, 128). Economic interests entered on the scene about the same time in John Davidson and Alexander Gray, *The Scottish Staple at Veere: a study in the economic history of Scotland* (London, 1909). A preliminary sketch by an able scholar appeared with A Francis Steuart, *Scottish Influences in Russian History* (Glasgow, 1913), which looked at the era from the end of the sixteenth century to the beginning of the nineteenth. The inter-war years, in this as in other aspects of Scottish historical research, saw very little solid advance, although John R Elder, *Spanish Influences in Scottish History* (Glasgow, 1920) intelligently covers the period 1488-1603 and does not deserve the neglect which seems to have overtaken it.

In the post-war years the subject was fairly slow to develop, although studies of emigration have not surprisingly been fairly common. Ian C C Graham, *Colonists from Scotland* (Ithaca, 1956), handled that topic in relation to North America in the eighteenth century and many others have followed the emigrant story, most recently Marjory Harper in *Emigration from North-East Scotland* (2 vols, Aberdeen, 1988). A soundly-based popular survey of *The Scots Overseas* was produced by the ever-prolific Gordon Donaldson in 1966; and from the 1960s onwards books on more distant areas and more specialised interests began to emerge: for example, David S MacMillan, *Scotland and Australia, 1788-1950: emigration, commerce and investment* (Oxford, 1967), W Turrentine Jackson, *The Enterprising Scot: investors in the American West after 1873* (Edinburgh, 1968), Hoh-cheung and Lorna Mui, eds, *William Melrose in China, 1845-55: the letters of a Scottish tea merchant* (Scottish History Society, 1973), and John D Hargreaves, *Aberdeenshire to Africa: North-East Scots and British overseas expansion* (Aberdeen, 1982). A fresh impetus to investigation of the long-existing and varied European links has recently been provided by the set of twelve essays edited by T C Smout as *Scotland and Europe, 1200-1850* (Edinburgh, 1986). And his introductory question (p.vi) is apposite: 'Have we done more than skim the surface of the European archives that might yield material on the Scots, and on Scottish history itself? The horizon for scholarly endeavour is almost limitless'.

The contributors and editor who have created this volume affirm that Christopher Smout's comment is sound. This element of Scottish historical studies is amply worthwhile and distinctly in need of further development. Contacts abroad are a fundamental aspect of Scotland's history from the earliest days of the creation of the kingdom and the nation. Edward J Cowan has put the point crisply: 'It may be doubted whether any country of comparable size anywhere in Europe had to contend with so many different ethnic groups in the early middle ages' (*Scottish Historical Review*, lxiii (1984), 135). And relationships with the rest of the world remain an issue in the questions of what Scotland is and what Scots are in the last decade of the twentieth century. European influences were built into Scotland from the arrival of the earliest prehistoric peoples, especially the Celtic-speaking colonists. Conversely, too, from at least the fourteenth century onwards there has existed a Scottish diaspora notable both for its social variety and for its vigorous penetration to the most distant lands.

Those of us in the University of Aberdeen who were involved in planning the First Mackie Symposium had no real difficulty in deciding that Scotland and Scandinavia would be a very appropriate choice of subject. Scotland has been for centuries (and still is) truly a part of the world of Northern Europe; and there exists a long and honourable tradition of scholarly study of this set of linkages. Through the enterprise of W Douglas Simpson and others the University of Aberdeen was closely involved in the First Viking Congress, held at Lerwick in Shetland, and the

University subsequently published the papers from that occasion as *The Viking Congress, 1950* (Aberdeen, 1954). The subject has been most recently investigated from the eighth to the eleventh century in a penetrating survey by Barbara E Crawford: *Scandinavian Scotland* (Leicester, 1987). But it remains important to make clear the thinking which lay behind the balance of topics selected for the Symposium and this volume. The Vikings represent an important and indeed striking chapter near the outset of the story of Scoto-Scandinavian relations. But study of that aspect is a fairly well-developed and active realm of scholarship; and it seemed most fitting to take a broadly-based look at them, through the eyes of Magnus Magnusson, an Icelander, and then to investigate the saga sources for later Viking activities by means of a survey by Rosemary Power, who is based in Ireland. For the periods thereafter our aim has not been to produce comprehensive coverage, but to try to select new viewpoints or to mount new assaults on partly-known material. The editor and authors have tried to point to gaps that need filling and to stimulate further research. In addition to the chapters on direct contacts, we also attempt illumination by means of some parallel studies. Rikke Agnete Olsen and Geoffrey Stell have looked at later medieval castles in two separate national contexts and some notable points of similarity and of difference emerge. Castles have to fit not only into a landscape, but also into a political, social and economic climate. And it is perhaps helpful to note in passing that those historians who feel that the Scottish monarchy in later medieval times was often subject to undue pressure from an obstreperous baronage should look seriously at some of the political developments in contemporary Denmark. The parallel approach has been usefully employed again in Lee Soltow's statistical analyses of landed wealth, as seen when set against different social backgrounds. We should all surely cast our eyes beyond our borders; or, to paraphrase Kipling: what should they know of Scotland who only Scotland know?

As editor I am particularly grateful to my colleague, David Ditchburn, Mackie Research Fellow, who at very short notice agreed to contribute, as an additional chapter, his preliminary investigations into the important but ill-documented matter of Scandinavian trade with Scotland in the later middle ages. For their careful assistance and support in the processes of editing, I am much indebted to Elizabeth Riddell and Sonja Väthjunker.

Aberdeen, 1990   *Grant G Simpson*

Contents

		Page
Introduction *Grant G Simpson,* Department of History, University of Aberdeen		*v*
1	The Viking Road *Magnus Magnusson,* writer and broadcaster, Scotland	1
2	Scotland in the Norse Sagas *Rosemary Power,* Institute of Irish Studies, The Queen's University, Belfast	13
3	Shetland, Scandinavia, Scotland, 1300-1700: the changing nature of contact *Brian Smith,* Shetland Archives, Shetland Islands Council	25
4	Orkney Bishops as Suffragans in the Scandinavian-Baltic Area: an aspect of the late medieval church in the North *Troels Dahlerup,* Historical Institute, University of Aarhus	38
5	Kings, Nobles and Buildings of the Later Middle Ages: Denmark *Rikke Agnete Olsen,* independent scholar, Denmark	48
6	Kings, Nobles and Buildings of the Later Middle Ages: Scotland *Geoffrey Stell,* Royal Commission on the Ancient and Historical Monuments of Scotland, Edinburgh	60
7	A Note on Scandinavian Trade with Scotland in the Later Middle Ages *David Ditchburn,* Department of History, University of Aberdeen	73
8	Scottish Soldiers in the Swedish Armies in the Sixteenth and Seventeenth Centuries *Alf Åberg,* formerly Swedish Military Records Office, Stockholm	90

                                                                    Page

9   Boards, Beams and Barrel-hoops: contacts between Scotland and
     the Stavanger area in the seventeenth century   100
     Arnvid Lillehammer, Stavanger Museum

10   Gothenburg in Stuart War Strategy, 1649-1760   107
     Göran Behre, Historical Institute, University of Gothenburg

11   Some Eighteenth-century Intellectual Contacts between Scotland
     and Scandinavia   119
     John Simpson, Department of Scottish History, University of
     Edinburgh

12   The Distribution of Private Wealth in Land in Scotland and
     Scandinavia in the Seventeenth and Eighteenth Centuries   130
     Lee Soltow, Department of Economics, Ohio University

Index   148

1

THE VIKING ROAD

Magnus Magnusson

This volume is dedicated to the study of Scotland's links with her Scandinavian neighbours from the time of the Norsemen to the early nineteenth century. The burden of the study is outward-looking, as is proper: the traffic of men and ideas and trade *eastwards* across the North Sea; the Scot overseas.

But in these introductory remarks I am thinking about the reverse direction — thinking Norse rather than nineteenth century. From my happy and privileged personal position of having a foot in both camps, I want to look inwards, *towards* Scotland, westward and southward; for I have always been entranced by the delicious geographical anomaly that called the northernmost county in Scotland 'Southland' — Sutherland — thanks to my ancestors. And since I was brought up with the Icelandic sagas at my mother's knee, as it were, my thoughts are both personal and peripheral.

I should perhaps have entitled my theme *Brattir hamrar blálands Haka strandar* ('Steep cliffs of the shore of Haki's dark land'), a poetic kenning coined by Kormákr Ögmundarson, hero of the Icelandic *Kormáks saga*, to indicate 'the sea': what the Anglo-Saxons in their rudimentary kennings called *hwælweg*, 'the whale's way', and which I have chosen to call 'The Viking Road'; because for the Scandinavians of the Viking age, the sea was to all intents and purposes the only road they knew, the only highway they had.[1] Indeed, the very name of Norway itself was not so much for a land as for a sea-route, *Norvegur*, the 'North Way'.

I shall be using the term 'Viking' somewhat indiscriminately, in the way that it has come to be used in the popular prints, for anyone who happened to be a Scandinavian in the middle ages, whether he was a seaman, a farmer, a merchant, a poet, an explorer, a warrior, a craftsman, a settler — or a pirate. And I shall use the term 'Viking Age' as it affected the West equally loosely, to cover some three centuries of dynamic, determined expansion from Scandinavia from around 800 AD onwards. In the pages of history it is usually represented as a clearly defined period of high drama. First there came a curtain-raiser, in the shape of a quayside brawl at Portland harbour in Dorset, in which a Customs and Excise officer, a royal official called Beaduheard, was killed — an untoward occurrence which was noted with casual indignation in an editorial in the *Anglo-Saxon Chronicle;* and this was followed by a theatrical and well-publicised First Act: the raid on the island monastery of Lindisfarne, off north-east England, in 793.

These preliminaries were succeeded by a long Second Act of escalating power as the Vikings assaulted the commanding heights of the coastal economies of Europe and mounted military invasions intent on imperial conquest, which culminated with a Danish king, King Knut Sveinsson (Canute) sitting on the throne of England and ruling a North Sea empire for twenty peaceful years early in the eleventh century. And the Third Act ended in a spectacular finale on a battlefield in England when the Viking-descended Normans conquered England in 1066. Here in Scotland one should perhaps stretch the final end of the Viking age as far as the battle of Largs in 1263, and push the onset of the Viking age back to the start, rather than the end, of the eighth century; for archaeology has shown that colonists from Norway had been moving across the North Sea for at least a century before the raid on Lindisfarne, taking over farmland and assimilating, apparently peacefully, with the native population.

Oddly enough we do not even know for certain what the word 'Viking' actually means, because the derivation is still disputed. It may be related to the Old Norse work *vík*, meaning a bay or creek, suggesting that a Viking was someone who lurked with his ship in a hidden bay. Some think it may come from the Old Norse verb *víkja*, meaning 'to turn aside', so that a Viking was someone who turned aside from his main business of voyaging in order to indulge in raiding on the side. The only certainty about the word is that for centuries it has been used as a term of opprobrium and dread. The Vikings have always had an appallingly bad press, even though their behaviour was, as Peter Sawyer disarmingly put it, simply 'an extension of normal Dark Age activity, made possible and profitable by special circumstances'.[2] To put it more crudely, in an age of rampant piracy the Vikings were better at it than most; and obviously, it was the sensational and the lurid that made the shrill headlines in the chronicles of their victims.

Modern studies are taking a more enlightened view, certainly a more relaxed view, of the Vikings: as entrepreneurs and explorers, as traders rather than raiders; scoundrels and opportunists, perhaps, but rather engaging ones, like Raleigh and Drake. The thrust of recent scholarship and archaeological discovery has tended to highlight the constructive rather than the destructive effect of the Scandinavian impact on the British Isles — the impact of their craftsmanship, their artistry, their language, their ethos, their commercial flair, their agricultural skills, their marine technology. And it was this marine technology in particular that made the North Sea into the crucible of the 'old' Viking age; and I say 'old' Viking age because for the last twenty years or so it has been the crucible of a 'new' Viking age, in which the North Sea has been used once again as a major arena of raw energy. For the Vikings of old, their main energy resource was, quite simply, manpower: highly-skilled, self-confident, shrewd, ambitious manpower. They exported this energy to the other North Sea lands, and that energy helped to develop and revitalise the economy, the life-style and the culture of the countries which absorbed it.

To me, the oilmen of today are the direct descendants of the Viking pioneers of old who dared to invest their all in the great adventure, the great challenge, of the North Sea. Indeed, it has always struck me as singularly appropriate that the capital of the Norwegian oil economy should be the town of Stavanger; for it was in the waters of the fjord where Stavanger now stands that Norway itself was born as a unified Viking nation, when King Harald Fine-Hair defeated a confederacy of sea-kings in the great naval battle of Hafrsfjörd, 1100 years ago.

The exploitation of that North Sea energy was made possible by a major technological revolution, in the same way as the exploitation of North Sea oil and gas today has come about through a modern technological revolution. The technology of the Viking ship, which had been developing for centuries, was just as spectacular to medieval minds as the technology of energy extraction is to the twentieth century. The Viking ship was the finest craft in the northern world of its time, as functional and awe-inspiring as a modern oil-rig; and it was the Viking ship that made the conquest of the North Sea not only possible, but inevitable.

The Viking ship came in all shapes and sizes, from small 'six-oarings' to the enormous *drekar*, the 'dragons' of the sagas. In between came a versatile variety of cutters, ferries, pinnaces, plump cargo-boats, ocean-going ships and galleys. But the pride of the fleet, the boat that has become the universal symbol of the Viking age, was the lordly longship, master of the seas — long, lean and predatory, the equivalent of today's destroyers. According to that great Icelandic saga-historian, Snorri Sturluson, in his monumental 'History of the Kings of Norway', familiarly known as *Heimskringla,* this is how Thjóðólfur Árnarson, an Icelandic court-poet in the service of King Harald Sigurðarsson (Hardraada) in the middle of the eleventh century, hymned the launch of a magnificent new flagship:

> Skeið sák framm at flœði,
> fagrt sprund, ór ǫ hrundit.
> Kenndu, hvar liggr fyr landi
> long súð dreka ens prúða . . .

> I saw the mighty vessel
> slide from the stocks, my maiden.
> See how the lithe serpent
> sits lightly in the water.
> The mane of the glistening dragon
> glows over the deadly cargo,
> its arched neck gilded,
> gleaming with golden carvings.

> Men will quake with terror
> ere the seventy sea-oars
> gain their well-earned respite
> from the labours of the ocean.
> Norwegian arms are driving
> this iron-studded dragon
> down the storm-tossed river,
> like an eagle with wings beating.[3]

That longship reminds us of the largest longship we know of from the Icelandic sagas, the *Long Serpent* of King Olaf Tryggvason, in the dying years of the tenth century; it had 34 pairs of oars and was said to have been carrying a complement of more than 200 warriors when the king leapt overboard to his death at the battle of Svold in the year 1000.

When we think of Viking ships today, we think inevitably of the Gokstad ship, which was excavated from a burial mound in south-western Norway in 1880. Whenever I see the Gokstad ship in the Viking Ship Hall in Oslo, it makes me think of W B Yeats and his memorable couplet about the abortive Rising in Dublin in his poem *Easter 1916*:

> All changed, changed utterly:
> a terrible beauty is born.

What deadly grace of line! What dangerous latent power in every curving plank! Oak-hulled and pine-masted, they were built for strength and speed, and could make 12 knots under sail. The shipwright used no blueprint; he worked entirely by eye and by instinct. With their extraordinary shallowness of draught (less than a metre even when fully laden) they could steal up rivers and through channels where no warship had ever gone before, giving them access to rich inland cities like Paris, Hamburg and Dorestad; the effect was like dropping paratroops behind enemy lines. They needed no harbours, for they were designed to be beached on any shelving sandy shore, where they could land men and horses with ease; and in retreat they could reach islets in shallow waters of estuaries that other boats could not navigate. They could be dragged overland on long portages, using wooden rollers under the hulls. It was this versatility that gave them perhaps the most important factor in warfare, the element of surprise, indeed of shock. It was shock rather than outrage that prompted the first reactions to the Viking raid on Lindisfarne in 793, when the Northumbrian scholar Alcuin penned his letters of condolence to the king of Northumbria:

> Lo, it is nearly 350 years that we and our forefathers have inhabited this
> most lovely land, and never before has such terror appeared in Britain as
> we have now suffered from a pagan race; nor was it thought possible that
> such an inroad from the sea could be made.[4]

In an age of ocean cart-horses, the Viking longships were thoroughbreds: beautiful and terrible. And that image of terror was deliberate: those ornate dragon-prows, carved and gilded, snarling menace as the ships skimmed into action. Princes loved them; peasants took profound pride in them. And poets like Thjóðólfur Árnarson poured praise on them. They were ships fit for heroes.

Through the Vikings, the world became a larger place than it had been. They were insatiable explorers, and pioneers of their Viking sea-roads in search of new trade opportunities to exploit, new lands to settle, new horizons to cross. The North Sea was only the first of their oceanic conquests.

From south-western Norway to the Orkneys was only a short sail, a relatively easy voyage by dead reckoning due west along the latitude. Soon the Northern Isles had become the stepping-stone for further voyages north-west into then-uncharted waters. First they made their way to the Faeroes, rocky and forbidding; the Vikings found them uninhabited, apparently, and peopled them. From the Faeroes north-west again, to Iceland, which was also uninhabited, to all intents and purposes. Here they founded an enduring Nordic state which has left us the greatest cultural monument of the Viking age — the Icelandic sagas, from which we derive so much of our knowledge and so many of our conceptions and preconceptions of the history and achievements of the Northlands.

One of the Norwegian settlers in Iceland was a man called Eiríkr *rauði*, Eric the Red, who had been outlawed from Norway 'on account of some killings', as his saga laconically puts it. It was he, in the 980s, who extended the Viking reach farther to the west when he discovered and subsequently colonised the huge and empty island of Greenland. And it was his son, Leifur *heppni*, Leif the Lucky, who pressed on even farther west across the Atlantic, and became the first European to explore the littoral of North America, five hundred years before Christopher Columbus stumbled across South America. Leif the Lucky called his New World *Vínland*; and from Vínland the Vikings brought back choice timber and dried grapes for making wine, and a treasure-chest of tales to tell. Two centuries later, these tales would be transmuted into two Icelandic sagas that recorded the first undisputed European discovery of the New World. The story of the accidental discovery and attempted colonisation of North America — an attempt that was thwarted by the hostility of the indigenous Red Indians — used to be considered mere legend, a fable; but now archaeology has unearthed authenticated evidence of a Viking settlement at L'Anse aux Meadows, in Newfoundland, and the saga accounts have been vindicated.

Nowhere, it seems, was too far, too unlikely, or too dangerous for these Vikings to venture. It is the sheer range and scale of the Viking expansion that is so astonishing. But why did they do it? What drove them ever onwards and outwards?

It is a difficult question, because all major historical shifts have complex causes. Personally, I tend to agree with the thesis that the major cause can be traced back to a considerable expansion in the production of iron in Scandinavia in the seventh and eighth centuries. The development of any primary commodity has a huge impact on history, whether it be stone, bronze, iron or oil. The effects of improved iron production in Scandinavia seem to have been electrifying. It led to the production not only of better weapons but also of better agricultural implements. Better agriculture meant better food; better food meant less infant mortality; and since only the eldest sons inherited a farm, through primogeniture, we find large families of younger sons all looking to make for themselves a place in the sun. (And it pleases me to reflect that the name of the main centre of oil development in Shetland by the new oil Vikings still contains an echo of this idea; for Sullom Voe, which is derived from the Norse *sólheimar*, means, quite literally, 'a place in the sun'.)

We know that new farms were being carved out of higher forest-land in Scandinavia in this pre-Viking period; so it is reasonable to deduce that the effect of the iron boom was a growing pressure on land, caused through over-population. And as a side-product, it would leave Scandinavia with a surplus of iron to export, thus providing a boost to the mercantile trade.

It was not because conditions were so bad in Scandinavia that they were forced to flee their homelands to seek a better life elsewhere, as their descendants would do in the second wave of Scandinavian emigrations to the New World in the second half of the nineteenth century. On the contrary, it was because things were so good in Scandinavia that they wanted to capitalise on what they had. It was a measure of their self-confidence, not an index of their despair. They left because they believed they had the ability to make good. They wanted to make their own way in the wide world; and above all they admired achievement. They went everywhere there was to go, until there were no more seas to cross, no more Viking roads to travel.

This encomium of the Viking age is, of course, a distinctly biassed and even prejudiced account. My view of the Vikings is, I confess, that of an Icelander looking at things from a northern viewpoint. And from the same viewpoint I want to consider more closely now the colonisation of the northern islands of Shetland and the Orkneys, much of mainland Scotland, and the Hebrides; for that period of colonisation brackets both the beginning and the end of the Viking road, as I have suggested.

In Shetland and the Orkneys, according to the sagas, the Vikings created a splendid Golden Age of power and prosperity such as the islanders were not to experience again until the new influx of oil-energy from the North Sea. They also infiltrated and took over the Western Isles, but never to the same absolute effect, apparently; the native culture there was never subsumed by the newcomers, and the Viking hold was always more tenuous. The political connection with Scandinavia was much more equivocal. Norway claimed both the Northern and the Western Isles as Norwegian fiefdoms that owed allegiance and annual tribute to the Norwegian crown; but exacting that allegiance, imposing that subservience, was a different matter. It depended very much on the individual temper and temperament of the Norwegian kings, and of the earls and chieftains who held sway in the Isles.

Whenever the Scottish islands showed signs of truculence the king of Norway, if he had the inclination and resources, would send a task force west over sea to remind them who was lord. King Harald Fine-Hair did it in the 890s. My namesake, Magnus Barelegs, so called because he abandoned Viking trousers in favour of the kilt, did it with devastating effect in the 1090s. In 1263 another great Norwegian king, Haakon the Old, did it again, or rather tried to do it again; but this time the exploit failed, partly because of what is known to history as the battle of Largs.

Looking back on it with the advantage of historical hindsight, we can see something inevitable about the failure. The Scottish crown was becoming stronger and more effective as a sense of Scottish nationhood asserted itself. The pure dynamic of the Viking age had long been weakening. The island chieftains were feeling their oats, sensing the slackening of Norwegian power and the growing authority of mainland Scotland. And so, as in all power-struggles, the Scots were beginning to play politics, to change sides either covertly or overtly, weighing up their own prospects for the future. Both geographically and politically, Scotland now seemed a better bet than Norway.

Haakon Haakonsson, King Haakon IV of Norway, Haakon the Old (for he was then nearing sixty), decided to try to turn the clock back. He assembled a massive expedition of 150 ships and some 20,000 warriors, and set sail from Bergen early in July of 1263. The old king insisted on taking charge himself; but everything went wrong. Reinforcements he had expected failed to turn up. Former allies and vassals smelled failure in the air. There were endless delays. Haakon wanted to intimidate the young king of Scotland, Alexander III, by the mere threat of force, but Alexander out-thought him and out-manoeuvred him. Even as that formidable

Norwegian fleet was cruising slowly down the Western Isles, exacting tribute from recalcitrant island chieftains and cuffing sullen island populations, Alexander was negotiating, or *apparently* negotiating. He kept sending envoys to the Norwegian king to try to patch up their differences, and reach agreement about their respective spheres of influence; but always some obstacle would crop up, some hitch would develop, which meant that the negotiations would drag on a little longer. And all the time, autumn with its storms was approaching.

It was late September by the time Haakon reached the Ayrshire coast. He was getting impatient, and so were his men. He had never intended actually to invade the mainland of Scotland — just to threaten to invade it. He had always intended to go to the conference table with a mailed fist, without actually having to use it. Then one night, when the Norwegian fleet was at anchor off the Cumbraes, just across from Largs, an autumn gale arose from the south-west. Three longships and a merchantman dragged their anchors and were hurled on to the beach at Largs. The Scottish army, which had been monitoring the progress of the fleet down the west coast, hung back; it was not Alexander's intention to do battle. Instead the local militia moved in to see what pickings were to be had. As the storm raged, a skirmish developed on the beach. Volleys of stones and arrows were exchanged. The merchantman was half-looted before the Norwegians managed to send in reinforcements in the teeth of the gale. Not many were killed, only a handful at the most on either side; but many, I suspect, were sorely bruised. By the end of the day the Scots had withdrawn from the beach, no doubt pleased with their spoils, and the Norwegians were no less relieved to be able to withdraw to the safety of their ships off the Cumbraes.

It was an indecisive, brawling, messy encounter. No one enjoyed it, and no one could claim a clear victory (except, of course, the chauvinists on both sides). It solved nothing; but it underlined the inexorable fact that Norwegian power in the Western Isles was no longer a potent political factor. The Norwegians, who were sick of the whole business by this time, decided to go home. Old King Haakon, caught in another storm as they passed the Orkneys, planned to stay there for the winter; but there, in Kirkwall, just before Christmas, he died — not of battle wounds, but of old age and exhaustion. The tried and trusted Viking road had failed him, at the last.

His son and successor, King Magnus the Lawmender (*Lagabœtr*), bowed to the inevitable, and soon agreed to sell the Western Isles to the Scottish crown. In a way, the battle of Largs, the *non*-battle of Largs, was the ideal outcome. It had been a flexing of muscles without too much violence, or too many deaths to poison future relations. It led to a realistic acceptance of the inevitable: the Western Isles passed peacefully into the geo-political realm where they clearly now belonged, and two centuries later the Northern Isles went the same way, pawned to the Scottish crown by a Scandinavian king who apparently could not afford a marriage dowry for his daughter.

That is one version of the battle of Largs. It hardly squares with the perceived Scottish version that still finds its way into too many careless encyclopaedias, based on George Buchanan's Latin *History of Scotland*, published in 1582, which claimed that Haakon had landed a force of 20,000 men who were routed to the tune of no fewer than *16,000 dead*, with *5,000 dead* on the Scottish side! I have relied far more on the Icelandic sagas, specifically the account given in the near-contemporary Icelandic *Hákonarsaga*: the Saga of Haakon, written only two years after Haakon's death by Sturla Thórðarson, nephew of the great Snorri Sturluson himself.

I have referred to the sagas as 'the greatest cultural monument of the Viking age'. Indeed, I believe they represent the outstanding achievement of European medieval literature. I am sure that many literary critics would agree with that sentiment; but a problem always arises with the sagas if one is tempted to confuse their literary merit with their validity as historical sources.

In English, the word 'saga' has come to have rather pejorative connotations: 'Oh, what a *saga* it's been!' In Icelandic the word simply means 'something said', and is cognate with the English word 'saw', meaning 'a saying', but it has come to have the more specialised meaning of 'prose narrative'. In that sense it covers the same ground as the Latin word *historia*, which means both 'history' and 'story'; but it is also analogous to a word like 'legend', which comes from the Latin *legenda*, meaning 'things to be read'. And that is what the word 'saga' has come to mean: it is a comprehensive term that encompasses reading-matter that is both history, and story, and legend.

In the same way, what are known collectively as the Icelandic sagas encompass several different kinds of saga writings. The earliest in time were saints' lives (*heilagra manna sögur*). Then came *konungasögur* — kings' sagas, synoptic or individual biographies of kings of Norway, a genre that started in the middle of the twelfth century. Then, in the thirteenth century, came the Golden Age of what we think of as the 'classical' sagas, the sagas proper: *Íslendingasögur*, the sagas of Icelanders, or family sagas as they used to be called. They tell about people and events in Iceland during the formative years of the nation, some two or three centuries earlier. Some forty of them are now extant, including the celebrated five that are familiar to most serious readers — *Njáls saga, Egils saga, Laxdœla saga, Eyrbyggja saga*, and *Grettis saga*. And to complete this outline catalogue: the fourteenth century saw the growth of another saga genre, the so-called 'legendary sagas' (*fornaldarsögur*, meaning 'sagas of ancient times'): fantastical tales of adventure and magic, set in Scandinavia and on the continent in prehistoric times, long before the settlement of Iceland or the Norse occupation of Scotland. Some of them are great fun, but they are not so highly rated as literary achievements; they were, in effect, the popular pulp-fiction of their day, almost a pastiche of the classical saga style.

So the Icelandic sagas are really a sprawling mass of material which constitutes a unique blend of learning and entertainment, fact and fantasy, history and story-telling, literary endeavour and family pride, pagan past and Christian present; and one has to be careful to try to differentiate these disparate elements.

How much credence can we put on the evidence of the sagas? The short answer is that it depends on the saga. The legendary sagas, for instance, were deliberate works of fiction and recognised as such: 'lying sagas' (*lýgisögur*), as King Sverrir of Norway cheerfully called them. The saints' lives would no doubt like to be taken as gospel truth, but stretch credulity further than most. The great classical sagas compellingly embody very real truths about human behaviour, but should, I think, be treated as historical novels about early Iceland rather than history proper.

It is in the historical sagas that we meet the greatest problems of verisimilitude and veracity; for here the twin strands of learning and saga-entertainment come together in disconcertingly brilliant fashion, especially in the person of the great Snorri Sturluson, who ushered in the Golden Age of saga writing in the first half of the thirteenth century. Snorri was an archetypal Renaissance man long before his time: scholar, poet, historian, politician, statesman, saga-writer and saga-maker. He wrote perhaps three, certainly two, outstanding works, any one of which would have earned him immortality: an encyclopaedia of Norse mythology and poetic diction known as the *Prose Edda*; one of the greatest of the Icelandic family sagas, *Egils saga* (although that is an educated assumption, not a known fact); and his monumental *Heimskringla*.

Snorri Sturluson lived in an age of violence and civil lawlessness, at a time when the unique parliamentary commonwealth established by the early settlers of Iceland was disintegrating in a welter of savage power-struggles between half a dozen ruling families; and Iceland was being drawn irresistibly into the ambit of the Norwegian crown. In fact the end of the commonwealth came in the year 1262, the year before the battle of Largs, when the Icelanders swore fealty to King Haakon the Old himself. Snorri was one of the leading protagonists in that sorry story, and paid for it with his life when he was assassinated at the behest of Haakon the Old, in 1241. It is an extraordinary irony that when Genghis Khan was trying to conquer the eastern world by force of arms, Snorri Sturluson the scholar was trying to subjugate the northern world to the discipline of history. His great *History of the Kings of Norway* begins with the words 'The orb of the world, which mankind inhabits . . .'; and it is from its first two words, *Kringla heimsins*, that his history was given the title *Heimskringla*.

It is a prodigious work: nothing less than the story of Norway from prehistoric times to 1177, told in a series of biographical sagas of all the kings who had occupied the throne of Norway. Snorri was a scrupulous, erudite European rationalist, trying to impose his sense of order on the chaos of the past in order to understand it better. But he was also a great journalist. His history is a sweeping portrait gallery of individual monarchs, depicted with immense skill and authority. He saw history as a linear flow of events which he explained in terms of individual personalities and their aspirations, achievements and failures, not economic factors or trade statistics. He was also a humanist: he saw 'destiny' as a force that could be controlled by great men through their greatness, but which would ruin lesser men through their weakness and incapacity. He would no doubt have agreed with Thomas Carlyle's dictum that 'the history of the world is but the biography of great men'. To the writing of *Heimskringla*, Snorri brought not only his outstanding literary ability but also his deep insight and experience of princes and peasants as a protagonist in the power-struggles of his own times that were to cost him so dear. He interpreted the past in terms of his own present, as we all tend to do: history not in the sense of what actually happened, but as a composite perception of the past.

In his introduction to *Heimskringla*, Snorri modestly makes no explicit claim to total historical accuracy:

> In this book I have had written old stories about the chieftains who held sway in the northlands and who spoke the Norse tongue, according to what I have heard learned men tell, and also of their descendants, as I myself have been taught them. Some of this is to be found in the genealogies wherein kings and others of noble birth have traced their descent, but some of it is written according to old poems or historical lays which people have used to entertain themselves with. And although we cannot be sure what truth there is in them, we do know for a fact that old and learned men have held them to be true.[5]

It is the business of professional historians to analyse Snorri's sources and the use to which he put them; but whatever flaws can be shown, the work has a feel of authority that compels credence, and an entertainment value that disarms critical scepticism. It is Snorri above all who has shaped the *way* in which I, for one, look back at the Viking age. He gave the Viking world its style.

Orkneyinga saga gave the same sense of style to the story of the Norse occupation of the Northern Isles, through a series of vivid personality-pictures. It was written earlier than *Heimskringla*, perhaps around 1200, and lacks its awesome authority; but it, too, has put its indelible stamp on how we perceive the Viking age in Scotland.

By a quirk of history, it was Snorri Sturluson's nephew, Sturla Thórðarson, another distinguished saga-historian, who was commissioned to write the official biography of the king who had had his uncle murdered: Haakon the Old. The man who commissioned it was the king's son and successor, King Magnus. Sturla Thórðarson had the advantage of access to the Norwegian state archives, and to eye-witnesses of the great events of Haakon's reign, such as his final ill-fated expedition. As a historian, Snorri Sturluson had never enjoyed such advantages. Yet his works read so much better than Sturla's saga of King Haakon. It is a cautious, circumspect document, one that had to be politically acceptable to his royal patron. Sturla could not afford to be as objective, or as subjective, as he would no doubt like to have been. He could not write, as his uncle had written, primarily for an Icelandic audience.

Snorri himself was very aware of this Icelandic bias in his own writings. Indeed, he was almost apologetic about it in his Prologue to *Ólafs saga helga*, the saga of St Olaf; but he was prepared to justify it nonetheless:

> I realise that if this account should reach other countries, it will be thought that I have spoken rather too much about Icelanders, but the reason for this is the fact that the Icelanders who witnessed the events, or heard about them, brought to this country the stories which later generations have since learned.[6]

In Snorri's view, as a historian of the past, the most reliable source of historical information was the vast corpus of court poetry composed by the Icelanders who had monopolised the posts of court poets in Scandinavia since the tenth century:

> The best evidence we have is that which is contained in the poems which were composed for the kings themselves or their sons. We accept as true everything which is to be found in these poems concerning their journeyings or their battles. It is, of course, the way of court poets to lavish the most praise on the people for whom the poems were composed; but no one would dare to tell the king himself about deeds which everyone present, including the king, would know to be nonsense and lies; that would be mockery, not praise . . .[7]

Knowing, as we all do, the infinite capacity of rulers to absorb praise and ignore mockery, we might regard that as rather naive on Snorri's part. But we should not forget that amongst Icelanders of those times, and indeed of today, it has always been considered a matter of pride and importance to be able to give a good account of events at which one had been a participant or an eye-witness. This is neatly illustrated by an episode in *Orkneying saga* itself, when Earl Rögnvaldr of Orkney was leading a bold company of Orcadians on the Viking road through the Mediterranean on their way to the Holy Land in the year 1152. Just off Sardinia they attacked a huge Saracen merchantman known as a 'dromond', which they only managed to overcome with the greatest difficulty. Afterwards, Earl Rögnvaldr's men talked about the engagement:

> They began to talk over what had just happened, each describing what he thought he had seen. One point of argument was who had been first to board the 'dromond', and on this they could not agree. Some now felt that it was silly not to have the same account of such a great event; and in the end they decided that Earl Rögnvaldr should have the last word, and that everyone should then stick to that version.[8]

Whereupon the earl summarized the information in a verse that would become the received account of the fighting.

Snorri's good opinions of Icelanders as sources had already, much earlier, been voiced by the Danish historian Saxo Grammaticus in his Preface to his massive *Gesta Danorum* (History of the Danes), written around the year 1200:

> The diligence of the men of Iceland (*Tylenses*) must not be shrouded in silence; since the barrenness of their native soil offers no means of self-indulgence, they pursue a steady routine of temperance and devote all their time to improving our knowledge of others' deeds, compensating for their poverty by their intelligence (*inopiam ingenio pensant*). They regard it a real pleasure to discover and commemorate the achievements of every nation; in their judgement it is as elevating to discourse on the prowess of others as to display their own. Thus I have scrutinised their store of historical treasures and composed a considerable part of this present work by copying their narratives, not scorning, where I recognised such skill in ancient lore, to take these men as witnesses.[9]

Ultimately, the past is not a stable entity which can ever be wholly recovered. It is an inconstant amalgam of contemporary evidences and testimonies, of images and documents, constantly under review in the light of new theories, new interpretations, new methodologies. But let us not forget the *voice* of the past in all this: the voice of the story-teller, the saga-writer. When people ask, 'Are the sagas true? Did they really happen?', the questions fade into insignificance in the face of the power and passion of the narratives they contain. The sagas are 'true' in the one way that matters: true to something deep within us all as human beings, true to the great imperatives of human action and feeling.

So let me end with an enigmatic quotation from a fellow Scandinavian with no more qualifications to pontificate than I have. It comes from Isak Dinesen (Karen Blixen), in 'The Blank Page' in her book of *Last Tales*: 'If the story-teller is faithful to the story, in the end the silence will speak; but if the story-teller is not faithful to the story, in the end there will be nothing but silence'. I am not sure that I fully understand it. But I like it.[10]

NOTES

1. *Kormáks saga* (Íslenzk fornrit viii, Reykjavik, 1939), 269.

2. Peter Sawyer, *The Age of the Vikings* (2nd edn, London, 1971), 203.

3. *Haralds saga Sigurðarsonar* (*Heimskringla III*, Íslenzk fornrit xxviii, Reykjavik 1941), 141. Translated by Magnus Magnusson and Hermann Pálsson in *King Harald's Saga* (Penguin Classics, 1966), ch 60.

4. Dorothy Whitelock, ed., *English Historical Documents, c.500-1042* (2nd edn, London, 1979), 842.

5. *Heimskringla I* (Íslenzk fornrit xxvi, Reykjavik, 1941), Prologus, 3-4. Translated by the author.

6. *Heimskringla II* (Íslenzk fornrit xxvii, Reykjavik, 1945), Prologus, 422. Based on a translation in *King Harald's Saga*, 28-29.

7. *Heimskringla I*, Prologus, 5. Translated in *King Harald's Saga*, 24-25.

8. *Orkneyinga Saga* (Íslenzk fornrit xxxiv, Reykjavik, 1965), 227. Translation based on that by Hermann Pálsson and Paul Edwards (Hogarth Press, London, 1978), ch. 88.

9. Saxo Grammaticus, *History of the Danes*, ed. H E Davidson, transl. Peter Fisher (2 vols., Woodbridge, 1979-80), i, 5.

10. Karen Blixen, *Last Tales* (Random House, New York, 1957), 100. I am indebted to my old friend Richard Luman for drawing my attention to this quotation and its relevance in a TS article he sent me, entitled *The "Historical Question" as a Problem in the Interpretation of Ancient Literature.*

2

SCOTLAND IN THE NORSE SAGAS

Rosemary Power

I

To the Norse writers of the late twelfth and thirteenth centuries, Scotland was a reasonably well-defined region, both geographically and culturally. In accounts of the events of the Viking age Scotland is referred to fairly often as a place in which raids took place, and also as the home of Norse, or partly-Norse, individuals. But the areas which the saga-writers and annalists knew most of were naturally those within the Norse sphere of influence, the Northern and Western Isles and the adjacent parts of the mainland, and it is these that figure most in the accounts of events in the twelfth and the first part of the thirteenth century. There is relatively little said concerning the kingdom of Scotland itself in this period, and by the time of increased contacts between the kingdom and Norway in the late thirteenth century, sagas were no longer being composed on contemporary events.

Shetland is served poorly by the northern writers, but in contrast Orkney is frequently mentioned in Norse literature, and is fortunate in having a saga composed on its earls and their contemporaries which covers its history up to about the year 1200.[1] Later sagas concerning Norwegian monarchs cover events of the thirteenth century up to 1265. Together with its rich archaeological evidence and documentation from other sources the history of Orkney in this period is relatively easy to piece together.

Records for the Western Isles are far more sparse, and none are native. A great deal more reliance must be placed on the Norse material. Irish annals and the thirteenth-century Manx *Chronicle of the Kings of Man and the Sudreys*[2] gives us some further information on the kingdom of Man and the Isles from the mid-tenth century onwards, and these can be supplemented from the late twelfth century onwards with diplomatic and similar records which concern the kingdom and the bishopric. Even so we need to rely heavily on what can be pieced together from various sagas and other works for the period up to 1266, during which the kingdom ostensibly owed allegiance to Norway. However, the various sagas give no straight-forward chronicle of events in the Isles and Man. Throughout the period they were culturally and linguistically less Norse than the Northern Isles, and events there impinged far less on the Norse world. On the whole we are told of matters concerning the Western Isles only when they do affect events in the Northern Isles or Norway, or when they are visited by inhabitants of these lands. There is little curiosity about the Isles for their own sake.

The Norse sagas are primarily literary works, most of them composed in Iceland,

and intended for a home, and, in the case of the histories of the Norse kings and similar works, for a Norwegian audience. Written in the late twelfth and thirteenth centuries, they contain an account of the Norse world as seen through Norse eyes, composed for the purposes of entertainment and edification, and subject to certain literary conventions. They deal with events from the Viking age onwards, and the farther back in time are the events they record the greater was the freedom of the author to arrange his material according to the demands of taste and literary structure, and the desire to point to examples of the noble and ignoble in human character. The sagas are full of literary techniques such as echoes; the use of dreams to foreshadow events; the interweaving of stories, perhaps at the expense of chronology; standard episodes; literary clichés; and other devices that hold the material together. As such their authenticity as historical documents must always be in question, but, generally speaking, the nearer their authors were to the period in which the events they describe took place, the more they may be trusted historically. Sagas dealing with events of the twelfth century often use poetry composed at that time. The prose can vary in historical value, as far as can be determined from comparison with other source material, but it is far too important to be dismissed without careful consideration. The sagas written in the thirteenth century on contemporary or near-contemporary subjects may be taken as fairly good records of events, as seen from a purely Norse perspective. While the saga material is uneven, the Icelandic annals are a trustworthy, if sparse, source for the events of the twelfth century onwards.

II

The political history of the Western Isles is the aspect most thoroughly covered in the sagas, most through anecdotes concerning its kings and other colourful characters. There is a distinctively different treatment given to these from that accorded to the earls of Orkney, which reflects the difference in situation. The Western Isles were allegedly conquered by the Norwegian king Harald Finehair in the late ninth century, who destroyed at least temporarily the power of Vikings who made them their base. But in spite of Norse settlement in the Isles they remained distinct, and their rulers were styled 'king' as in the Gaelic fashion, unlike the Norse earls of Orkney. We hear of the Isles in the Viking age either because of Viking activity or because individuals of Norse or partly-Norse backgrounds settled in Iceland in the late eighth and ninth centuries. The first sustained account concerns the sudden descent in 1098 on both the Northern and Western Isles by the Norwegian king, Magnus Barelegs. The Orkney earls were taken off guard, captured and sent to Norway. Magnus proceeded west to pillage, and a number of verses, said to be contemporary, are eloquent on the violence of his onslaught. He raided Lewis, Uist, Skye, Tiree, Sandey, left Iona intact, then pillaged in Islay, Kintyre, on both sides of the North Channel, and went on to Man, which he made his base. In Anglesey he brushed with the Norman invaders. On his return north he is said to have made a treaty with the Scots king by which he was to have all the islands west of Scotland if he could sail between them and the mainland with a rudder set. Thus Magnus gained the entire area which was reckoned as belonging to the kingdom, and later the bishopric, of the Isles and Man. Magnus returned to Norway by way of Orkney that autumn. He reasserted his authority in a later expedition in 1102, but was slain the following year in Ireland.

The verses which eulogise Magnus's depredations are paradoxically the first indication we have from Norse literature that the Isles had a population other than Vikings — though it is not until the *Orkneyinga saga's* description of the death of Saint Magnus in about 1117 that we hear of any occupation as mundane as 'farmer' attributed to someone from the Western Isles.[3] The verses themselves appear first in the history of the kings of Norway known as *Morkinskinna*,[4] but the Icelander Snorri Sturluson, writing some twenty years later, had new information about the kingdom, perhaps obtained from a Hebridean visiting Norway, for he rearranges the verses he takes from *Morkinskinna* so as to give the Isles named (with the exception of Sandey) in their correct order from north to south.[5] Snorri is also responsible for the information that Magnus received his cognomen as a result of this expedition. We are told that on his return to Norway Magnus wore the clothes common in the West in his time, a short kirtle, which left his legs bare, and a cloak.[6] Perhaps again this knowledge of Hebridean dress came from an informant from the Isles whom Snorri met in Norway.

After Magnus's death three of his sons ruled Norway. But in about 1128, when only one of them, Sigurd, was still alive, a man from Ireland came to the Western Isles claiming that he was a son of Magnus Barelegs. He was taken to Norway, and after undergoing trial by ordeal he was accepted as a brother of Sigurd. Gillikristr, or Harald *gilli* as he was known in Norway, reigned for six years after Sigurd's death.[7] Snorri again describes a form of Gaelic dress which he says that Harald wore on the occasion of a race he ran with incredible swiftness against a horse.[8] This race is a motif in Gaelic tradition, and perhaps this too Snorri got from his contemporary Hebridean informant — and from him too perhaps he took the notion he attributes to Harald, that he spoke Norse haltingly. Harald died at the hands of yet another claimant to be a son of Magnus Barelegs, who himself met a violent end. But before he had come to Norway, Harald had had a son, Eysteinn, and in 1142 he too came to claim his inheritance. He had no difficulty in being accepted as the son of Harald *gilli*, perhaps because his kinship was well known in the Western Isles and he could be vouched for by Hebrideans visiting Norway.[9] Eysteinn was no peace-lover. In the summer of 1151, when one of the Orkney earls, Rögnvald, was away preparing for a pilgrimage, Eysteinn harried his domains, and went on to Caithness, where he caught the other earl, Harald, unawares, and forced him to ransom himself. Eysteinn also raided Aberdeen and pillaged in England, giving the excuse for the latter that it was to avenge the death at Stamford Bridge of Harald Harðraði, his great-great-grandfather, some eighty-five years previously.[10]

For life in the Hebrides in the mid-twelfth century we have another source, the story of the flamboyant Orkneyman Sveinn Ásleifarson, which is told some thirty years after his death in *Orkneyinga saga*.[11] For the most part we have little independent corroborative evidence for the story of Sveinn, but from the saga account we can get some idea of conditions in the Northern and Western Isles at the time.

Sveinn is introduced in the saga when his father is burnt in his house, an event ascribed to about 1136. Shortly afterwards Sveinn slays a certain man named Sveinn brjóstreip, by this earning the gratitude of the bishop of Orkney, who sends him for safety to a great chieftain in Tiree named Holdboði. Here Sveinn is out of the reach of Earl Rögnvald, and resides in comfort for a year, before going to another safe haven with friends in Scotland. When in 1139 he avenges his father's death, only one of those responsible escapes from Orkney, like Sveinn before him to the Western Isles, where we may presume he too had friends.

Two years later Holdboði is raided and chased from his home by a Welsh chieftain, and applies to Sveinn for help. Earl Rögnvald, who is now reconciled with Sveinn, warns him against getting involved. 'Most Hebrideans are treacherous', he says, stating not only a Norse cliché on those of other races, but also perhaps the need of Hebrideans to make a life either as mercenaries or by accommodating with the neighbouring rulers. But when Sveinn insists on setting out Rögnvald gives him two ships. He meets up with Holdboði in Man, and the two set out on an indiscriminate raiding tour of Wales. On one occasion, we are told, Sveinn burns six farms before breakfast. The inevitable Icelander is present to record the deed. Sveinn winters on Man that year, and gets married. In the spring he asks Holdboði for his company in raiding that summer but Holdboði, who has made a secret agreement with the Welsh chieftain, refuses on the grounds that his men are busy or away trading. Sveinn goes raiding with three ships, but gains little at first except a trading vessel owned by monks of the Scilly Isles. He turns his attention to Ireland, where he does better. In the autumn he returns to his base in Man, and, in spite of warnings, continues to trust Holdboði, until he is attacked one night and barely escapes with his life. He returns to Man with a large band of followers, but sells his possessions in the spring and makes for Lewis. He hears that Holdboði is in the Western Isles, seeks him out and pursues him, killing and burning in his wake. Holdboði, we are told, never dares to return.

Sveinn goes on with his career as a Viking. We even hear that on one occasion he takes shelter from the weather in an abbey, and raids it on leaving. Yet in spite of such deeds, when he arrives in Edinburgh he is made welcome at the court of the Scots King David, of saintly repute. David is so taken with Sveinn that he wishes to keep Sveinn with him, but he declines. Sveinn retains his Hebridean friends in spite of the episode with Holdboði. In 1151 he sends his brother Gunni to safety in Lewis, out of the reach of Earl Harald Maddaðarson of Orkney, whose mother is pregnant by Gunni.

Two years later Sveinn is raiding in eastern England. He is chased back to Edinburgh by the men of Berwick and King David intervenes on Sveinn's behalf. In 1155 he raids the west coast of Scotland, and is said to be the guest of a friend, a great chief named Sumarliði. Then the next year, we are told, he kills another Sumarliði in these parts. Both episodes may refer to the Hebridean chieftain of that name, who married into the family of the kings of Man. As a result the kingdom was split and, while the northern Hebrides remained in Manx hands, the southern

Hebrides went to his family and were divided among his sons in 1156. Sumarliði was slain at Renfrew in 1164, not by Sveinn. But these events in the Gaelic world are noted only in the confused account in *Orkneyinga saga* and by a reference to kings of the Sumarliði line in *Hákonar saga Hákonarsonar*,[12] a chronicle of the reign of the Norwegian king Haakon IV (1217-63), written shortly after his death by the Icelander Sturla Thorðarson.

Sveinn came to organise his raiding with the percipience of a good farmer from his home in Orkney. When the winter's work was over he went out on his 'spring viking', but returned in midsummer for the corn-harvest. Then he went on his 'autumn viking' and did not return until a month of winter had gone by. In 1171 he went on his spring viking, as usual to the Western Isles, where the people are said to have been so afraid of him that they hid their possessions. He went on to Man, where he had little luck, but off Ireland he came across two trading vessels, laden with fine English cloth, wine and mead. He took everything except the clothes the traders stood in, and then let them sail on, while he returned to Orkney. That autumn Sveinn set out on what he intended to be his final voyage. It was: he was slain in Dublin, an incident also recounted, though with considerable variation, by Giraldus Cambrensis.[13]

The story of Sveinn shows something of the strife and absence of centralised authority in the Western Isles, which make the Northern Isles seem reasonably controlled by comparison. Yet, as in many troubled societies, there is not strife in every part, all the time, and ordinary occupations go on. People harvest their crops and go trading in summer, and winter on their farms, doing, it seems, the normal round of work. And, if it is true that Sveinn raided the Western Isles as frequently as it is claimed, this shows that the inhabitants had some small moveable property worth the taking.

Nor was Sveinn their only raider. Sverrir Sigurðsson, who came to reign in Norway in 1177, is said in his saga to have considered raiding the Hebrides in order to raise funding for this enterprise.[14] Raiding traders seems to have been one way of making wealth in Orkney, and doubtless in the Hebrides too. When in the 1190s the leading men of Orkney go to Norway to be reconciled with Sverrir on account of having plotted against him, Earl Harald complains that not all his people obey his behests: many take off to Scotland or Ireland, or raid traders against his will.[15]

In 1209 members of the two factions known in Norway as Baglar and Birkibeinar, erstwhile enemies, planned together to raid the Hebrides the following year, in order to raise finance for a pilgrimage to Jerusalem. One of their number, named Óspakr, is himself a Hebridean. This group arrives in twelve ships in 1210 and harries successfully, even pillaging the holy isle of Iona. The next winter two ships carrying the pilgrims are lost at sea: and this is the nearest the saga gets to a condemnation of such practices.[16]

Another occupation open to the men of the Isles was that of mercenary soldier. In 1161, Guðröð Óláfsson, a king of the Isles, is in Norway. He fights for King Ingi Haraldsson, but flees as prearranged from a decisive battle, taking with him an alleged 1500 followers, presumably men from the Isles. Another Hebridean leader actually takes his men to join the opposing faction.[17] And in 1196 we find

Rögnvald, king of Man, acting for the Scots King William, against Earl Harald of Orkney, who has taken possession of Caithness without William's permission. For this expedition Rögnvald gathers followers not only from the Isles, but from Kintyre and Ireland as well.[18] We know too, though not from the sagas, that Rögnvald visited England several times, and that, while formally the subject of the king of Norway, he became the vassal of both the English King John and the pope. For King John he was required to keep the coasts of England and Ireland free from pirates — no easy task if the story of Sveinn Ásleifarson is to be believed, but one best undertaken from Man. In return the English had to supply Rögnvald with corn and beer from Ireland, which Rögnvald made sure he received. He also got occasional gifts of money from John, and in 1212 received a fief in the Carlingford area of the eastern Irish coast. His successors as kings of Man made similar arrangements with the English monarchs, which drew them further into the English sphere of influence.[19]

From 1217 until 1263 we have *Hákonar saga Hákonarsonar* as a fairly trust-worthy source of information on how events were seen from a Norse perspective. From the start Orkney is engaged in Norwegian politics and the Western Isles are embroiled in internal strife, by now so extreme that we are told that already by the 1220s many Hebrideans are found at the Norwegian court, seeking aid for their land. Haakon is able to exert considerable influence in determining the succession of the kings in the Isles. By this time there were a number of kings reigning simultaneously, and Haakon seems to have made no attempt to reduce their number or permit any of them to increase their powers notably, but kept them, rather, dependent upon his goodwill. He did however assist them in various ways, probably as much because of the growing interest in the western seaboard from the kingdom of Scotland as for the maintenance of any form of order in the Isles.

One of Haakon's trusted followers, the Hebridean Óspakr, whom we met raiding the Hebrides in 1210, is a son of a king of the Isles, and in 1230 he is given the title of king himself and sent home to assert Haakon's authority. This is a hopeless task, which would have required him to fight his own brothers, and he achieves nothing before his death at the end of that summer.[20] Another trusted candidate of Haakon's was King Harald Óláfsson of Man. He had acceded in 1237, without Haakon's permission, but was soon brought to heel and came to Norway in 1240 to make peace. He goes home but returns to Norway in 1247 and marries a daughter of Haakon the following year. He is sent back home the same year to keep control, but his ship sinks with all hands, it is thought off Sumburgh Roost south of Shetland.[21] This event echoes a tragedy of 1231, when a ship carrying the chief men of the Northern Isles sank with all on board on return from attendance at Haakon's court.[22] When Haakon learnt of the loss of Harald and his wife, he sent another Hebridean then in Norway, Jón, known in Scotland as Eoghan of Argyll, to take charge, for the Scots King Alexander II, who had been unsuccessful in his offers to buy the Isles from Haakon, was now gathering a large army to invade the Isles. Jón met Alexander, who attempted to win him over, unsuccessfully, though Jón later switched allegiance to his successor. Alexander's invasion got no further than the island of Kerrera, for there in 1249 Alexander took sick and died, according to the saga as a punishment visited on him by Saints Olaf of Norway, Magnus of Orkney and Columba.

There is a lull while Alexander III is in his minority, and then he too asks Haakon for the Isles, which he regards as rightfully Scots. When his ambassadors arrive in Haakon's court in 1261 we are told they fail to impress him with their honeyed speech. They make matters worse by trying to leave without permission, and are held in Norway that winter. Letters from Henry III of England show that he tried to intervene on their behalf and to negotiate between Norway and Scotland.[23]

A showdown was inevitable, and in 1262 there was Scots violence in the Isles. Alexander, who had recently attained his majority, was ready to invade. In 1263 Haakon decided to go in person to assert his authority. At this time he was at the height of his powers, the sole ruler of a country in which he had ensured there would no longer be a divided monarchy. He had even persuaded most of the independent Icelandic chieftains to submit to his authority in 1262, and it was perhaps his waiting for word from the Icelandic Parliament held in late June concerning the others (who submitted that year or the following) that prevented him from leaving Bergen until July 5, somewhat late in the year for a major expedition. He took a great fleet with him, that sailed first to the Northern Isles, and then to the Western Isles, where he was joined by Magnus, king of Man, Duggáll or Dufgall, king of the Sumarliöi line (called Eireksson in the saga, but in fact the son of Ruairidh). Alexander's army was in the Isles and the usual depredations of the locals were made by both parties. They met at Largs on October 2, and there was a skirmish from which the Norwegians retreated. The next day they suffered from a storm. Haakon felt in no way defeated. Shortly before, the saga tells us, emissaries had come to him from Ireland, asking him for aid against the English. Haakon had sent a Hebridean follower to gain further information. He now wished to turn his attention to Ireland. To have done so would have broken his long-standing friendship with Henry III of England, but it may still have been an old ambition. Forty years previously, just after Haakon had written to Henry offering friendship, Henry's sister, Queen Johanna of Scotland, had written to warn him of a rumour that Haakon would come to Ireland to assist the rebellion of Hugh de Lacy.[24]

In all events Haakon was persuaded to retreat to Orkney for the winter, and here he took sick and died on 15 December. From Scots documents it is clear that the writers considered the victory to be Scots, but the Norwegians considered it to be theirs. The writer of the *Chronicle of Man* thought that Haakon had achieved nothing, while the *Annals of Ulster* record merely that Haakon died on his way to Ireland.

Certainly there was no peace as a result, but harrying on both sides. But the new Norwegian king, Magnus, was willing to negotiate, and ambassadors passed between the two monarchs. Matters were simplified by the death of the warlike King Magnus of Man in 1265, and the following year the Treaty of Perth was concluded. This treaty gave Alexander the Western Isles and Man, but not the Northern Isles. The bishopric remained under the archdiocese of Trondheim, as it had been since 1152, but Alexander was given rights in the election of the bishop, a right he exercised in 1275. In return, Scotland was to pay to Norway 4,000 marks sterling within four years, and then 100 marks sterling a year in perpetuity. The 4,000 marks were paid with considerable delay, but little of the rest ever found its way to Norway, in spite of attempts by its later kings to get the treaty honoured. Superficially the sum seems enormous, but the position of the Western Isles, controlling Scandinavian trade to the North Sea area, may have made the price seem reasonable at the time to both parties. But changes in trading patterns in the Northern world may have later lowered their value. Furthermore, the Scots were to have little more success than the Norwegians in controlling the Isles.

All but one Hebridean leader, Duggáll mac Ruairidh, submitted to Alexander and no longer used the title of king. Duggáll died in 1268, and his son Eric took advantage of a clause in the Treaty of Perth, and left for Norway.[25] The leaders of the Isles proved loyal to Alexander in 1275, when an attempt was made to re-establish the kingdom of Man, and they were in fact used to suppress it.

Sturla Thorðarson's saga on Magnus Lawmender, probably written in about 1275, is the last of the sagas on the Norwegian kings, and survives only in two fragments, one of which contains a record of events leading up to the Treaty of Perth. With the loss of the Western Isles from the Norse world we have to rely on the odd reference in Icelandic annals to understand political contact between Scotland and Scandinavia. These are scrappy and do nothing to replace the full-blooded accounts of the saga-writers.

III

The sagas have little to say on the religious history of the Isles. A few bishops are referred to, as they are in the annals, but there is nothing on the setting up of the metropolitan at Trondheim in 1152, or on the difficulties of running the diocese from such a distance. It is in the other sources that we hear most of the problems caused by turbulence in the Isles, and by the difficulties of travel, which were considerable but nothing in comparison with the journey to Greenland, which was also subject to Trondheim.

The Hebrideans differed notably from the inhabitants of Orkney and Shetland in their attitude to saints. The latter, like the people of Scandinavia, acted as new converts to Christianity in need of local saints. In about 1117 they acquired a suitable candidate in Earl Magnus, whose cult became a popular one. It is notable that the accounts of pilgrims who visited his shrine contain scarcely a reference to Hebrideans among their number. This may be evidence that the Norse in the Hebrides had mingled more fully with their neighbours, and had more readily adopted Christianity and the visitation of local shrines.

IV

We know a little more about the economic life of the kingdom. References to ship-wrecks are one reminder that the passage through the Western Isles was a well-used, if dangerous, pathway to the Irish Sea, with its busy ports of Bristol, Chester, and

Dublin with its Norse community. Dublin had close contacts with the Isle of Man during the eleventh and early twelfth centuries, and there was also trade between England and Ireland. After the Norman invasion of Ireland the English kings went to great lengths to protect shipping and military interests in the Irish Sea. There seems to have been trade from Norway even in the early twelfth century. The Englishman Ordericus Vitalis, writing in the 1120s, speaks of the wealth of Norway which is brought from all over the world. Norway itself teems with fish, birds and the flesh of wild beasts.[26] Ordericus's contemporary, William of Malmesbury, indicates that fish may have been an item of trade. Writing on the call to the First Crusade in 1095 he says: 'The Welshman left his hunting; the Scot his fellowship with fleas; the Dane his continual drinking; the Norwegian his raw fish'.[27]

We also have a number of references to shipwrecks, and we know that treaties were drawn up to protect shipwrecked persons from slaughter by the locals, though these were not always believed to be enforced. In 1258 the Icelandic ship *Grobuzán* was lost at sea, but legend had it that she was wrecked on the coast of Scotland and the men and women aboard slain.[28] Taking the benefit of shipwrecks may have aided the economy of the Isles. And in addition there was straightforward piracy.

Orkneyinga saga gives an account of trade on the east coast of Scotland, said to take place in the 1120s. A young Norwegian named Kali travels in the company of other traders and with a good cargo to Grimsby in England. Many others had come there too, from the Orkneys, from Scotland and from the kingdom of the Isles. Here Kali meets Harald *gilli*, the supposed son of Magnus Barelegs, who is assured by Kali that he will be welcomed if he comes to Norway. We do not know what the Norse sold, but they may have bought cloth in England — on his return to Norway Kali gets the reputation of a dressy man, while the tale of Sveinn Ásleifarson's capture of English ships in 1171 specifically mentions fine cloth as an item looted by him. It is also referred to in a speech attributed to King Sverrir of Norway (1177-1202) on the evils of drink. *Sverris saga* is practically contemporary and was composed by people who knew him well. Sverrir begins by thanking traders from various lands: the English, who bring wheat and honey, flour and clothing; and all those who bring linen and flax, wax and kettles. He then refers to traders from Orkney, Shetland, the Faeroes and Iceland, and all those who bring to Norway necessary goods that improve life there. Unfortunately he does not state what they bring. He then goes on to condemn the Germans with their big ships, destructive trading practices and importing of drink.[29] Perhaps there was trade too with the Western Isles and Man though it is not mentioned here, nor in the Norwegian laws of 1276.

We know little else directly of trade. The Icelandic annals record that the Black Death of 1349 affected Shetland, Orkney, the Faeroes and the Western Isles,[30] news that may have come by trade, by chance travel or through the contacts between the bishopric and Trondheim, which remained the metropolitan for both Northern and Western Isles until 1472.

Not all travel was for trade, nor all visits to the Isles intentional. The saga of the Icelandic Bishop Guðmund Árason preserved in Sturla Thorðarson's compilation *Sturlunga saga*, was written in Guðmund's lifetime or shortly afterwards by one Lambkar, who knew him well, but was not with him on the voyage he made with certain traders to Norway in 1202 for his consecration as bishop of Hólar in northern Iceland. The journey was begun in the autumn, and it was not long before the travellers were blown off course. They sighted the Hebrides but did not come to land until they were driven to 'those islands which are called Hirtir', or Saint Kilda, forty miles to the west of North Uist. Here they heard that King Sverrir was dead — proof that this remote Hebridean community had some contact with the Norse world, and perhaps an indication that the language of communication was Norse, though Latin or sign language would have done as well. When they leave, the voyagers are storm-driven again, this time south of Ireland. They are in extremes when they hear the waves breaking on all sides, Guðmund tells them all to confess their sins and the clerics to shave their tonsures. Then they make an oath to give an ell from every sack of wadmal (woollen cloth) on board and to send a man to Rome and give half a mark of wax for each person on board to the church. The weather improves and they sail to Norway.[31] In a later version the storm-driven travellers see Saint Kilda but do not land, and are then, as in the earlier version, driven south of Ireland, where they make their oath. They are then blown back north to Scotland in the improved weather and finally sail into good harbour at Sandey, probably the Sandey which, with Canna, makes a large natural harbour.[32] When Guðmund goes ashore he meets King Óláf of the Isles, who invites him to a meal.[33] A still later version of the tale adds that on coming ashore the Icelanders are met by the king's bailiff, who demands landing tax of 120 ells of wadmal for each of the 20 Icelanders aboard, in accordance with the law of the Isles. The Icelanders do not wish to pay it as they will have to part with the same amount again in Norway. Trouble is averted for a while when King Óláf invites Guðmund to dine with him, but when he is ready to leave the king tells the bishop-elect to fulfil his obligations or he will keep him there. A fight is only just averted and a settlement is reached by which the Icelanders pay six *hundraðs* of wadmal, about 360 yards, instead of the 1,200 demanded.[34] Presumably the Hebrideans intended the wadmal for re-export, as they would have produced it themselves, as indeed would the Norwegians. Wadmal lengths were themselves recognised as units of value, which reflects the importance of this product for northern trade.

The Icelanders needed no interpreters in the Hebrides. While Gaelic must have been the dominant language in the Isles by the thirteenth century, the leaders of society at least must also have spoken fluent Norse. None of the Hebridean chiefs and kings who visited Norway is said, like Harald *gilli* in Snorri's account, to have had language difficulties. The Western Isles were visited in 1258 by the Icelander Gizurr Thorðarson, who had been given the title of earl in Norway and sent home to persuade his fellow countrymen to submit to Norwegian rule. He not only wintered in the Isles, but also spent the summer there, an indication that his stay was voluntary and not determined by the weather. As in Norway, Gizurr must have spoken Norse with his hosts. Five years later when King Haakon heard that the Irish would welcome his presence in their country, he sent a Hebridean, who was surely bilingual, to gain further information. The Icelandic authors knew that in their own time the same language was spoken in the Western Isles and Ireland, and they believed, perhaps erroneously, that the same had been true in the Viking age.

V

We hear little of the kingdom of the Isles after 1263 from the Icelanders. Ship-wrecks still occurred and traders were robbed, as was an Icelandic ship in 1332,[35] but most of the sparse references that occur are to political events in mainland Scotland. In the Western Isles life may not have changed too dramatically, though the Isles became increasingly Gaelicised and contacts with Man diminished. The Western Isles supplied mercenary soldiers to Ireland as late as the 1590s, but concerning other ways of life there are few records. The Norse sagas tell us a little about daily life before 1263 only: that there was farming and fighting, a limited trade and a widespread use of shipping. But about the culture, the loss of the Norse language, and the breaking of ties with Norway, they give us no account. Their interest was in the Norse kingdom, and with the loss of that kingdom to Scotland and the decline in saga-writing, the Isles sank into the mists, to be sighted only occasionally by some storm-driven voyager.

Acknowledgement

My thanks are due to Anne Johnston for numerous helpful comments on the text of this paper, and for her assistance with preparing the footnotes.

NOTES

1. Finnbogi Guðmundsson, ed., *Orkneyinga saga* (Íslenzk fornrit, xxxiv, Reykjavik, 1965) (hereafter *Orkneyinga saga*); Alexander B Taylor, trans., *The Orkneyinga Saga* (Edinburgh and London, 1938). Some of the relevant material from this and other Norse works can be found in Alan Orr Anderson, *Early Sources of Scottish History, AD 500 to 1286* (2 vols, Edinburgh, 1922).
2. P A Munch, ed., *Chronica Regum Manniae et Insularum* (Christiania/Oslo, 1860). A more accessible edition is P A Munch, ed., and Rev. D Goss, trans., *Chronicum Regum Manniae et Insularum: The Chronicle of Man and the Sudreys* (Manx Society, vols xxii-iii, Douglas, 1874).
3. *Orkneyinga saga*, 109, names Holdboði, 'a truthful farmer from the Isles', as the source for the account of the death of Magnus.
4. Finnur Jónsson, ed., *Morkinskinna* (Samfund til udgivelse af gammel nordisk litteratur, vol. 53, Copenhagen, 1932).
5. Snorri Sturluson, *Heimskringla*,ed. Bjarni Aðalbjarnarson (Íslenzk fornrit, vols xxvi-viii, Reykjavik, 1941-51), iii, 219-21.
6. *Heimskringla*, iii, 229.
7. See 'Magnússona saga' and 'Magnúss saga blinda ok Haralds gilla', in *Heimskringla*, iii, 265-302.
8. *Heimskringla*, iii, 267-8.
9. There is a Gaelic tradition that a woman of the Sumarliði family of the Hebrides married a King Harald of Norway at about this time. See David Sellar, 'The origins and ancestry of Somerled', *Scottish Historical Review*, xlv (1966), 129-30.
10. *Orkneyinga saga*, 239-40; *Heimskringla*, iii, 327-30.
11. *Orkneyinga saga*, 150-289. The story of Sveinn is interwoven with numerous other events and is used by the author to help to hold the saga together.

12. In C R Unger, ed., *Konunga Sögur: Sagaer om Sverre og hans efterfølgere* (Christiania/Oslo, 1873). It is also printed, as *Hákonar saga gamla*, in Guðni Jónsson, ed., *Konunga sögur* (3 vols, Reykjavik, 1957), iii, 1-463, where the reference to kings of the Sumarliði line is on p.190.

13. A B Scott and F X Martin, eds, *Expugnatio Hibernica: The Conquest of Ireland* (Dublin, 1978), 76-9.

14. *Sverris saga* in Unger, *Konunga Sögur*, and Jónsson, *Konunga sögur*, ii, 1-342; the reference is p.140.

15. Jónsson, *Konunga sögur*, 232-3. It is on this occasion that Sverrir takes the Shetlands from the earls of Orkney.

16. Jónsson, *Konunga sögur*, ii, 388-9; Icelandic annals for 1209-10, in Gustav Storm, ed., *Islandske Annaler indtil 1578* (Christiania/Oslo, 1888).

17. *Heimskringla*, iii, 367.

18. *Orkneyinga saga*, 293.

19. C A Lange and others, eds, *Diplomatarium Norvegicum* (21 vols, Christiania/Oslo, 1849-1976) (herafter *Diplom. Norv.*), vol. 19 (1900), nos. 84 (1205), 87-9 (1206), 90 (1207), 93-7 (1212), 115-18 (1218), 123-8 (1219), 129 (1220), 131-2 (1220), 145 (1223), 168 (1225), 178-9 (1226), 185 (1227), 188 (1228), 216-17 (1235), 220-1 (1235), 223-4 (1236), 238 (1246), 247 (1248), 262-3 (1255), 265-6 (1256), 270 (1259). Vols 19 and 20 (part one) (ed. Alexander Bugge) contain records of Norway's relations with the 'British Isles' in the middle ages.

20. Jónsson, *Konunga sögur*, iii, 189-95; see too Goss, *Chronicle of Man*, 92-3.

21. Jónsson, *Konunga sögur*, iii, 339-42; see too Goss, *Chronicle of Man*, 94-101.

22. Jónsson, *Konunga sögur*, iii, 199.

23. *Diplom. Norv.*, vol.19, nos. 271-3 (1262-3).

24. *Diplom. Norv.*, vol.19, no. 153 (1223-4) for the offer of friendship; no. 157 (March 1224?) for the rumour. No.167 (1224-5) mentions gifts sent to Henry by Haakon.

25. David Sellar, 'The Western Isles c.1095-1286', in Peter McNeill and Ranald Nicholson, eds, *Historical Atlas of Scotland c.400-c.1600* (St Andrews, 1975), 52.

26. Marjorie Chibnall, ed., *Ecclesiastical History of Ordericus Vitalis* (6 vols, Oxford, 1969-80), v, 218.

27. William Stubbs, ed., *Willelmi Malmesburiensis Monachi de Gestis Regum Anglorum* (Rolls Series 90, 2 vols, London, 1887-9), ii, 399.

28. Jón Jóhannesson, Magnús Finnbogason and Kristján Eldjárn, eds, *Sturlunga saga* (2 vols, Reykjavik, 1946), i, 523. Laws were passed and treaties made in attempts to stop such activities. See *Diplom. Norv.*, vol.19, nos.51 (before 1170), 63 (1185-8 original of 1182). In 1227 a ship was robbed by the English, and those aboard, including a Norwegian bishop-elect, were slain. See vol.19, nos. 186 (1227) and 188 (1228).

29. Jónsson, *Konunga sögur*, ii, 193.

30. The Western Isles are mentioned together with Shetland, Orkney and the Faeroes. See Storm, *Islandske Annaler*, under 1349.

31. *Sturlunga saga*, i, 159.

32. This identification was made by Ian Fisher.

33. Hið Íslenzka Bókmenntafélag (publisher), Jón Sigurðsson *et al.*, eds, *Biskupa sögur* (2 vols, Copenhagen, 1858-78), i, 483-5. The texts are reprinted in Guðni Jónsson, ed., *Byskupa sögur* (3 vols, Reykjavik, 1948); the episode is in vol. ii, pp.274-7. This account is followed in a later version: *Biskupa sögur*, ii, 48-51; Jónsson, *Byskupa sögur*, iii, 228-32.

34. *Byskupa sögur*, ii, 562-4; Jónsson, *Byskupa sögur*, ii, 397-402. (The visit is not mentioned in this account.) For a further discussion of the episodes see A B Taylor, 'The Norsemen in St Kilda', *Saga-Book of the Viking Society*, xvii (1966-9), 116-44, esp. pp.120-3. The 'hundrað' I have assumed to be a unit of 120. The ell is calculated at 47.4 cm, that is, approximately half a yard.

35. Storm, *Islandske Annaler*, under 1332, and incorrectly in *Flateyjar-annáll*, under 1334.

3

SHETLAND, SCANDINAVIA, SCOTLAND, 1300-1700: THE CHANGING NATURE OF CONTACT

Brian Smith

> Stranger and visitor, she has learnt to live with things.
> William Trevor, *The News from Ireland* (1986)

During the sixteenth and seventeenth centuries Shetland's contacts with her overseas neighbours changed fundamentally. Her relationship with Scandinavia became increasingly tenuous after the impignoration of royal rights in the islands to Scotland in 1469, and her relationship with Scotland, formerly non-existent, grew correspondingly closer. So much is well-known. Everyone knows, also, that the pre-1469 period in Shetland was a Golden Age. In the popular account Shetland was either a passive recipient of 'influences' from Norway, or was, equally passively, ground under Scotland's heel.

This interpretation is barren. Shetland had an economy, a local government and other local institutions *of her own*. Administrators, landowners and traders came to Shetland from other countries from time to time, but these visitors had to come to terms with Shetland, and if they lived and operated there Shetland society moulded them as much as they moulded Shetland. To suggest that Shetland society in 1300 or 1700 was a replica of Norwegian or Scottish society at the same time is nonsense.

The main difficulty in telling this story is the lack of documentary evidence. The first Shetland documents, documents written in the islands by Shetlanders, date from 1299 and 1307. There are only two dozen references to Shetland in the Orkneyinga Saga, most of them trivial. As a result, we know next to nothing about Shetland in the high middle ages, when Shetland was quintessentially Norse, and most of what we know has been deduced from highly technical place-name and archaeological material during the last hundred years.

It was not until the nineteenth century that enthusiasm for things Norse began to sweep through Shetland. Just as Norwegian historians of that period, irked by the union with Sweden, idealised the independent Norway of the middle ages, Shetland antiquarians, confronted with the squalid details of local landlordism, looked back to the quite unrecorded Shetland of the twelfth century.[1] Some Shetlanders regarded the lack of evidence as a virtue. 'During all that long period', wrote Charles Rampini in 1884, 'Shetland had literally no history . . . Yet we have one consolation. Happy is the land that has no history'.[2]

What I have to say will be, I hope, an antidote to such obscurantism. I want to look at concrete institutions and relationships, in Shetland and between Shetland, Scandinavia and Scotland, during specific periods. To be precise, I want to look at administration, landownership and trade in the islands, between 1300 and 1469, 1469 and 1611 and 1611 and 1700, always with the local society in the forefront of the picture.

I

My starting point, then, is Shetland at the beginning of the fourteenth century: a small country, a distant appanage of Norway; 550 square miles of rather poor land, with about 700 farms, compared with 35,000 or so in Norway; with a population of, perhaps, 10,000 (although all such estimates are more or less inspired guesswork).

As I said, the first Shetland documents date from the period around 1300. Few as they are, they throw a great deal of light on the Shetland administrative system of that period. A century previously King Sverre had removed Shetland from the earl of Orkney's control, and from that date onwards local governors, later called fouds, collected the kings' fines and taxes in the islands.[3]

At the beginning of our period the governor of Shetland was Thorvald Thoressøn, lord of the island of Papa Stour, representative of Duke Haakon Magnussøn in the islands. Some events occurred in Papa Stour in Passion Week in the year 1299 which show the extent of Thorvald's power in Shetland, and the checks on it. On Monday of that week a woman in the island, Ragnhild Simunsdatter, accused Thorvald to his face of cheating the duke. She did so in front of two witnesses from the Shetland Mainland, in Thorvald's own living room. She repeated her allegations the following day in a field adjacent to Thorvald's house, this time before a priest. 'Thou shalt not be my Judas', Ragnhild warned Thorvald, 'though thou be Judas to the duke'.[4] Although we do not know precisely who Ragnhild was, it is clear that she was not afraid to speak her mind. Nor did Thorvald feel able to deal with her allegations peremptorily. He called the onlookers as witnesses to Ragnhild's words, and in due course brought the case to the lawthing or head court of the islands.

Eight years later we find him at odds with another woman, and on this occasion we can see the machinery of the Shetland legal system at work even more clearly. On the Friday of Whitsuntide week in 1307 Thorvald and Bjorg, the mistress of the house of Cullivoe in the island of Yell, came to the lawthing to plead their cases concerning a point at issue between them. In charge of the proceedings were the lawmen of Shetland, Hauk and Ivar, with their parochial representatives, the lawrightmen; also in attendance were the king's representatives, later simply called underfouds. Bjorg seems to have been in the wrong, but when Thorvald tried to argue that she should pay her fine in coinage of high quality the lawmen 'advised that for leniency's sake' he should not persist with his stringent claim.[5]

These local deliberations are not without general significance. They remind me of the recent virulent debates, among Norwegian historians, about the Norwegian crown and its function in Norse society. Was the crown simply parasitic on that society, in league with the nobility and the church to extract taxation, rent, tithes, and fines from the people? Or was it, as the veteran historian Andreas Holmsen has come around to thinking, a much more complex and relatively autonomous institution, let down on occasion by its local representatives?[6] There seems to me to be nothing very controversial in the second formulation, and it fits the Shetland situation well. The Shetland lawthing, in inspiration at least, existed to administer justice, to protect the interests of the poor and defenceless as well as powerful men like Thorvald Thoressøn. As a British historian has remarked, about an entirely different (but equally patrician) society:

> the essential precondition for the effectiveness of law, in its function as ideology, is that it shall display an independence from gross manipulation and shall seem to be just. It cannot seem to be so without upholding its own logic and criteria of equity; indeed, on occasion, by actually *being* just . . . Even rulers find a need to legitimize their power, to moralize their functions, to feel themselves to be useful and just.[7]

Good or bad, the Norwegian crown representatives in Shetland, and later those of the Scottish crown, had to come to terms with the local legal system.

I turn now to landownership, the second main area where foreigners made themselves felt in Shetland. Here we have to confront the myth that property in Shetland in the pre-1469 period was largely in the possession of small peasant proprietors, holding land in udal tenure or absolute ownership. As in Norway itself there is no doubt that many Shetlanders were tenants. It is difficult in the absence of rentals to estimate the size of the Norwegian crown estates in the islands. In any case the question is theoretical, because it is likely that Thorvald Thoressøn's descendants and their relatives gradually took full possession of any royal estates they had in lease. Meanwhile, they were making their own acquisitions of land in Shetland: we have records of three separate purchases of land, in widely separate parts of Shetland, by Thorvald's daughter Herdis in the 1350s, probably in the midst of the chaos following the Black Death.[8] By the mid-fifteenth century this Shetland estate was bigger than any other estate in the islands, and dwarfed the royal estates there.

There is no evidence, however, that the 'Lords of Norway' (as the Shetlanders later called them) wielded extensive lordly power over the Shetlanders. Herdis Thorvaldsdatter certainly lived in Shetland, but Jon and Sigurd Haftorssøn, to whom her estates passed after her death, lived in Norway, as did their descendants. After all, these lords were the cream of the Norwegian nobility, and their attention was fully occupied in Scandinavia. No doubt the Lords of Norway employed bailiffs in Shetland, and likely some of them were rapacious, but there is little sign in Shetland of big manorial farms: the only clear example is Papa Stour itself, with only a handful of other possibilities. Herdis Thorvaldsdatter amassed a great deal of land in Shetland, but most of her acquisitions were tiny parts of townships; and when we first have detailed descriptions of the Norwegian estates in Shetland, in the sixteenth century, it is the fragments which stand out.[9] Nothing could have been more discouraging to magnates — people, I repeat, who had far more fertile and extensive estates, and lucrative political offices, elsewhere — than fragmentary and ill-favoured lands like those in Shetland.

The same is true, to an even greater extent, of another Norwegian landowner in Shetland, the Munkalif cloister in Bergen. Many of the monastery's acquisitions in the islands were made as late as the fifteenth century, and they were without exception fragments of farms rather than whole townships.[10] The church itself had minute estates in Shetland, in striking contrast to its huge possessions in Norway and Orkney.[11] In other words, the Norwegian landowners were fitting into the Shetland landholding system: they were not dominating it or modifying it.

The only likely exceptions to this rule are the fouds of Shetland, who were more or less permanent fixtures in the islands, perhaps founding dynasties: I have no doubt that they formed large estates, as their counterparts did in Shetland in the sixteenth century.

Finally, trade. Here we are almost completely in the dark about the relationship between the two countries. We have to proceed by inference. Shetland's main export commodity was fish, and the destination of Shetland and Norwegian fish in the late middle ages was of course the Hansa, channelled as they were through the *kontor* at Bergen.[12] The question is: how was this trade organised at the Shetland end? Thomas Gifford, a reliable Shetland informant, writing in the early 1730s, provides a clue. Prior to 1469, he says, the people of Shetland

> were miserably oppressed by the . . . Fowd, and kept under, being
> forbidden all sort of commerce with foreigners . . . so there was no such
> thing as money among them; and what they had of the country product
> more than paid the crown rent, they were obliged to bring to the
> governor, who gave them for it such necessaries as they could not be
> without, and at what prices he had a mind, wherewith they were obliged
> to rest content, having no way to be redressed. Kept under this slavery,
> they were miserably poor, careless, and indolent.[13]

There is not a trace of sentimentality in Gifford's account of Shetland's Scandinavian past: the contrast with the nineteenth century antiquarians could not be more marked. There is no good reason to reject his reconstruction out of hand. Knowing what we do about the power which the fouds wielded, their administrative and judicial power, tax and rent collecting power, and their status as major landowners in the islands, the rôle which Gifford assigns to them is perfectly believable. The type of commercial organisation Gifford describes was not unlike the arrangement which he and his fellow landowners themselves practised in Shetland, and his Faroese contemporaries would have recognised it immediately. Once again the foud of Shetland was at the centre of things: not a foreign interloper but a local magnate, 'forbid[ding] all sort of commerce with foreigners'.

II

For the Shetland antiquarians of the late nineteenth century there was little or no difference between the high and the late middle ages. There was no awareness of the depressions of the later period, the collapse of the European economies in the fourteenth and fifteenth centuries, even the Black Death. For them everything was political, and everything before 1469 was a golden age. 1469 was the only date that mattered, the moment which inaugurated 'the ruin of the native race', as Gilbert

Goudie put it in 1887.[14] There have been attempts since then to look at the 1469 impignoration in more detail, mainly from the point of view of international diplomacy and law.[15] I shall not go over that ground again here. But I do want to look at the results of the impignoration in Shetland society.

At the level of administration there were relatively rapid changes in personnel, more so than has sometimes been realised. Gilbert Goudie, arguing that Shetland administrators and officials continued to write documents in Norse until the beginning of the seventeenth century, published a long paper on the subject, illustrated by 18 Norse documents.[16] Historians since Goudie's time have tended to cite this article rather uncritically. The fact is that 13 of Goudie's documents were written in Norway and two in Denmark. Only one of the post-1469 documents, dated 1545, can be said with certainty to have been written in Shetland.

Scots professional men came into Shetland in large numbers after the impignoration, and the lexicon of administration and to some extent law (and of course religion) became Scots rapidly. What we have to consider, however, is the substance in that change. In the field of conveyancing the new Scots lawyers deliberately introduced Norse, or rather local Shetland words and phrases, into their deeds. In particular, they invariably incorporated the key concepts of udal landholding: on one occasion, as late as 1595, a notary even inserted a udal term which he had omitted, as an addition for the parties to sign in the margin.[17]

More important for our purpose, there is impressive evidence that the Shetlanders' expectations and suspicions concerning local administration remained static. Almost exactly a century after 1469 a particularly rapacious foud, Laurence Bruce of Cultmalindie, took up office in Shetland. There is no space here to discuss Bruce's sins in detail; the important thing to consider is the Shetlanders' remarks about his administration, which were transcribed by two commissioners appointed by the Regent Morton to investigate complaints in February 1577.

> The hail comownis and inhabitantis of Yetland [they said] hes beine in tymes bygane, as thai ar instantly, grevuslye rubbit, oppressit and spoliat of their gudis and substance, be sic men as hes borne and beiris authoritie and offices above thame, sic as chalmerlanis, fowdis, under fowdis, officiaris and utheris prevat personis . . . pairtlie throw wrangus . . . messur . . . of their dewities . . . [and] pairtlie be wrangus and negligent ministratioun of justice.[18]

Note that there is not a word here, or elsewhere in the document, about Scots administrators. In fact many of the 1577 complainants were themselves Scots, and the 'leader of the patriots', as Gilbert Goudie put it,[19] was called Arthur Sinclair. The problem for the Shetlanders was *private persons*, people who made decisions and rules behind closed doors, people who used 'wrong' laws and 'wrong' weights and measures. Far from distrusting the king of Scotland as a foreign interloper the Shetlanders regarded him and his servants in precisely the same way that they regarded any king. They implored the regent and nobility, 'for Goddis saik, and the zeil thai beir to justice, according to the dewitie of thair commissioun under God', to send commissioners to the islands every four or five years, to prevent further abuses. For the Shetlanders the problem of oppression was a problem of human nature, unaffected by mere changes in personnel.

This Shetland system of local government was tenacious. As late as the early seventeenth century Earl Patrick Stewart, the tyrannical Scotsman of twentieth-century guidebooks, was still presiding over it. Take the case of Henry Wardlaw, a servant of a local landowner, who fell foul of Patrick in 1602: there is ample evidence, from Wardlaw's own account, that Patrick failed to persuade the Shetland courts and juries to punish him (on a charge which may or may not have been trumped up).[20] In 1602, again, the Shetland lawthing consulted the old Shetland lawbook in a murder case, thus disposing of the myth that Earl Patrick had personally consigned it to the flames and introduced a Scots alternative.[21] There were, indeed, changes: there is no sign of a local lawman after the 1530s, for instance, and I suspect that the lawrightmen played a less important part in Shetland society from the 1570s onwards, and the underfouds played a more active one.[22] On the other hand, Earl Patrick was still playing much the same role in Shetland that Thorvald Thoressøn had played 300 years previously: unable to act utterly arbitrarily, using the local law book whether he liked it or not.

Another traditional belief about 1469 and its alleged results is that Scotsmen immediately acquired large amounts of land in the islands. Once again the reality is far more complicated. As we have seen, the biggest estate by far in the islands in 1469 belonged to the 'Lords of Norway'. Twenty years afterwards, following the death of Hans Sigurdssøn without heirs, that estate was split into three.[23] The resultant thirds were given the names of three Shetland islands which were prominent parts of the original estate: Papa Goods, Vaila Goods and Noss Goods. I suspect, without detailed proof, that each of these thirds was still a pre-eminently large Shetland estate.

If Scots immigrants wished to acquire large amounts of land in Shetland, there were not many opportunities to acquire extensive feus of crown or church lands, since (as I have pointed out) the royal and ecclesiastical estates were very meagre. The main plums in Shetland were the Norwegian estates, and, not surprisingly, there was competition for leases of them. In the 1580s, for instance, Earl Robert Stewart adjudicated in a dispute between Andrew Hawick of Scatsta and Robert Cheyne of Ure, concerning a lease of Vaila Goods.[24] Although the Hawicks had long been associated with the estate — Andrew's father, Vincentius, had been collecting the rents for the proprietor, Gorvel Fadersdatter, in 1563[25] — Robert Cheyne produced a letter of tack by the king of Denmark (to whom Gorvel had given the estate in a transaction of 1582), along with a confirmation by the king of Scotland. As far as we can tell, there was no successful misappropriation of lands here: quite the reverse. The kings of Scotland and Denmark, Earl Robert and the local law courts were co-operating to protect landowner and lessee, and perhaps to prevent an international incident.

There are other examples of the same scrupulousness. In 1561 a Shetland law court adjudicated in a case concerning a disputed lease of Noss Goods, carefully perusing an assedation of the lands by the owner, Erik Ottessøn Rosenkrantz.[26] Five years later Mary, queen of Scots, wrote to Jens Spliid, the then proprietor of Papa Goods, and son-in-law of the famous Inger of Austraat in Norway (the eponymous hero of a play by Ibsen). Mary was acting on behalf of Ursula Tulloch and Andrew

Mouat, daughter and son-in-law of William Tulloch, who had been tenant of the estate since the 1540s, and implored Spliid to continue the lease in their favour. Once again Robert Cheyne was in the wings, anxious to secure the lease, but on this earlier occasion, thanks presumably to the queen's intervention, he was unsuccessful.[27]

We can see a variety of Scotsmen at work in these transactions. All of them were interested in acquiring land. The question is: were their attempts kept in check by the local administration? There is every indication that they were. I have no doubt that the local fouds, as always, were building up large personal eatates. David Sinclair of Sumburgh, Thorvald Henderson of Brough, Edward Sinclair of Strom and Olla Sinclair of Broo are four good examples, spanning the period from the 1480s to the 1570s.[28] But despite Olla Sinclair's Scottish surname, and despite his lands, the Shetlanders who complained against Laurence Bruce in 1577 looked back to 'Olla Sinclair's time' as a halcyon era.[29] The question is: were Scotsmen increasingly riding roughshod over the Shetlanders and their institutions? No, they were not. In the second half of the sixteenth century the Shetlanders were still capable of looking after themselves, something they had had to do before 1469 as well.

As far as trade is concerned, there were major changes during the fifteenth century, especially after 1469, changes which sharply curtailed Shetland's contacts with Norway. They were changes for the better. Previously, as I have shown, Shetland fish had been channelled through Bergen as part of the Hanseatic economic system, probably with the active involvement of the Shetland foud. By the early fifteenth century merchants in North Germany were already ignoring this system, much to the impotent rage of the Bergen merchants. After 1469 the Danish kings lost political control over the Shetland trade, and brotherhoods of merchants from Hamburg and Bremen began to sail directly to Shetland in flocks.[30]

These events were crucial for Shetland society. First, the relationship between administration and trade in the islands changed radically. In the 1550s and 1560s Olla Sinclair paid a great deal of attention to the local trade with German merchants. Now, however, trader and administrator had completely different aims. Sinclair's avowed intention was to ensure that the visiting merchants were spread evenly throughout the islands, so that all communities in Shetland could have access to them.[31] With other Shetlanders he set the prices for import and export goods at the beginning of each season, and inspected the Germans' weighing equipment.[32] In the early seventeenth century Earl Patrick Stewart was still using local courts to regulate the Germans: banishing an unfortunate Hamburg merchant from Northmavine to Papa Stour on one occasion, and threatening the Germans with dire penalties if they used false weights and measures.[33]

There was a rupture in communications between Shetland and Norway, but it was not a complete rupture. In the second half of the sixteenth century several Shetlanders, some with local surnames, some with Scots names, most of them from the North Isles of Shetland, began to fit out their *own* boats, to travel from Bergen and its environs to get timber. They took home boat kits and on occasion even house kits (called stockstoves in Shetland),[34] presumably in return for the money brought to Shetland by the German merchants. Here I have to take issue with Dr Hance Smith, author of a massive work on Shetland trade: Dr Smith argues that the Norway trade of the sixteenth century was organised and carried out by big Shetland landowners.[35] My strong impression is that there is a distinctively plebeian flavour about the trade, organised as it was by people like John of Windhouse, the Nisbets of Kirkabister and David Sanderson Scott of Reafirth, all in Yell.[36]

All this activity has to be seen in the light of the upturn in economic life and prosperity in Europe in the late sixteenth century. Shetland in that period became a society characterised by intense entrepreneurial activity in a small way. Thanks to the activities of the Germans there was no local merchant class, but, paradoxically, everyone in his or her own way became a merchant. One small but striking proof of this is the sudden appearance on Shetland documents of what were called 'merchant usit marks': authenticating marks which were sometimes incorporated into paper seals. The people who affected these marks were not the type of person who normally used such marks in towns and cities. They were native small landowners and tenants.[37] There is no sign of any such affectation in Orkney, a pre-eminently agrarian society: in Orkney seals of any kind were few and far between, owned by big landowners and jealously preserved by their owners.[38] Orkney was a patrician, Shetland a plebeian society.

When I look at Shetland society a hundred years after 1469, I do not see 'the ruin of the native race', as Goudie put it. I see a flourishing society with a vigorous local government, with a trilingual population, full of fructifying influences from Scotland, Norway and Germany. If I did not dislike the phrase so intensely I might refer to the late sixteenth century as a Golden Age in Shetland history.

III

In 1700 Shetland did not have a grassroots local government or a vigorous plebeian culture. What had happened?

I have argued throughout this paper that the health of local administration in Shetland is a touchstone for the vigour of the society. In 1611, thanks to disorders in Orkney, the Scottish Privy Council abolished 'foreign laws' in the Northern Isles.[39] As a result, the system of local government over which Thorvald Thoressøn and Patrick Stewart had presided was dismantled. The bishop of Orkney convened Sheriff Courts in Shetland in 1612 which differed not merely in terminology but also in substance from the courts held there only a few years previously. Nothing more was heard of the local lawbook or the lawthing. Bishop Law swept away the local testamentary arrangements, and his apparatchik Harry Aitkin arrived on the scene with a commissary court book.[40]

Bishop Law and his successors as stewarts principal and crown chamberlains in Shetland were Scotsmen. More important, however, there was now a self-confident class of local landowners in Shetland, men who had been Earl Patrick's opponents. All these men had Scottish surnames; many, on the other hand, were members of families who had been in Shetland for at least a century. Under their control Shetland, far from turning to Scotland, became increasingly parochial. In part this must have been due to economic disaster: the dreadful famines of the 1620s, for instance, and later the long drawn out crisis of the eighties and nineties. It would not be correct, however, to argue that the local landowners were very successful at subverting the old local order, snapping up land or monopolising local trade. I have argued elsewhere that they simply took over the administrative system which Bishop Law had handed them, appropriated (as we shall see in a moment, the fragmented Norwegian estates, and counted on the Germans to continue their monopoly of trade.[41]

It was during this period that the theory and practice of udal law, which historians have seen as a quintessentially Norse aspect of Shetland society, finally withered and died. From 1620 onwards, for about twenty years, a feud raged in Shetland between members of several landowning families, concerning the method by which the Bruce family had acquired its estates. The main protagonists were Andrew Bruce of Muness and James Sinclair of Scalloway, the one a son of Laurence Bruce, the tyrannical foud of the 1570s, the other a son of Arthur Sinclair, Laurence Bruce's patriotic opponent. If the events of the 1570s were tragedy, the new controversy was farce, a squabble at the top of society rather than a grass-roots movement against oppression.

From our point of view the most instructive part of the argument concerned the status of property in Shetland. Andrew Bruce argued that his estates were udal property, 'quhilk', he said, 'is only a naicked possession without anie wreatten securitie'. James Sinclair argued in response 'that non cane clame the priviledg of ane udailler bot only the successours of old kyndly possessours' — 'quhilk', he said, '. . . Andro Bruce cannot alledge, because his father was the first and he is only the second man of his race that ever was in that countrie'.

> Thair is no lawe, statut or practiq [he went on] establisching or alloweing ane udaill ryght in this kyngdome . . . . It wer against all equitie to susteine such ane chimera that hes no truth nor substance aggrieing with the lawes . . . of this realme, under coulour and pretext quhairof the said Andro Bruce and his complices and manie other oppressours in that countrie have intended themselves in sundrie poor men's lands and appropriated the same to themselves.

And Sinclair further suggested that 'the Danisch lawes ought to have no respect heir now efter so long time since the annexation of the countrie of Yetland to the crowne of Scotland, bot ought to be altogether abolisched'.[42]

Here we have the world turned upside down: udal law wielded by oppressors, and the native patriots pleading for its abolition. In fact the whole argument was theoretical in the extreme. There was no way in which udal law could sensibly be abolished, since by that time only a few vestiges of it remained in the islands. What Sinclair was arguing for was a reform in conveyancing and testamentary practices, and by the 1630s that was well under way.

I argued above that in the late sixteenth century, with a little help from the kings of Scotland and Denmark, and from Shetland's local government, the Lords of

Norway managed to protect their interests in Shetland. By the 1620s and 1630s things had changed radically. Take Noss Goods, for instance. When Jakob Rosenkrantz died in 1616 his family sold the estate to the Company of Copenhagen, the famous Danish company which traded with Iceland. In March 1634 Christian IV of Denmark wrote to the Governor of Shetland, asking him to assist the Company in upholding its claims to its Shetland property and rents.[43] Clearly there were problems. Twenty-five years later, probably to make the best of a bad job, the Company sold the estate to John Neven of Luning, a Shetland landowner.[44]

The fate of Papa Goods and Vaila Goods was even more striking. In the early 1630s there were violent disputes between branches of the Mouat families in Shetland about Papa Goods. There was much breaking up of tenants' doors and 'bauche and blae straikes'. One of the parties wrote to the Lords of Norway to complain, but another stole the letter out of the messenger's pocket prior to the voyage while the latter was asleep.[45] This time, incidentally, the intruders did not invoke udal law to justify their actions: on the contrary, as James Sinclair wryly observed, they 'have banisched the udaillers therfra upon pretext that their ryghts ar not conforme to the lawes of Scotland'. In desperation the Lords of Norway complained to the Scottish Court of Session, apparently without result.[46] In 1661 the Danish Lands Commission wrote about Vaila Goods as follows: 'There should be paid from the Gidske estate which lies in Shetland 80 Rix Dollars, which however is seldom received'.[47]

In fact the Cheyne and Mouat families, who, we have already seen, had had leases of these estates in the sixteenth century, gradually came to regard them and dispose of them as their own property. In 1664 Thomas Cheyne of Vaila bought a feu charter of Vaila Goods from Alexander Douglas of Spynie, the viscount of Grandison's representative in the islands;[48] and Douglas himself, in his instructions to his commissioners, referred dismissively to 'those pretending to hold of the Lords of Norway'.[49]

At the level of trade, contacts between Shetland and Norway continued. It was still a relatively plebeian trade. Captain John Smith wrote in 1633 that 'the inhabitants of Ounst usually have a bark that they trade with to Norway where they may buy timber for houses ready framed; also deal boards, tar, ships, barks and boats of all sorts and other necessaries for their isle'.[50] He would not have written in that way if a big Unst landowner — Bruce of Muness, for instance — had been organising the trade. David Sanderson Scott's son or grandson Hosea was travelling to Norway with his own ship in the late 1620s, as David himself had done in the seventies.[51] But as in the sixteenth century this was a small and now probably contracting trade: Dr Frances Shaw has pointed out that timber imports from Norway are completely absent from Shetland customs returns of the late 1660s and early 1670, and has suggested that by that time most of Shetland's wood imports were coming via Orkney.[52] The trade flourished again in the eighteenth century, but that is an entirely different story.

There was one additional trading link between Shetland and Norway in the first half of the seventeenth century, and that too was going awry. Shetlanders paid part of their crown taxation and rents in wadmel, a rough cloth whose threads, according to one writer, were 'as thick as fishers' lines'.[53] Landlords and crown chamberlains disposed of it in Norway. In a letter of August 1642 by James Dishington, an agent in Bergen for the then stewart depute of Shetland, we get a vivid glimpse of the problems which were developing. 'Trewlie, Sir', says Dishington,

> in tymis bypast, it haithe bein ane verrie good comodittie heir, bot nu within sum few yeirs the Norland bours quho usethe to by it, complainethe mikill of the onsufficiencie thereof . . . and schawethe it is neather so thick or suo long by sex or 7 els as it usethe to be, quhairby they ar peis and peis and nu at the last quhollilly come out of use thereof.[54]

The trade lingered on for a while: in 1655 Jacob Tait of Laxfirth, one of the native shipowners, was still carrying wadmel to Norway for the laird of Brough.[55] By that time the crown chamberlains, sick to death of this bulky and inconvenient commodity, had commuted the payment into money.

IV

'Peis and peis and nu at the last quhollilly come out of use thereof.' James Dishington's remark is a good epitaph for Shetland's relationship with the motherland. By 1700 the traffic between Norway and Shetland must have been very slight indeed, and the cultural links, other than antiquarian ones, correspondingly tenuous.

Shetland's relationship with Scotland is more difficult to sum up. Most Shetlanders still spoke a Norse dialect in 1700, but they could speak Scots just as readily, and for 200 years the vocabulary of administration and religion in the islands had been Scots. It is unlikely that there was a large immigration from Scotland to Shetland during most of the seventeenth century; but the growth of Lerwick in the last quarter of the century, the first commercial centre in the history of the islands, meant that Scottish and North-European artefacts and fashions were arriving in Shetland in a steady stream.[56]

The great mistake the late nineteenth century antiquarians made was to misunderstand the force and pace of the Scottish contribution to Shetland history. I have tried to show that Shetland had its problems in the late middle ages, under the shadow of powerful local fouds, and also in the seventeenth century, when the local landowning class had the whip hand. But they were *local problems*. When conditions were right, particularly in the late sixteenth century, the Shetlanders managed to keep their masters in check.

How did they do it? I found a clue recently in Milan Kundera's remarkable novel *The Unbearable Lightness of Being.* Kundera is writing about a very different, twentieth-century, society, but has a theory which seems to me to throw light on Shetland and its relationship with governments overseas.

> Perhaps [says Kundera] it was the fact that no one wished to settle there that caused the state to lose its power over the countryside . . . . As a result of such apathy, the countryside had maintained more than a

modicum of autonomy and freedom. The chairman of the collective farm was not brought in from outside (as were high-level managers in the city); he was elected by the villagers from among themselves.[57]

Shetland is a long way from Bergen, and even farther from Edinburgh. This is one key to Shetland history, one reason why newcomers found it so difficult to prevail in the islands, so necessary to *change* when they came there. The nineteenth-century antiquarians did Shetland and her local institutions a disservice. Foreigners occasionally ground Shetlanders under their heels; far more often Shetland magnates oppressed other Shetlanders, and in the eighteenth and nineteenth centuries they did so with ever-increasing competence and vigour.

NOTES

1. Bronwen J Cohen, 'Norse imagery in Shetland: an historical study of intellectuals and their use of the past in the construction of Shetland's identity' (PhD, University of Manchester, 1970), 315ff.
2. Charles Rampini, *Shetland and the Shetlanders* (Kirkwall, 1884), 32.
3. Barbara E Crawford, 'The pledging of the islands in 1469', in Donald J Withrington, ed., *Shetland and the Outside World* (Oxford, 1983), 33.
4. Alfred W and Amy Johnston, eds, *Orkney and Shetland Records*, i (London, 1907-13) (hereafter *OSR*), 37-40.
5. J Storer Clouston, ed., *Records of the Earldom of Orkney* (Edinburgh, 1914), 69-70.
6. These debates are pungently described in Knut Helle, 'Norway in the High Middle Ages' (hereafter Helle, 'Norway'), *Scandinavian Journal of History*, vi (1981), 172-86.
7. E P Thompson, *Whigs and Hunters* (Harmondsworth, 1977), 263.
8. *Diplom. Norv.*, i, 270; iii, 234-5, 250-1.
9. Ludvig Daae, 'Jørdebog over fru Gorvels gods paa Hjaltland', *Historisk Tidsskrift* (Norway), 3rd series, iii (1895), 264ff.
10. *Diplom. Norv.*, xii, 105-6, 123-5, 162-4, 204.
11. *OSR*, 179-80; compare Helle, 'Norway', 172, and William P L Thomson, *History of Orkney* (Edinburgh, 1987), 62.
12. John A Gade, *The Hanseatic Control of Norwegian Commerce during the Later Middle Ages* (Leiden, 1951), 59ff.
13. Thomas Gifford, *An Historical Description of the Zetland Islands* (London, 1786) (herafter Gifford, *Description*), 37-8.
14. Gilbert Goudie, 'The Danish claims upon Orkney and Shetland', *Proceedings of the Society of Antiquaries of Scotland*, xxi (1887), 237.
15. Barbara E Crawford, 'The pawning of Orkney and Shetland: a reconsideration of the events of 1460-9', *Scottish Historical Review*, xlviii (1969), 35-53.
16. Gilbert Goudie, *The Celtic and Scandinavian Antiquities of Shetland* (Edinburgh and London, 1904) (herafter Goudie, *Antiquities*), 78-131.
17. Shetland Archives (hereafter SA), Lerwick Sheriff Court records, SC.12/65/1/31.
18. David Balfour, ed., *Oppressions of the Sixteenth Century in the Islands of Orkney and Zetland* (Edinburgh, 1859) (herafter Balfour, *Oppressions*), 84.
19. Goudie, *Antiquities*, 203.
20. Scottish Record Office (hereafter SRO), Court of Session records, CS.7/203, folio 157.
21. Gordon Donaldson, ed., *The Court Book of Shetland, 1602-4* (Edinburgh, 1954) (herafter Donaldson, *Court Book*), 42-3.
22. Gordon Donaldson, *Shetland Life under Earl Patrick* (Edinburgh, 1958), 3-4.

23. *Diplom. Norv.*, viii, 436-9, 489.

24. SA, Vaila papers, D.10/10/1.

25. Per-Øivind Sandberg, *Gørvel Fadersdatters Regnskap over Giske og Giskegodset, 1563* (Oslo, 1986), 30.

26. Orkney Archives, Balfour papers, D.2/33/13.

27. *Register of the Privy Council of Scotland* (hereafter *RPC*), xiv, 259-60.

28. For example, David Sinclair's estates on the Mainland of Shetland are listed in the middle section of a rental of Shetland c.1500, SRO, GD.1/366/1.

29. Balfour, *Oppressions*, 67.

30. Klaus Friedland, 'Hanseatic merchants and their trade with Shetland', in Donald J Withrington, ed., *Shetland and the Outside World* (Oxford, 1983), 86-90.

31. Herman Entholt and Ludvig Beutin, eds, *Bremen und Nordeuropa*, i (Weimar, 1937), 58-60.

32. Balfour, *Oppressions*, 39-42.

33. Donaldson, *Court Book*, 17, 74.

34. Brian Smith, 'Stockstove Houses', in J Graham and J Tait, eds, *Shetland Folk Book*, vii (1980), 22-7.

35. Hance D Smith, *Shetland Life and Trade, 1550-1914* (Edinburgh, 1984), 32.

36. Balfour, *Oppressions*, 7, 66-7, and, generally, Atle Thowsen, 'The Norwegian export of boats to Shetland', *Sjofartshistorisk Arbok* (1970), 148-50.

37. For example, SA, Lerwick Sheriff Court records, SC.12/65/1, 16, 20, and Bruce of Symbister papers, GD.144/21/13; compare Elizabeth P D Torrie, ed., *The Gild Court Book of Dunfermline 1433-1597* (Edinburgh, 1986), ix.

38. J Storer Clouston, 'Three more seals', *Proceedings of the Orkney Antiquarian Society*, viii (1930), 33.

39. *RPC*, ix, 181-2.

40. Robert S Barclay, ed., *The Court Book of Orkney and Shetland, 1612-13* (Kirkwall, 1962).

41. Brian Smith, ' "Lairds" and "Improvement" in 17th and 18th century Shetland', in T M Devine, ed., *Lairds and Improvement in the Scotland of the Enlightenment* (Glasgow, 1978), 13.

42. SA, Lerwick Sheriff Court records, ms. information for James Sinclair of Scalloway, SC.12/65/3.

43. *Norske Rigs-Registranter*, vi (Christiania, 1877), 633.

44. SRO, Particular Register of Sasines, Shetland, RS.44/3, folio 466.

45. RPC, 2nd series, v, 220-1.

46. SA, Lerwick Sheriff Court records, ms. information for James Sinclair of Scalloway, SC.12/65/3.

47. Ludvig Daae, 'Om berøringer mellem Otknøerne og Hjaltland og moderlandet Norge efter 1468', *Statsokonomisk Tidsskrift* (1895), 52.

48. SRO, Particular Register of Sasines, Shetland, RS.44/4, folio 130.

49. Gardie House, Bressay, Shetland, ms. instructions for Thomas Leslie, 21 June 1664.

50. Cited in Gifford, *Description*, x-xi.

51. Albert Joleik, 'Names of 17th-century Shetland shipmasters', *Shetland News*, 8 May 1947.

52. Frances J Shaw, *The Northern and Western Isles of Scotland* (Edinburgh, 1980), 179.

53. J Bruce, ed., *Description of ye Countrey of Zetland* (Edinburgh, 1908), 40.

54. SRO, Smythe of Methven papers, Orkney and Shetland documents.

55. Society of Antiquaries Library, Edinburgh, letter by Andro Greig to Laurence Sinclair, 4 July 1655.

56. John Brand, *A Brief Description of Orkney, Zetland, Pightland-Firth and Caithness* (Edinburgh, 1701), 66-7, 69-70.

57. Milan Kundera, *The Unbearable Lightness of Being* (London, 1984), 283.

4

ORKNEY BISHOPS AS SUFFRAGANS IN THE SCANDINAVIAN-BALTIC AREA: AN ASPECT OF THE LATE MEDIEVAL CHURCH IN THE NORTH

Troels Dahlerup

A medieval bishop was a most important person. Notwithstanding peculiar jurisdictions of exempt abbeys or the judicial claims made by archdeacons, the bishop was the central figure in the medieval church. Even papal claims of supremacy were often more of an ideological nature than practical politics. In short, the bishop was the linchpin in his diocese, the *ordinarius*.

A medieval canon lawyer described the bishop and his considerable power in this charming way: 'It might be claimed that the bishop possessed the omnipotence of Christ'![1] 'Unfortunately', he goes on, 'he does not possess the Lord's omnipresence' — meaning that even if the bishop's power inside his diocese might be absolute, for very practical reasons he had to delegate. Accordingly chapters, archdeacons, officials of every sort, commissaries, etc., took over more of the heavy episcopal obligations, especially administrative and jurisdictional matters.

But one power the bishops kept for themselves, which effectively prevented the episcopal power from dwindling away in the manner in which central powers waned in the age of feudalism. Thanks to the apostolic succession, only consecrated bishops could confer holy orders (that is, on deacons and priests) and exercise many other rights (of confirmation, consecration of churchyards, etc.); and, even if several of those lesser rights could be delegated, the consecration of priests (and of course of new bishops) was kept as an episcopal privilege.

In the high middle ages many bishops became more and more involved in the secular politics of their countries. Royal chancellors generally were (or at least became) bishops, and we may often wonder how such bishops were indeed able to administer extensive dioceses, since at the same time many were highly influential royal councillors. But canon law and growing papal influence could provide a legitimate power of dispensation, permitting minor clergy to perform, for example, the consecration of churchyards. But at the same time papal pretensions were often followed by secular resentment, and the fight in the high middle ages between temporal and spiritual power sometimes resulted in the election of several competing popes. And in the same way many episcopal elections were disputed, which produced a 'surplus' of bishops, where the unhappy losers had to look for employment. This explains why an unlucky Danish bishop of Odense in 1168 is found in Cologne, whose archbishop belonged to the same political group and who could use the fraternal help of his unsuccessful colleague.

In particular, the energetic missions of the eleventh and twelfth centuries to

Scandinavia and the Baltic area initially met such strong opposition that many missionary bishops gave up the unequal strife and settled peacefully in their home countries, giving the local bishop some help and thereby returning his hospitality. In German research the Baltic area has aptly been called 'the cradle of the medieval suffragan', and even if this view might not be wholly correct from a purely legal and theoretical viewpoint, it has some basis in fact.[1a]

As we have practically no written evidence from Denmark before 1100, it is no wonder that most of our knowledge of the earliest Danish bishops comes from northern Germany. But, of course, it is difficult to distinguish between a dispirited missionary and an honoured guest who merely made an accidental visit.

To take an instance: careful research in Belgium has provided for us the names of several Danish bishops present in the Low Countries;[2] but there is generally a very simple reason for this. The regular route from Denmark to Rome, for example, went via Bruges, and during their travels Danish bishops may often have repaid the hospitality they received by an action such as consecrating an altar. On the other hand, when during the Danish schism in the thirteenth century a papal legate consecrated a French Cistercian to the see of Odense, the new bishop wisely left Denmark together with the inept legate; and this Cistercian bishop is never heard of again in Danish history, as he spent the rest of his life all over Europe, for a time as a suffragan in Liège.[3]

With the Crusades we arrive at a turning-point in the history of suffragans, as suddenly a host of oriental and Palestinian bishops appear throughout Europe, collecting help for continued support, for example. Before the end of the thirteenth century the Holy Land was lost. But popes went on appointing new bishops of places such as Bethlehem and Nazareth, Ephesus and Laodicea. And, as the spirit of the Crusades dwindled, these bishops ended up as the regular supply of suffragans for ordinary bishops in need of help and assistance. And in the later middle ages ecclesiastical princes, such as the electors of Cologne and Trèves regularly had the use of such *episcopi in partibus infidelium*, whose distant and often rather spurious titles were never seriously investigated. Later, it was even possible to appoint a bishop *in ecclesia universalis*, if a vacancy among the usually inexhaustible supply of oriental bishops was not readily found.

But the market was not solely furnished by 'middle-eastern' bishops. Many poorer dioceses held little appeal for ambitious clerics, and Irish bishops especially (or perhaps better: English clerks with Irish titles) very often gave up the idea of settling in that wild and troublesome island, choosing instead a comfortable berth in the service of the English episcopate, whose members were generally all too busy with matters of state to undertake regular visitations and consecrations.[4] And with the arrival of the Great Schism of 1378 we reach a veritable *embarras de richesses* of bishops, as Europe became divided between rival popes, of Rome and Avignon, and for a time even a third pope, of Pisa.

At last we begin to enter upon our Scottish-Scandinavian scene. As the kings of France naturally supported their own nominees in Avignon, most reasonably Germany, Scandinavia and England preferred the Roman pope; whereas Scotland in accordance with 'the Auld Alliance' joined Avignon as one of the most loyal and persistent supporters of the anti-pope.

As far as I have been able to discover, suffragans as such never played any significant part in Scotland. We have the charming incident of the Greek bishop of Dromore (in Ireland), who in 1484 consecrated an altar in the diocese of St Andrews, and even if he seems to have spent most of his life as a suffragan in England, at his death in 1529 he did leave property in Edinburgh.[5] And in 1483 a James Lindsay is found in St Andrews with the 'Arabian' title of *Dionysiensis*.[6]

This apparent lack of suffragans in Scotland might possibly be explained by the enormous differences in the sizes of Scottish bishoprics. Occasionally bishops of Argyll are commissioned to do episcopal work in the diocese of Glasgow, and the strange geographical position of Brechin 'inside' the extensive diocese of St Andrews might perhaps be explained in this context too. On the other hand, the Scandinavian bishops, who in the later middle ages were *ex officio* members of the royal council, had to get all possible help; and, as I shall show, this came not only from oriental bishops, but especially by employing their less fortunate colleagues from north Atlantic sees.

The Schism of 1378 made a considerable impact on the church in Scotland. Not only did an awkward Dunkeld bishop prefer the Roman pope, for which reason he of course had to leave Scotland, but as a line of Avignon-appointed bishops resided in Dunkeld, the Roman popes went on appointing Dunkeld bishops, who had to find a living as English suffragans.[7]

But while this was a minor problem, the situation on the northern and western borders was more serious, as the sees of Sodor and Orkney belonged to the ecclesiastical province of Nidaros (Trondheim) in Norway, which of course followed Rome.

The Avignon pope deposed the Sodor bishop in 1387, but as his appointee only became recognised in Scotland, whereas Man continued to obey Rome, the diocese at last was divided, and even after the end of the Schism this *ad hoc* solution was preserved (even if most bishops of Man are to be found as English suffragans).

In Orkney too we now find two lists of bishops,[8] one Roman (and supported in Scandinavia), another belonging to the observance of Avignon (and of course supported by the Scottish authorities of this time). I find it impossible, and probably unproductive, to discover for certain which of the contenders were, in fact, in possession, if any. But at least it is possible to outline a tentative picture of the problems of Orkney-Shetland and their bishops. (An elegant but erroneous solution is found in a German historical atlas, which places Shetland under Rome, but Orkney proper under Avignon).

To understand the position of the Orkneys fully we must for a moment take a look at the broader context. Most probably the general European crisis of the fourteenth century was felt especially hard among the originally Norse settlers in the north Atlantic islands; and, as the system of suffragans comes into use at the end of this century, just as Irish bishops are very often found working as suffragans in England, bishops from the northern islands are constantly found in Danish and Norwegian sources performing consecrations and carrying out other episcopal functions.

Still, there must have been many cases where this was not a matter of formal appointment as a suffragan, as bishops from Iceland or the Faeroes, for example, might simply be returning received hospitality. But, incidentally, we do possess rather impressive materials which illustrate the visits of bishops from those distant parts. As the Union of the three Scandinavian kingdoms was established at the end of the century, the sovereigns tried to govern by a sort of conciliar rule. Accordingly, both spiritual and lay magnates from all three realms assembled, and duly marked their presence by placing their seals on the accepted decisions. Of course, only real bishops took part in such council sessions, even if suffragans were often present. And this is a well established fact, thanks to the special privileges of a bishop. Among others he had the right to grant forty days of indulgence. If, for instance, a church fabric was in sore need of repair, the church-wardens might petition a bishop for a letter of indulgence, granting forty days to all who visited the church in a pious frame of mind and gave alms to the fabric. Precisely in this case there were no differences between bishops, archbishops and suffragans. Accordingly church-wardens and members of the mendicant orders gathered around those Union Councils, where with some luck they might get a patent from perhaps a dozen bishops, thereby gaining grants of indulgences out of all proportion: with ten to fifteen bishops present they might get from 400 to 600 days of indulgences at one and the same time, and this is in an age when indulgences caused a great deal of competition.

Unfortunately these sources are especially rich after the end of the Great Schism in 1417, and the first unquestionably and undisputed residing bishop of Orkney, Thomas Tulloch (1418-61), is best known through his numerous visits to Denmark. As he is found there between 1419 and 1423, it seems possible that he started his term of office with a visit to Denmark to pay homage to King Eric.[9] As he did not visit Bergen during the provincial Council of the Norwegian Church in 1425, but was influential in bringing about the Scottish-Norwegian treaty of 1426, it is reasonable to suppose that with the return of King James I to Scotland in 1424, Bishop Thomas spent some time acquainting himself with the affairs of both the Orkneys and Scotland.[10] As late as 1433-4 he paid another visit to Denmark, both taking part in Union Councils and granting indulgences. But I think it possible that the deposition of King Eric, late in the 1430s, might have deepened the gap between these islands and Scandinavia.

As Scotland in the early fifteenth century was isolated both by having no functioning monarch at home and by following Avignon, we find a rather extraordinary contact between Scandinavia and England (both belonging to the Roman observance), which in 1405-6 resulted in a marriage between young King Eric and the Lancastrian Princess Philippa. Of course, much historical research consists of a rather hopeless attempt to bring some sense and reason into a lot of muddled and confused material; but still we have to make the attempt, notwithstanding our everyday experiences with modern politics. The fifteenth century is among others interesting, as in this period we find a short but hectic English spell of activity in the north Atlantic waters, centred around the cod-fishery that grew up in these northern seas, especially around Iceland. This royal marriage might signify an attempt to come to some sort of understanding about English fishing rights, especially as the complaints mentioned not only illegal trading, but piracy too.[11]

In the first half of the fifteenth century every second bishop in Iceland was an Englishman, probably with a futile hope that an English bishop might be in a stronger position to try to get a semblance of discipline and legality in the behaviour of the English fishermen and traders (and perhaps pirates). But this connection between England and the northern dioceses goes further back, as a Roman pope had already in the 1380s appointed an English bishop of the Faeroes. It seems that he perhaps never visited his distant see, but apparently spent the whole of his life as a suffragan in various English bishoprics. Correspondingly most of his successors are found as suffragans in Denmark or Norway, and in 1431 a Faeroese bishop even exchanged his title with the purely titular (and rather spurious) name of *Tranquiliensis*, which until then had been used by a Greyfriar, who from his provision in 1414 is only found in Denmark-Norway as suffragan. And even after their exchange of titles, no one seems to have considered it necessary to reside.[12]

And at last to the Orkneys. We are in the 'dark and drublie days' of Scotland, with royal power at a low ebb. Besides continuous border wars, the north especially was troubled, for example, in the burning of Elgin Cathedral in 1390, and the semi-independent Lords of the Isles repeatedly tried to establish themselves as earls of Ross, a feud that did not end until the forfeiture of the Lordship in 1493. Besides such troubles as the battle of Harlaw (1411), the Orkneys were continuously harassed by the Lewismen, who made rather outdated Viking raids even as late as the 1460s,[13] which, together with English fishing-traders-cum-pirates, must have made life in the Orkneys rather difficult.

Power in these islands must, of course, have been centred around earl and bishop, and no doubt most royal 'fouds', who ought to have been local men, soon had to ally themselves to one of the parties. No wonder that the long period when the title of earl lay dormant, and with several claimants in dispute, must have given the earlier bishops a free hand. Accordingly, an agreement between Bishop William and the royal official ('sysselmand') in 1369 indicated earlier troubles.[14] And when at last in 1379 Henry Sinclair is recognised as the earl, he commits himself to supporting the royal interests against the bishop.[15] We do not know the details, nor what sort of problems existed, but they were not solved thereby, as the bishop was killed about 1382/3, and probably antagonism between earl and bishop continued, as both the Sinclair earl and the pretender Malise Sperra were present at a Council in Helsingborg in 1389, but the Orkney bishop was not.[16]

After the slaying of Bishop William, the cathedral chapter nominated the rector of Fetlar, John, who was provided as bishop of Orkney by the Roman pope, whereas the Avignon pope provided Robert Sinclair, and for most of the period of the Schism we have a double line of Orkney bishops.

It is my considered opinion that the Avignon bishops never had much of a chance of getting real possession of the diocese. Already in 1391 Robert Sinclair had been transferred to the more lucrative — or at least safer — see of Dunkeld (his Roman opponent in which, as already mentioned, wisely spent his life in England); and notwithstanding his elevation to the rank of bishop he prudently kept his remunerative prebend as dean of Moray as long as possible.[17]

In the same way one of his Avignon successors wisely accepted a papal privilege letting him keep his otherwise incompatible benefices 'until he got real possession of the Orkney see', and, as none of them went to the trouble of being consecrated, until they became appointed to more unproblematic bishoprics, this indicates that the title of bishop-elect in the Orkneys was of little real value for a Scotsman loyal to Avignon.

Probably as late as 1407, the Avignon pope provided one Alexander Vaus to the see, who in 1414 was translated to Caithness, but probably he kept the archdeaconry of Caithness until then. His consecration took place in 1417, and in 1422 he was elevated to the much more important see of Galloway. As late as 1415, when most European states had given up any allegiance to Avignon, one William Stephenson was provided as bishop of Orkney with the express privilege of keeping his benefices, until he got possession of the disputed see (meaning, of course, if ever he succeeded). And his translation to Dunblane was eventually made in 1419 by the now undisputed Roman pope Martin, who in this way moved a small but probably irritating problem from the new Orkney bishop, Thomas Tulloch (from 1418), who now at last had an undisputed title.

Even if I have little reason to suppose that the appointments from Avignon ever had any influence in Orkney and Shetland, on the other hand I must stress that neither did their Roman counterparts necessarily lead an easy life. The kings of Scotland of course withheld the traditional allowance of £5 from the crown revenues of Aberdeen, and Thomas Tulloch did not receive this gratification until 1426.

But the old problems also went on: disputes with the earls and the royal officials, the harassments of English fishermen and the traditional raids from Lewis (probably connected with the continuing fight about the earldom of Ross) gave the bishops no soft bed. Very early Bishop John went to Denmark, where, as we shall later see, he played an interesting part in solving a great dynastic problem, and about 1389/90 he is often mentioned in Roman sources, interestingly enough in connection with both a Faeroese and a Greenland bishop.

I have already quoted the problems of the Faeroese bishops, but they were nothing to speak of compared with those of poor Bishop Henry of Gardar. His predecessor died in the late 1370s, the last residing bishop, as Greenland trade stopped and in time the title of Gardar became just another convenient fiction for a suffragan.

Many nineteenth-century historians of Greenland in the middle ages have tried to make the most of the totally unknown last years of the Norse settlement in Greenland by using the often detailed narrative elements in the papal letters of provision: 'No bishop has visited Greenland for generations (eventually a specified number of years), and accordingly the inhabitants are in great danger of becoming heathen, as there are few priests left, and the people cannot get the Holy Sacraments', etc., etc. But these are stories with a purpose, or rather two purposes: first they identify the humble Greenland bishop as poor, that is, too poor to pay the traditional fees to the Roman *curia*: secondly, like other bishops *in partibus infidelium*, he must have the extraordinary privilege of being permitted to use his episcopal powers (especially the power of consecration) 'as long as he is travelling to his distant see'! With a stiff upper lip everybody of course understood that this was a permanent and lifelong travel, as nobody expected him ever to reach Greenland, and very soon the exact location of this distant land was completely forgotten.

But, thanks to the episcopal title and ordination, this extra privilege made him sure of an occupation as suffragan, and as both Rome and Avignon (later Rome and Basle) went on appointing Gardar bishops, it is possible to find up to half a dozen Greenland bishops functioning all over Europe at one and the same time.

Now we go back to the first absentee Bishop Henry, to whom we may give the benefit of the doubt, as he at least in the beginning may have hoped to be able to join some of the last Greenland expeditions. He is said to have been a friar, but neither his order, nor his nationality is known. In 1386 he was present during a council session in Denmark, as he among other bishops granted many indulgences.[18] Most appropriately, he was present among the Norwegian clergy in 1388, when Queen Margaret was proclaimed regent:[19] there could be no doubt about a Greenland bishop's right as a full member of the ecclesiastical province of Nidaros. But if he had gone to Rome, he might have met his Orkney colleague, as they did some business together. He promised John, the Orkney bishop, to pay his fees to the papal *curia* and to visit his diocese in order to institute a new archdeacon in Shetland.

It is, however, not possible to prove if either of them ever reached the bishopric, even if Henry did show some interest in Orkney, which at least is indicated, since the two bishops with papal permission simply changed titles in 1394.

The native Shetlander, John from Fetlar, now abandoned any interest in his origin: already some years earlier we find him in Pomerania, and he must have realised the opportunities of a new and easier life as suffragan to the bishop of Cammin (now Kamien Pomorski). In this position he did not need a 'real' bishop's title, and, perhaps for a consideration, he was willing to change his see to the eventually rather mythical one of Gardar. Soon he must have been completely forgotten both in his home country and in Scandinavia, where a new Gardar bishop (of the Roman observance, of course) is provided as early as 1401, and is known especially through numerous grants of indulgences.[20] As he is mostly found in Norway, this might be the reason why the Pisa pope, John XXIII, in 1411 provided still another Gardar bishop, who became *vicarius in spiritualibus Roskildensis*, and accidentally met the new Orkney bishop, Thomas Tulloch, as they both gave indulgences in Copenhagen in 1419.[21]

It is extremely doubtful if the former Greenland Bishop Henry ever visited his new diocese of Orkney. In 1394, six months after his translation, he gave indulgences to churches in Denmark,[22] but must have died a short time later, as the Roman pope in 1396 provided to Orkney an Englishman, John Pak, a Benedictine of Colchester. This is, perhaps, another indication of the previously mentioned Danish-English contact, which culminated in the dynastic marriage, and at least signifies a rather cold relationship between Scotland and Scandinavia, if indeed Scotland in those difficult days could be said to have much consistent foreign policy. Apparently this bishop met, or at least inherited, considerable opposition in the Orkneys, as a son-in-law of the Sinclair earl as late as 1422 is said to have had difficulties, being a loyal supporter of Bishop John of Colchester.[23] As John's

Avignon opponents never seem to have got possession, we are left with a vacuum for this period. When at last the Schism ended, and the new and undisputed Pope Martin in 1418 provided Thomas Tulloch, his predecessor was said to be dead, but against normal custom his name is not stated. Could no one remember 'the English bishop' or even his name? Only money leaves a certain trail: as late as 1419 an optimistic Hanseatic merchant was in Bergen trying to get the chapter of Orkney to pay the debts of Bishops Henry and John.[24]

With the arrival of Thomas Tulloch these problems were at last over. When in 1424 the young King James of Scotland arrived in his country, a new period began, in which the Tulloch bishops especially played quite an important part. With some hesitation I tend to consider Thomas Tulloch a loyal supporter of King Eric and of the Roman *curia*. But when this king was deposed at the end of the 1430s, and the new government flirted with the Basle pope, it is no wonder that Bishop Thomas Tulloch became estranged, and in time the traditional relationship between these islands and Scandinavia cooled off. Perhaps the importance of the Tulloch bishops in the gradual and very peaceful process through which these islands went from Scandinavian to Scottish domination should not be underestimated.

But still, however often we recognise the Orkney bishops as only humble suffragans, they were never completely without some influence: indeed two of them took some active part in highly significant events in the history of Scandinavia around 1400.

The founder of the Scandinavian Union was the great Queen Margaret, but characteristically she was never queen of Denmark. As her late husband Haakon was king of Norway, she was, of course, only Queen Dowager. But, in fact, her reign was based on her position as guardian of their son, Olaf, a minor. When her father King Valdemar of Denmark died in 1375, she placed her young son on the throne of Denmark by a veritable *coup d'état*.

Wisely she realised the advantages of the humble rôle of a guardian. A 'proper' king had to give privileges, both to whole estates and to individuals, and royal rights existed which no guardian could encroach upon. Every nobleman might to his own cost have learned the heavy obligations of a guardian. At some point the day of accounting would arrive, and the guardian was responsible for everything he had held in trust. Accordingly the queen, with great regrets, could inform her troublesome aristocracy that personally she would like to give them everything they wanted, but unfortunately such things had to wait, until the king came of age.

A very critical situation then developed when in 1387 the boy king suddenly died, at a time of continuing problems with the Hanseatic League, and of war with Sweden. In this situation Queen Margaret took power with doubtful legitimacy, under the extraordinary title of 'Lady Protector and Guardian of the Realm' (whereas in Norway at least she might claim the title of Queen Dowager).

But to be guardian it was necessary to have a minor, in order to give the guardianship some semblance of legality. Fortunately Queen Margaret had a late sister, whose daughter had married a duke of (part of) Pomerania, and they had a minor son. In 1388 the boy Eric was, therefore, proclaimed king-elect in Denmark and in the following year recognised in Norway too; and as Sweden had also been conquered, the Union was founded with Eric as titular king. But as long as she lived (until 1412) Queen Margaret was the mighty regent. No wonder that a delegation from Lübeck once accidentally addressed her as 'Lady King'!

In this time of crisis we find our Orkney Bishop John in Pomerania of all places, where in April 1389 he functioned as *vicarius in pontificaliis ecclesie Camynensis*,[25] i.e. he was a regular suffragan notwithstanding papal letters indicating a (personal?) visit to Rome. As from now on he is a regular figure in north German church life, it is tempting to suppose that this Fetlar rector played at least some part in the negotiations between the duke of Pomerania and Queen Margaret, resulting in the elevation of the boy Eric to Union monarch-to-be. Bishop John's translation to Gardar could be seen as a consequence of his success in Pomerania. As a suffragan he had of course no use for a 'real' title, and as Gardar bishop he continued to function as *vicarius in pontificaliis* for the Cammin bishop. It is probable that he lived for more than twenty years after, as his death is mentioned as late as 1431, when he was said to have founded several altars in the cathedral.[26]

In 1397 the young King Eric was considered to have come of age. Accordingly a magnificent spectacle was performed in the south Swedish town of Kalmar, where the spiritual and temporal magnates of all three kingdoms assembled to crown King Eric. This was witnessed by a great charter with 67 seals, whereas the strange and to this date hotly debated 'Union document' (on paper!) only states some principles for a 'union government'.[27]

Thanks to later independence movements in Norway it was for ages a dogma that Norway had no part in establishing a real union. It is true that no bishops from Norway proper were present, even if the provost of Oslo (*ex officio* chancellor of Norway) and the bishop of Orkney were both there, and our 'English' Bishop John of Colchester was legally a full member of the Nidaros province, however doubtful his real position in the Orkneys might be.

Greenland was soon forgotten, and in Iceland more and more English bishops are found. How spiritual care was ordered in the Orkney diocese, we have no idea. But at least these two Orkney bishops must have played some part in two of the most crucial events in Scandinavian history, in 1389 and in 1397.

Around 1800 the Danish historian Suhm wrote his *History of Denmark*, based on a wealth of documents. Here he raised the interesting point: 'It is unknown why an Orkney bishop ended up in Pomerania'.[28] The story is, inevitably, a bit long-winded, but I have tried to give a tentative answer to his problem.

NOTES

1. See Troels Dahlerup, 'Den gejstlike jurisdiction i dansk middelalder,' *Fortid og Nutid*, 23 (1966-8), 301.

1a. On suffragans in general, see H E Feine, *Kirchliche Rechtsgeschichte* (4th edn., Köln Graz, 1964), 371ff. On Scandinavian suffragans, see *Kulturhistorisk Leksikon for Nordisk Middelalder*, viii (Copenhagen, Oslo, Stockholm, 1963), col.619ff., with cited literature.

2. Ursule Berliére in *Revue Benedictine*, 20, 21, 24, 29 (1903-12).

3. (Dansk) *Historisk Tidsskrift*, 13/VI (Copenhagen, 1979), 137, n.8.

4. A Hamilton Thompson, *The English Clergy in the Later Middle Ages* (Oxford, 1966), 48-9.

5. David McRoberts, 'The Greek bishop of Dromore', *Innes Review*, xxviii (1977), 22-38.

6. C Eubel, *Hierarchia Catholica Medii Aevi, 1431-1503* (Münster, 1914), 275.

7. D E R Watt, *Fasti Ecclesiae Scoticanae Medii Aevi* (Scottish Record Society, 1969) (hereafter *Fasti*), 97; cf. A Hamilton Thompson, op.cit., 48, n.4.

8. Most relevant material on these bishops is found in *Fasti* and in *Diplom. Norv.*, xvii.

9. In Copenhagen in 1419: *Kjóbenhavns Diplomatarium*, 1st series, iv (Copenhagen, 1879), no.33; and again in 1423, *Diplom. Norv.*, ii, no.676, cf. ibid., ii, nos. 657 and 670 (1420 and 1422), and *Repertorium Diplomaticum Regni Danici Mediaevalis*, 1st series, iv (Copenhagen, 1906), (hereafter *Repertorium*), no. 5854 (1420).

10. The complaints about David Menzies' misrule in the Orkneys (about 1424) mentioned that the young earl was in Scotland, while the bishop was studying at St Andrews (J. Storer Clouston, ed., *Records of the Earldom of Orkney* (Scot. Hist. Soc., 1914) (hereafter *Records*), 44ff.), and it is important to remember that the 'classical' excuses for non-residence were (1) being on the king's business, which was appropriate for the Sinclair Earl, who held estates in Scotland proper, but not for Bishop Thomas, whose sovereign was king Eric; so it was necessary to fall back on excuse (2): studies abroad!

11. P A Munch, *Det Norske Folks Historie, Unionsperioden*, i-ii (Christiania/Oslo, 1862-3) (herafter Munch) gives some information in i, 379ff. On the English influence see Eileen Power and M M Postan, eds, *English Trade in the Fifteenth Century* (London, 1933).

12. On these bishops see *Diplom. Norv.*, xvii (suppl.), 290ff, and 353ff.

13. See complaints as late as 1461 in *Records*, 51ff.

14. Ibid., 15ff.

15. Ibid., 21ff.

16. Munch, ii, 321.

17. *Fasti*, 251ff.

18. *Repertorium*, no.3534, and numerous others.

19. *Diplom. Norv.*, iii, no. 477.

20. 1401: see *Diplom. Norv.*, vii, nos. 208-9; 1426: see ibid., xiii, no.91.

21. *Diplom. Norv.*, xvii, nos. 356-7; *Kjóbenhavns Diplomatarium*, iv, no. 23.

22. Jacob Langebek, ed., *Scriptores Rerum Danicarum Medii Aevi* (Hafnie, 1772), i, 317.

23. *Records*, 34.

24. *Diplom. Norv.*, i, no. 665.

25. P F Suhm, *Historie af Danmark*, xiv (Copenhagen, 1828), 256ff., citing Martinus Rango, *Pomerania Diplomatica* (1707 ?); see Munch, ii, 381, n.1 (with some confusion about the two bishops named John).

26. R Klempin, *Diplomatische Beitrage zur Geschichte Pommerns aus der Zeit Bogislafs X* (Berlin, 1859), 335, 338 and 438ff.; cf. *Diplom. Norv.*, xvii, nos. 431, 491, 1004, and H Heyden, *Kirchengeschichte von Pommern*, i (2nd edn., Köln, 1957), 108. In 1431 the pope provided a new bishop of Gardar after the death of Bishop John (*Diplom. Norv.*, xvii, nos.491 and 492).

27. The Union problems are still hotly debated; see Aksel E Christensen, *Kalmarunionen og nordisk Politik 1319-1439* (Copenhagen, 1980), 138; Kai Hørby, 'Tiden 1340-1513', in (Gyldendals) *Danmarkshistorie*, ii (Copenhagen, 1980), 126ff., 174ff.

28. See above, n.25.

5

KINGS, NOBLES AND BUILDINGS OF THE LATER MIDDLE AGES: DENMARK

Rikke Agnete Olsen

In discussion of the relative power of king or crown in proportion to the nobility in late medieval Denmark, two sources are often mentioned, and both deal with building activities. One is Queen Margaret's ban on private castle-building in her ordinance of 1397.[1] The other is the provision in the coronation charter of King Hans in 1483 which says that no one — meaning the king, of course — may legally prevent noblemen from fortifying their homes as they like.[2] So in both cases the buildings in question are private castles, and within their contexts the two sources give clear evidence of the state of the crown.

After twenty years as regent of Denmark, first in the name of her son Olaf and after his death for her nephew and adopted son Eric (in Denmark called 'of Pomerania') Queen Margaret was by 1396 enjoying the zenith of her increasing power. She had completed the work of her father and predecessor, Valdemar IV Atterdag, and restored the crown completely after its power had been severely impaired since the beginning of the century. When King Valdemar acceded to the throne in 1340 there had been no king even in name for eight years, and for a considerably longer time there had been no central power worth mentioning either. Now, however, after forty-six years of unremitting royal efforts, certainly not always in accordance with the ideas of the nobility, the queen could look forward to stable government with Eric VII as king in both Denmark and Norway. Besides, she had excellent hopes of getting him placed on the Swedish throne as well, and thus the three Nordic countries would be united under the Danish king.

This became reality under the Union of Kalmar the year after (1397) but it turned out as frail as its legal basis was doubtful, and all through the period until the early sixteenth century Denmark and the Danish kings fought eagerly but with changing and in the long run bad luck, against the absent desire of the Swedes to submit to Danish supremacy.[3] This process was only possible with the benevolent support of the Danish aristocracy and as long as at least part of their Swedish colleagues favoured the union, but as time went by, and the wars became increasingly futile, both became more and more difficult to obtain. In spite of the influence won by their support, in the end even the Danish nobility lost interest in this course. In the meantime both King Hans in 1483 and his son and younger brother who followed him on the throne as Christian II in 1513, and Frederick I in 1523, had to sign coronation charters intended to limit their power in favour of the council of the realm and the aristocracy, on the whole.[4] It is not too much to say that the last three medieval kings of Denmark paid with their acceptance of the charters for the ambitions of Queen Margaret and among the provisions in all three documents was the legal right of noblemen to fortify their homes.

48

In 1536 a civil war made way for the Reformation and put an end to the middle ages in Denmark. The new king and victorious warlord, Christian III, did sign a coronation charter, but from a more favourable position than his predecessors and at the very beginning of the charter he declared himself in possession of the castles and fortifications of the realm and thus the master of his own house. There is no mention of private castles then or ever after.[5]

This very brief survey of the political history of Denmark between 1375 and 1536 leads us now to concentrate on kings, nobles and buildings at about the same period. To shed light on the course of events in that field, however, it is necessary first to go back in time to cast a glance on the role of the castle and study older building regulations still valid in the later middle ages.[6]

A combined study of written and archaeological sources shows that castles in the medieval sense came late to Denmark. Even royal strongholds were not common before about 1200, when they appear fully developed with ringwalls, towers, moats, ramparts and other details of fortification known in the rest of Europe and wherever castles were in use. With few exceptions the towers were of the German *Bergfried* type, and this remained so during the whole of the middle ages. These castles were defences of the realm, and it was not until the beginning of the fourteenth century that the crown built castles to control the subjects of the country. Not all royal property was actually fortified. Large areas remained under administration from manors, *curiae*, and there are cases where a *castrum* loses its military importance and becomes a *curia*.[7] From about the middle of the thirteenth century prelates and members of the royal house, who over the years had been made dukes or counts of different parts of the country, also built themselves castles, some of them entirely up to royal standards. The archbishop's 'Hammershus' on Bornholm, though now a ruin, still gives an impression of their grandeur.[8] The number of both royal and private fortifications increases, throughout the century, but it is not until about 1300 that we get more widely spead castle-building activity also among the nobility of lower rank. From then rivalry for the power in the country spread from the upper layers in society and caused generally unstable conditions, which in the end led to the pawning of the royal lands, with legal rights, prerogatives and income, to magnates in general and the two counts of Holstein in particular. The result was a total splitting up of central power, and when in 1332 Christopher II — the Danish 'King Lackland' — died in a house in the town of Saxkøbing on Lolland all he had left was that very house, and after his death the throne was left vacant. Naturally this development was followed by the building of many new castles all over the country and by members of all aristocratic layers in society, but this almost feudal state of affairs was only to be temporary.

Compared with the old castles of the previous century most of the new ones were small, old-fashioned and in a way also temporary in shape. They were very much like the motte-and-bailey type of the oldest castles abroad with earthen ramparts and wooden palisades for defence. Ringwalls were seldom seen and stone houses almost never, though an occasional tower more or less of stone could be found on the castle-mound. The field of action of these fortifications was limited to the protection of the owner or residents against local enemies or passing gangs of robbers, and a few of them played a role on a higher level in the politics of the country, like Bjørnholm of the Hvide family on Djursland, even late in the reign of Valdemar Atterdag.[9] Such strongholds were built both by the 'village squire' who did not own much more than the manor he lived in, and by the wealthy magnates to defend specially chosen property, and they are extremely difficult to place socially, because our knowledge of the changing ownership of landed property is rather limited. Besides, like the crown, the magnates did not fortify all their property, perhaps not even the ancestral seat, and neither did every 'village squire', with one manor and a few copyholders, always fortify.[10] The bishops generally had strong castles of an older date, but like the lay magnates they now fortified some but not all of their properties.

On the whole, the castles tell us a lot about the state of the country and the ambitions, the need for defence and the economic capability of the owners. It is, however, not now always possible to judge why this and not that place was fortified. The strategy of the time is lost to us for want of knowledge of economic and political matters, but also the natural conditions are changed beyond our understanding. Most modern explanations of convenient strategic settings should indeed be taken with several grains of salt, the more so as they are often uttered by people with little or no military understanding at all. The fact that the castles became obsolete after a fairly short period, less than a hundred years, and gradually disappeared afterwards, in many cases certainly totally, does not make it any easier to estimate their importance. In the connection between the use of castles and certain political conditions there are, however, parallels to Scotland, although at a later date and with other building materials. This should remind us that castles are particular and expensive specialist's tools in which you do not invest unless it is absolutely necessary or very much to your advantage — and you can afford it.

Parallel with their actual constructional details castles appear also in the written sources, and in particular their role in decrees and other legal texts from the middle of the thirteenth century onwards reflects the effects of castle-building on the relationship between the king and his closest rivals in the fight for the power to rule and exploit the resources of the realm, hold privileges and take part in royal prerogatives. The provisions relating to castles illustrate the balance of power in the country, and well-known and often quoted are the coronation charters of 1320 and 1326 which obliged the respective kings to demolish several important royal castles.[11] It is doubtful whether any demolition actually took place, but that such claims could ever be written into legal documents shows the predominance of the nobility and a situation very different from 1397, when Queen Margaret issued her ban on private castle-building.[12] The statutes also emphasise the fact that a country may be conquered without the castles being won, but it cannot be governed if the central power is not in command of its fortifications.

The first provisions known about castle-building date from the middle of the thirteenth century and in reality they deal with the right to employ the labour force, the peasants.[13] Work had always been part of the tax system of the country, and regulations concerning the amount of work to be demanded legally by the king and/or the magnates do reflect the balance of power economically. When the work demanded has to do with the construction of fortifications, the ancient rules of mobilisation must also be taken into consideration.[14] One of the important original functions of the king was to defend the country, and as warlord it was his prerogative to call up an army in case of need, but in a farming country this right was always somewhat counteracted by the natural inclination of the people to stay at home at sowing and harvesting times and not to leave the crops alone for too long during the growing season. So here is another point where the relationship between king and aristocracy can be measured. Imagine, for instance, the impact on the whole province when at times the peasants of Funen were so busy building on the royal castle of Nyborg that they could not look after their farms for a whole season — and that at a time when the crop yielded three- to five-fold![15] This is more than taxation, it is a question of a right over the resources of the country, and also the right to decide which policy to pursue. Accordingly it is a point often at stake between the two contending parties, no matter how society and the ways of war changed during the middle ages.[16] And here it is interesting to note that the last three medieval kings, who had been bound considerably by their coronation charters and had had to allow the nobility to fortify, seem to have been able to make quite extensive use of the labour force.

The conditions here outlined are further emphasised by the political history of the reign of Valdemar Atterdag, who did win the country by conquering it castle by castle. Written evidence from his time illustrates the changing power and ambitions of the nobility and himself, and particularly the contemporary 'Chronicle of Sealand' gives a most vivid picture of the period down to 1359. Finally, the scales weighed down in favour of the king when even the traditionally obstinate and stubborn aristocracy of Jutland was defeated. That royal victory was also accepted by these adversaries to royal predominance appears from two documents, both dated 1373, two years before the king died.[17]

Two noblemen promised to rebuild two royal castles which they respectively had destroyed during the recent war with the king. The names of both sites are well known to historians, but neither has been subjected to archaeological investigation. One, Aggersborg, was the successor of the giant Viking-age fortress by the Limfjord, but the site of the king's medieval stronghold there is not known to-day. The other, Ørum in Thisted county, is most probably buried under the existing manor. Both documents describe the typical motte-and-bailey site with fortifications of earth and timber. The contents are not identical, but so similar that we are here obviously not confronted with 'portraits' of the two castles, but certainly with instruments of debt.[18] The document relating to Ørum even enumerates all the furnishings, animals and provisions owed to the king. Nothing indicates that the two sites were ever refortified, but rebuilt they certainly were, and they functioned as administrative royal centres for quite some time afterwards. So also royal castles could be rather simple and old-fashioned at the time of unrest in the fourteenth century, though we cannot of course be sure if these strongholds were indeed constructed by the king or his representatives, or by someone who had pawned the place. The 'Chronicle of Sealand' tells us how in the 1350s the aristocracy of Jutland pitied their social equals of Sealand, because they were forced by the king to fortify their homes with mire and mud only; but apparently at times the king did not have much better castles himself.[19] There is no evidence that such strongholds were built after the time of King Valdemar or even in his later years either by the crown, the church or the lay nobility, except in the border area between the kingdom of Denmark and the duchy of Slesvig, and here it was for campaigning reasons. The castles set up quickly here in the early decades of the fifteenth century, when Eric of Pomerania fought for his right to unite the duchy with the kingdom, are parallels to those used when William conquered England in 1066, and also to those built by the English in Ireland later on.

Another piece of evidence to which I would like to draw attention brings us nearer to Scotland, and Orkney, which in the fourteenth century was still part of the North Sea empire founded by Canute the Great. The document in question is a treaty of obligation dating from 1379, in which the earl of Orkney committed himself to Haakon VI, king of Norway and the husband of our often-mentioned Queen Margaret. Besides promising to be obedient and faithful the earl obliged himself not to build castles without the consent of the king.[20] This is, of course, not exactly a Danish case, but it shows how the idea of the king as master of the fortifications of the country was generally held to in Scandinavia as in the rest of Europe in the middle ages. There is no need here to elaborate on the English 'licence to crenellate', but it might be worth remembering that in France also, and as late as the sixteenth century, it was the king's prerogative to give his permission for castle-building.[21] For any ruler of Denmark it must have been quite in accordance with both ancient legal powers and general European ideas that control over the fortifications of the country, their use and their construction, was a royal prerogative to give, take or delegate, as when Eric of Pomerania in 1409 exempted 'his' citizens of Nysted on Lolland from building work on his castle of Aalholm on the same island.[22] Naturally, the nobility very much wanted to share his prerogative, and this is illustrated by provisions stating who was to command the castles of the realm in case of vacancy of the throne: the council of the realm or perhaps a candidate for the crown.[23] Provisions on this matter run parallel with the statutes annulling the ban on private castle-building. Thus, in the late middle ages the nobility obtained not only a general licence to crenellate, they also legalised their right to take part in an important royal prerogative, which implied a wide control over royal finances and the official policy of the country.

Against this background it is no wonder that the king tried to find himself allies among the commoners and place them as holders of the royal entailed estates, preferably the more important ones. His opponents were, however, too strong. The nobility found it strictly illegal and against their ancient prerogatives to have commoners put in charge of the royal castles, and this only happened in a few places. For the greater part of the later middle ages the most important castles of the country were in the hands of members of a very narrow circle of the uppermost layers of society, and, in several cases as hereditary mortgage.[24] Even Shakespeare knew about Rosenkrantz and Gyldenstjerne, as anybody who had the least idea of the state of Denmark at that time was bound to. These families and their equals sat on and lived in royal castles like Kalø on Djursland and Tranekær on Langeland,

and whatever building efforts they carried out there were financed by the income of the area administered from the castle.[25] The ancestral seats or principal manors of these people normally remained timberwork buildings until the sixteenth century, when a new political situation and much improved economic circumstances led to the construction of many unfortified stone houses and beautiful manor-castles which, although neither medieval nor strongholds, have contributed much to the general idea of what Danish castles were like in the middle ages.

Queen Margaret had attained her aim of getting rid of the private castles, but her successors had to suffer the fact that noblemen took over the castles of the realm. The queen's efforts concerning the redemption of the property of the crown have been studied with eager interest. Her talent for using legal means instead of military ones, as favoured by her father, has been greatly admired, but her interference in probate cases where widows and orphans — traditionally pitied groups — were involved, has led to reproachful emphasis on her ruthlessness. From the very beginning she worked in close collaboration with the church, particularly the bishops, and she always paid her debts to them either with royal incomes or privileges, as when her chancellor, the bishop of Roskilde, Jens Andersen Lodehat, got the income from the herring market by Øresund for several years, or with some of the land she got back for the crown.[26] If there was a castle standing on such property it was normally given with the obligation to demolish the fortifications, as was the case at Hald near Viborg, the seat of one of the most obstinate noblemen of Jutland during the time of King Valdemar.[27] It is not easy to see when the castles were demolished, but it certainly happened fairly soon, since the upkeep would mean expenses — in money or labour — and demolition might mean an income and even a substantial one. To my knowledge this is mentioned in only one written source, namely the document issued when Queen Margaret gave the castle of Tibrantsholm near Stockholm to Archbishop Henry of Uppsala, with the obligation to demolish the castle. What profit he gained from the demolition was to be deducted from the 2,000 mk the queen owed him.[28] Although unfortunately the only piece of evidence of its kind, this is certainly most illuminating. Re-use of building materials has a long history in Denmark, and exactly because of that there are very few old houses left to study, apart from the churches. Re-use applied equally to the relatively few and late stone buildings as to wooden constructions. Amusing stories about over-night thefts of wooden or timberwork buildings are known from an early date, and provisions about the building of houses and the stealing of them are stressed in the laws and repeated even in 1354.[29] By the end of the fourteenth century there was at least one moated site, and certainly more, where the main building was a traditional wooden hall with central fire and the posts dug into the ground. Houses of stone were not often found on the mounds. From the written sources one gets the impression that stone buildings are mentioned, where they exist.[30] Danish 'stone' houses are normally built of brick which was a very expensive building material to produce, as it demanded both specialist manufacturers and great amounts of wood. The transport of it was also expensive and certainly slow, considering that a load of bricks in the middle ages was only 100 stones of brick. So, although the use of brick had come to Denmark by the middle of the twelfth century, few could afford it until relatively late, and both on monastic sites and in the towns many of the buildings were of timberwork, perhaps with wattle and daub between the posts, until the very late middle ages. This was also the case for the town houses of the nobility.[31] Timber, particularly cut beams, could also be expensive and hard to get, and beams are sometimes known to have travelled quite a lot from building to building, including those of humbler scale, over the centuries.[32] Thus, where bricks and wooden building materials are concerned, it is not only a question of private economy, but also one of the control of the resources of the country, and again a source of rivalry between king and nobility.

The value placed on fine trees at an early date is illustrated by a statute in one of the old provincial laws of Denmark, which ordained that 'if anybody should possibly be so malignant as to hurt an oak tree' this person should be punished like a thief.[33] In the fifteenth century the effects of the misdeeds of such people were felt, for by then trees good enough for building purposes apparently began to be in short supply. Even without malignant hurting of trees this is not strange, if we consider the enormous exploitation of the woods and the number of big oak trees used for houses, boats and fortifications since the Viking age. For a long time, and certainly still in the fifteenth century, many houses were built without ground-sills and with the wall-posts dug directly into the ground, which in our damp climate makes them rot away within a few years. Besides, swine were left to pasture in the woods, cattle were fed on young leaves, and all-eating, all-devastating goats were quite common. It all wore on the forests, and ordinances and decrees from the fifteenth and early sixteenth centuries show the concern of the central power to protect the woods and limit the damage.[34] People were ordered to build on sill-stones and use timberwork instead of 'bole' houses (i.e. of vertical tree-trunk construction) to save wood. It was strictly forbidden to feed cattle on leaves and an abrupt end was put to goat-keeping. Even if the situation was not so bad at the time of Queen Margaret, no doubt then also good timber and ready-cut beams were wanted and could provide an excellent profit.

It was not only the church which sometimes demolished castles. Unfortunately lay examples are few, but not without interest, and of course the queen was involved, as in the probate case of the Grubbes of Gunderslevholm near Sorø on Sealand.[35] The family had been faithful supporters of the queen and her father, and the place must at one time have been a strong castle, since King Valdemar bothered to attack and conquer it in 1345. The founder died as a consequence of the siege, but he must have taken part on the king's side, for the place was pawned and forfeited. This is one of the few cases which can make us feel the horrors of medieval warfare in Denmark, for we are told that the seneschal who led the royal army had the garrison slain.[36] However, time went by, and the son of the founder sat happily in Gunderslevholm until he died around 1390. The queen supported the widow in the probate case which followed, and had it written into the document settling the case that all fortifications should be demolished. From the point of view of the monarch it is, of course, always fine to get rid of a private castle, particularly if you cannot be sure of the intentions of the holder. But in this case, as certainly in others as well, the threat does not seem alarming, and the idea of profit from demolition appears to be more relevant. But it is difficult to tell who benefited: the widow, or perhaps Queen Margaret herself? If so, it would be two birds killed with one stone, and when profit is not mentioned here, and in the other examples from Denmark, it may have been because it was a matter of course.

For this indicates that, on the sites where demolition is known to have taken place, only the buildings and the palisades were pulled down. Mounds, moats and ramparts were left more or less untouched. This is true at Hald near Viborg, where two castle sites from the fourteenth century, and one from the early sixteenth, are still preserved, and at Nørholm near Varde in south-western Jutland the site was sold or let or pawned as good grazing land several times during the later middle ages.[37] It is in some ways contradictory to say that the castles were pulled down, when the really defensive elements remained standing, but that is no doubt because it was too complicated and expensive to move all the earth, and not through some idea of 'still having the castle in case . . .' From an agricultural point of view there was no need to demolish the earthworks since they provided fine grazing which was desirable at a time when cattle-breeding was expanding. The new owners, the bishops, already had better and stronger castles than the ones they received, and besides, with the strengthening of central power, peace and order reigned again in the country, and the private castles became obsolete without any fighting. So people gave up their mouldy strongholds in swamp and bog, which are the easiest places to fortify in the Danish landscape, and came back to civilisation to live in peaceful manor-houses as the queen wanted them to, and as their ancestors had done in the past, not so very long before. For the rest of the middle ages central power was able to maintain peace and order in the country except for two short intervals, one around 1440, when a rebellion harassed Jutland, the other in the 1520s, when the same happened in Skåne as a consequence of the dethroning of King Christian II. In both cases peasants were involved, but neither resulted in the building of any private fortification as peasant uproar never provoked such a reaction in medieval Denmark. Fear of angry peasants certainly did not motivate the annulments of the ban on private castle-building in 1483, 1513 and 1523, because then a host of new fortifications would certainly have been constructed over the years and that did not happen. We in fact know of only two private buildings worth being called castles from the period after Valdemar Atterdag.

But there was of course a lot of prestige attached to the dwellings of the nobility, and as class consciousness was growing in the later middle ages this became more and more characteristic. It is present already in a document from around 1400 concerning the manor of Hørsholm in north Sealand, which is described as a '*curia* that is also called *castrum*'.[38] It is also evident from all the moated sites created in the fifteenth and sixteenth centuries. The 'moating in' was really the Danish version of crenellation. It was used widely and for a long time even after the middle ages as the only thing resembling defences, but that does not make a castle out of a manor otherwise without ramparts and palisades or walls and towers, and with timberwork buildings on the mound: not even if there is a small stone house among these buildings as a kind of safe for the valuables of the owner in case of fire.[39] This way of building manors was partly due to tradition, partly to the bad state of the economy as the result of a century of unrest and crises, and partly also to the fact already mentioned that those who might have built on a grand scale were often holders, perhaps hereditary holders, of royal castles, and resided there.

There are, however, exceptions and the earliest and most magnificent is Gjorslev on Stevns at the south of Sealand, which was built around 1400 by the bishop of Roskilde, Jens Andersen Lodehat, chancellor and greatest supporter of Queen Margaret. This is a true palace, unique in shape and of royal status, which is no wonder, for besides being an immensely rich landowner the bishop had the royal income from the herring market by Øresund at the time when he had the palace built.[40] Gjorslev is not a castle: it is clearly not defensible, although there are gunloops at the top of the central part. It is a glorious example of the bishop's power and his obedience towards the queen. If he needed defence, he had the strong old castle of Dragsholm in the north-west of Sealand. In Skåne, the richest and most prosperous of the old Danish provinces, there are a few medieval stone houses, which are bigger and more decorated than the rest and are often not built of brick but of unhewn stone. One is Bollerup not far from Ystad, dating from the second half of the fifteenth century. Another, and best known of them all, is Glimmingehus nearby. The latter, often mentioned as one of two surviving medieval Danish castles, does look almost like a proper tower house, and its defences are the medieval dream come true; but when Glimmingehus was built, about 1500, it was an anachronism. It was too tiny to be lived in, and in fact never was, not even by the man who built it, Jens Holgersen Ulfstand, who resided at the royal castle of Visborg on Gotland. That Glimmingehus together with Bollerup was not burnt in the rebellion of the 1520s 'because they were of stone', as the source tells us, does not make the two of them castles.[41] Bollerup was a fine manor, and Glimmingehus could almost be called the rich man's folly, or a very early example of Danish Renaissance building because of the ancient elements deliberately used.[42] Thus Glimmingehus can be regarded as a forerunner of the manor castles of the sixteenth century, such as Borreby on south Sealand and Egeskov on Funen. How quickly economic capability improved and the demand for living standards of higher quality grew strong is illustrated by the example of the manor of Tjele near Vibord. Here a small but for its time fine stone house, from around 1525, is very well preserved, because it was soon outdated and replaced by a much bigger main building, also of stone.[43]

Most of the high prelates stuck to their old castles and manors but the only two genuine strongholds from the period were built by the bishop of Viborg in the 1520s: Hald near Viborg and Spøttrup in Salling. He was in opposition to the crown and very unpopular in his see, so safety was, of course, of great concern for him, and his two castles were, if not the biggest, certainly the most modern fortifications in the country, because they were defences against artillery. Spøttrup is still standing and is the other building always mentioned as a typical medieval castle, which, in fact, it is not at all. It is a combination of a medieval palace and modern anti-artillery ramparts, and thus it represents an early step towards the process of separation of dwelling and fortification, which put an end to the castle in the medieval sense.

Not even the crown built many new castles during the later middle ages and those it did build were very traditional: regular, rectangular and ringwalled. They obviously had the same functions as the old castles of the realm, placed as they were by the border, like Duborg in Flensborg, in newly-won areas like Visborg on Gotland, and at a centre of traffic like Krogen, later called Kronborg, by Øresund.[44] The kings modernised their old castles a little, but the real changes took place only after the middle ages, and it seems that the country must have appeared fully covered by fortifications of older date. The most extraordinary royal construction from the period is the fortified *warft* (dockyard) of King Hans on Lolland.[45]

All this leads us to the most important lesson about 'kings, nobility and buildings in the later middle ages' that we can learn from the study of buildings and building regulations and the statutes on the construction of castles. They do, of course, illustrate the balance of power between king and aristocracy. They also help to give a broader understanding of some of the royal prerogatives and their effects in society; and finally they show that more of economic life is involved than has previously been believed. These three aspects are closely connected, if not interlaced, but through them we get a better definition, not only of the state of affairs at particular moments, but also of the concept of kingship and the king's functions in society in general and over a longer period — the king seen as central power. This is in relation not only to nobility and church, the rivals of the crown, but to the inhabitants and the resources of the country as a whole. It is characteristic that the king issued decrees against the exploitation of the woods and repeatedly reminded holders of royal estates not to overcut, and preferably not cut at all, at the same time as they were being told about their obligation to see to the upkeep of the place they were in charge of.[46] The decrees became building regulations as well, when people were told to build on sill-stones, etc. The king appears really to be the master of the natural resources of the country when we see him in control of the building stones from the cliff of Stevns. He could order special trees from Holsten and the monastery of Herridsvad in Skåne, and through his local representatives he could, to some extent, decide who might have timber, stones and other building materials in the district.[47] The king — or central power — also controlled fiscal conditions by being able to call up peasants to work on fortifications, mills or other important constructions.

To return to the two sources from 1396 and 1483: they are indeed testimonies to the balance of power and rivalry between king and nobility about who is to rule and reign and be the steady, regulating and controlling power in society. To use modern terms, it is in reality a fight for the right to control the production potential of the country and decide whether it should be public or private. It is interesting to note that the ancient royal prerogatives concerning 'what belongs to no man belongs to the king' are not assailed during the period in question. In a way they still exist, only the word 'royal' should be replaced by 'of the state'. It appears that a king was necessary at the time, if for no other purpose than to legalise decrees and ordinances by supporting them with his signature and thus symbolising central power. It is, indeed, amazing how far the central power of the late middle ages sought to extend its control over individuals in society and their building activities, whether or not as

a consequence of the wood-protecting decrees. For instance, an ordinance for Funen
from 1473 ordered the peasants to build privies on sill-stones beside their farms.
That was, indeed, the economy of a farming country and perhaps even an example
of environmental care.

NOTES

1. Erik Kroman, ed., *Den Danske Rigslovgivning indtil 1400* (Det Danske Sprog-og
Litteraturselskab, Copenhagen, 1971), 335, para. 3: 'Dronning Margrethes forordning i
Viborg' (24.1.1396).

2. *Samling af Danske Kongers Handfæstninger og andre lignende Akter, af Geheimearkivets
Årsberetninger København 1856-1858* (1974), 54, para. 43: 'Hans' Handfæstning, Halmstad,
1.2. 1483'.

3. Ibid., 28ff (13 or 20.7.1397, Kalmar document).

4. Ibid., 56ff (22.7.1513).

5. Ibid., 65ff (3.8.1523).

6. Rikke Agnete Olsen, *Borge i Danmark* (1986): the most important literature is collected
together in this work.

7. E.g. Haraldsborg by Roskilde from c.1130: in the fifteenth and sixteenth centuries called
curia, and sometimes *castrum*.

8. Hammershus on Bornholm by the archbishop; Egholm in Voldborg district,
Copenhagen county, by Count Jacob of Northern Halland; Gottorp by Slesvig by the duke of
Slesvig.

9. 'Chronica Sialandie', in Erik Kroman, ed., *Danmarks Middelalderlige Annaler* (1980),
142 (1359).

10. Rikke Agnete Olsen, 'Big manors and large-scale farming', *Château Gaillard*, xiii
(1987), 161.

11. *Rigslovgivning*: Christoffer II (1320), 185ff.; Valdemar III (1326), 213ff.

12. C M Smidt, *Kalø* (Nationalmuseets Arbejdsmark, 1944). Kalø, Ø. Lisbjerg district,
Randers county, constructed c.1313, demolished after 1670.

13. *Rigslovgivning*: Ordinances, Abel and Christoffer I (1251-9), 43ff.

14. *Rigslovgivning*: Vederloven c. 1180, p.1 ff.; Sven Aggesen about Vederlov, p.5 ff.; Saxo
on Vederlov, p.25 ff. (Statutes in the provincial laws).

15. Otto Norn, *Christian III's Borge* (Copenhagen, 1949), 61-71; Kr.Erslev and W
Mollerup, eds, *Frederik I's Danske Registranter* (1879), p.411 (1532).

16. *Rigslovgivning*: Erik Mendved's privilege to Skåne; on the king's right to cut wood,
p.184. para. 4.

17. *Diplomatarium Danicum*, Aggersborg, 3, 9, no.279; and Ørum, 3, 9, no.282.

18. This idea is supported by Professor in law dr. jur. Ole Fenger, Aarhus University.

19. 'Chron.Sialandie', 141.

20. *Diplom.Norv.*, nos. 459-60.

21. Talcy in the Loire Valley c.1520.

22. *Repertorium Diplomaticum Regni Danici Medievalis*, iii, 127 (no.5066).

23. The 'slotslov' mentioned in the late medieval coronation charters. Eric of Pomerania
tried to ensure that they went to his cousin Bugislavs, whom he wanted as his successor.

24. Harry Christensen, *Len og magt i Danmark 1439-81* (1983), 52ff.

25. Rikke Agnete Olsen, 'The Danish royal castles in the late middle ages: fortresses or
administrative centres?', *Château Gaillard*, xii (1985).

26. Kr. Erslev, *Dronning Margrethe og Kalmarunionens Grundæggelse* (Copenhagen, 1882),
311-12.

27. Vald.Andersen, *Hald Hovedgård* (1977), 17.

28. *Diplom. Norv.*, no.357; *Svenskt Diplomatarium*, no.168.

29. 'Chron.Sialandia', 128ff.

30. Rikke Agnete Olsen, 'The buildings on Danish moated sites', *Château Gaillard*, ix-x (1982), 510ff.

31. Rikke Agnete Olsen, 'Danish manor houses of the late middle ages', *Liber Castellorum* (1981), 154ff.; Ingrid Nielsen, *Projekt Middelalderbyen* (Ribe, 1985), 134ff.; Marianne Johansen, *Køge*, 64ff.; Aage Andersen, *Næstved*, 51ff.

32. Øm Monastery demolished in the 1560s, materials used at the castle of Skanderborg, later at the manor of Moesgaard, near Aarhus.

33. Erik Kroman, ed., *Danmarks Gamle Love på Nutidsdansk* (1945); *Eriks Sjællandske Lov*, ii, 112 (bk.3, chap.42).

34. 'Fyns Vedtægt, 1473', *Danske Magazin*, V/5, 146; Arild Huitfeldt, 'Lollands Vilkaar, 1446', *Danmarks Riges Kronike*, iii, 678ff.

35. *Repertorium Danici*, nos. 3828-35.

36. 'Chron. Sialandia', 124.

37. *Frederik I's Danske Registranter* (23.11.1523); *Repertorium Danici*, nos. 4809-11.

38. Ibid., no.3788.

39. Rikke Agnete Olsen, 'The buildings on Danish moated sites'.

40. Chr. Aksel Jensen, *Gjorslev* (1924).

41. A Heise, ed., *Skibykroniken Dan.* (1890-1), 103ff.

42. Rikke Agnete Olsen, 'The buildings on Danish moated sites', 512.

43. Hans Henrik Engqvist, *Tjele* (1974).

44. Rikke Agnete Olsen, 'Danish royal castles of the late middle ages', *Château Gaillard*, xii (1985), 65ff.

45. On Slotø in Nakskov Fjord.

46. *Frederik I's Danske Registranter* (many examples).

47. William Christensen, ed., *Missiver fra kongerne Christian I og Hans* (1912-14), e.g. vol.i, p.194 (no.272), p.245 (no.350), pp. 266ff. (nos.379-81); vol.ii, p.243 (no.199); and many others.

6

KINGS, NOBLES AND BUILDINGS OF THE LATER MIDDLE AGES: SCOTLAND

Geoffrey Stell

Following recent reappraisals of the political and social character of late medieval Scotland,[1] the limited purpose of this paper is to assess the wealth, power and relationships of the monarchy and nobility as expressed through the secular architecture of approximately the first century and a half of the Stewart dynasty, between about 1371 and 1542. The building works of the crown and the nobility are examined in turn, and there follows an analysis of the negative and positive aspects of their relationships that emerge through this body of evidence.

I

An architectural measure of the standing of the main branch of the Stewart family at the accession in 1371 of Robert II, son of Walter the Steward and Marjorie Bruce, is provided by a small number of residential strongholds in west central Scotland. By the fourteenth century the Stewarts had become the most powerful of the nobility in the region around the Clyde estuary, their empire having been founded upon great lordships in Ayrshire and Renfrewshire conferred by royal grants in the twelfth century.[2]

Dundonald Castle was the centre of their Ayrshire lordship of North Kyle, and the elongated tower which forms the major surviving portion of the castle is substantially the result of Robert II's modification of an earlier structure on this site.[3] Despite Dr Samuel Johnson's scornful derision in 1773 at 'the homely accommodation of "King Bob" ', this building is one of the largest of its kind in Scotland, measuring some 25 m by 12 m on plan and over 18 m high, its chief architectural glory being a grand, rib-vaulted upper-floor hall. The building was designed as a residential gatehouse block and the outer walls incorporate carved armorials which proclaim the royal status of the Stewarts and their family connections in the late fourteenth century.

Dundonald thus bears tangible marks of the family's elevation to royal status. Its general character and proportions are also faintly reflected in the excavated remains of the large elongated block (30 m by 9 m overall) that Robert II erected at Kindrochit in Mar, evidently a royal hunting-lodge in an area where there was no royal hunting reserve.[4] Among other Stewart strongholds, that at Rothesay on Bute also shows the later effects of the family's promotion, particularly at the hands of James IV and James V who added a chapel, gatehouse and barbican to the circular and moated enclosure-castle of their thirteenth-century ancestors.[5]

However, of the royal castles and residences that the Stewarts inherited as part of the crown patrimony in 1371 there is surprisingly little archaeological knowledge. At Edinburgh, for example, the only visible pre-Stewart remains comprise a twelfth-century chapel and, encased within the Half Moon Battery, the ruins of the tower erected for David II in 1367-8. The earliest surviving work which bears an unmistakable aura of royal majesty is at Linlithgow Palace where James I spent over £5,000 Scots on a major rebuilding programme between 1424 and 1435, following his release from captivity in England. Part of this large sum was probably derived from the great customs levied at Linlithgow's port of Blackness, but most of it probably came from the half of the £26,000 raised for James's ransom that was never used for that purpose.[6]

Substantial portions of James I's work survive in the east quarter of the palace, a hall-gatehouse range 53 m in length comprising a great hall on the first floor and an adjacent kitchen at the northern end: a similar general arrangement to that at Dundonald and elsewhere. At Linlithgow, prior to the reorganisation of access in the reign of James V, the central entrance-passage was originally fronted by a drawbridge, the cables for which were evidently worked from the hall itself, while the portcullis was operated from galleries that ran beside the great hall. It is possible that a regular quadrangular layout was part of James's original scheme, but as they now stand, the towers and ranges enclosing the central courtyard are largely the products of his successors.[7]

The palace constituted part of the dower of Princess Margaret of Denmark, and was clearly one of the favourite residences of her son, James IV. His main surviving contribution to the building fabric is in the south quarter, which includes a royal chapel, and he was probably also responsible for the king's hall and presence chamber in the west range. Further works were undertaken and completed in James V's reign, this and most of the preceding phases of building activity being marked by a wealth and quality of decorative sculpture and architectural detail, as much a measure of royal patronage as sheer size and sophistication of layout.[8]

Building programmes of similar refinement and scale were also undertaken by James IV and James V at Holyroodhouse,[10] Stirling Castle and Falkland Palace, where the quality is best represented by the French-inspired courtyard facade, part of a scheme of remodelling carried out between 1537 and 1541.[11] The influences of a Francophile court and a French-led office of works are no less evident in the palace block built within the precincts of Stirling Castle in the last years of James V's reign.[12] About fifty years earlier, James IV appears to have set out there a similar quadrangular layout around the inner square immediately to the north of the later palace, and his principal surviving contribution, the Great Hall, lies on the lower side of that square, a detached, free-standing structure, unlike that at Linlithgow. Completed shortly after 1500, Stirling Great Hall outclassed its near-contemporary in the Crown Square of Edinburgh Castle in size (38.5 m by 11.1 m, as opposed to 28.9 m by 12.5 m) and probably also in splendour, rivalling those at English establishments such as Eltham and Hampton Court.

Stirling's defences were also the subject of attention in the reign of James IV (who was born there). Reconstruction of the main gatehouse and forework was begun in about 1500 and completed by about 1508. Following the line of an earlier screen across the front of the rock summit, these structures were of traditional design, the only concession to the advent of gunpowder firearms being a slightly greater ratio of wall thickness to height and the provision of so-called 'dumb-bell' gun-loops.[13] Interestingly, a loop of this type appears conspicuously in one tower of the curtain-wall of Stirling Castle as it is shown in the background to a fifteenth-century illustration of the battle of Bannockburn, the earliest known depiction of a Scottish castle.[14] Portions of the existing castle at Stirling date back to the late fourteenth century, but this illustration shows a complete and impressive multi-towered enceinte, an indication, perhaps, of the point that Scottish royal fortifications had reached by the later fifteenth century.

The needs of coastal defence constituted an important priority among other royal fortifications. One of the principal royal castles in the west of Scotland was on the rock citadel of Dumbarton, which overlooked the upper basin of the Clyde estuary and served as a base for west coast military expeditions. The site had been the centre of the British kingdom of Strathclyde from the fifth to the eleventh centuries,[15] and a 'new' royal castle associated with the establishment of a sheriffdom was erected here at some date before 1222, the castle lying within the earldom of Lennox but being specifically reserved to the king in a charter of 1238.[16] Serious difficulties in maintaining the status of this royal enclave occurred in 1489 when the earl of Lennox, despite having been granted custody of the castle, joined in a conspiracy against James IV, and the castle was twice besieged by royal forces.[17] In view of Dumbarton's considerable historical interest, it is unfortunate that the medieval remains of the castle are so slight and fragmentary, comprising only two lengths of plain walling.

On the east coast priority was given to the defences of the royal castles of Berwick, finally lost to the English in 1482,[18] Dunbar, focus of much activity in the late fifteenth and early sixteenth centuries but now a much-reduced ruin,[19] and Blackness Castle, an impressive promontory stronghold of distinctive ship-shape layout, situated on the middle reaches of the Forth estuary guarding the harbour and revenues of Blackness, the coastal port of Linlithgow. The earliest visible features of Blackness comprise a central tower, the so-called 'main mast', and a south frontal range which after 1537 was heightened, massively thickened and pierced by gun-holes to serve as an artillery fortification.[20] It is not clear whether the earliest remains belong to the 1440s, when the castle first comes on record, or to the reign of James III.[21] Nor is it clear how Blackness came to be a royal castle, for it first appears as a private stronghold of the Crichtons, and did not come into royal possession until 1453. To state simply that it was 'a gift by George Crichton to King James II' perhaps belies the circumstances under which James acquired Blackness for the crown.[22]

II

For about the first fifty years of the Stewart regime the political dominance of the widely ramified Stewart nobility expressed itself in a number of major buildings, the greatest of which, Doune Castle,[23] was of vice-regal status. The building of the castle in the later fourteenth century, probably from about 1380, followed the absorption through marriage of the earldom of Menteith by a member of a cadet branch of the main line of the Stewarts. Its builder, Robert Stewart, Duke of Albany, ruled the Scottish kingdom as regent for more than two decades until his death in 1420, and during his lifetime Doune probably rivalled the nearby royal castle at Stirling in scale and grandeur.

Albany was succeeded by his son, Murdoch, but in 1425 James I took a firm stand against the pretensions and troublemaking of his own kindred, and had all the Albany Stewarts executed. The development of Doune Castle itself appears to have been arrested by this event, and the windows in the south curtain-wall are indications of intended but incomplete ranges of buildings. Except for relatively minor additions and works of repair,[24] the castle remains much as it was taken over by the crown in 1425: a lofty four-storeyed tower-gatehouse adjoined by a long great hall range and linked kitchen tower, all backed by a courtyard enclosed within high curtain-walls.

Until the middle of the fifteenth century the family closest to the Stewarts in authority and influence was that of the earls of Douglas.[25] Their power-base at Douglas in upper Clydesdale retains no identifiable medieval remains, but their extensive acquisitions in the fourteenth century, many of them the rewards of service to the Bruce dynasty, are still marked by some powerful-looking buildings. The lordship of troublesome Galloway and the wardenship of the West March, for example, were bestowed in 1369 by David II on Archibald Douglas, who in 1388 succeeded as third earl of Douglas and in 1400 died in Threave Castle which he himself had erected.

Among the top dozen towers in Scotland in terms of its floor area and cubic capacity, Threave is a massive 26-m-high pile of five main storeys, its height still further emphasised by the fact that it stands on an island in a flat and watery landscape. Its design incorporates certain features that appear unusual in relation to Scottish towers of later generations, but it is possible that the work of Archibald's royal master, David's Tower in Edinburgh Castle, may have had an influence on Threave. Recent excavations have confirmed that Threave was associated with a group of ancillary buildings, possibly including a hall block, and that it had its own riverside harbour.[26] The site is surrounded by a low earthen bank, and the tower came to acquire a regular and close-fitting curtain-wall of stone and lime. But there are grounds for doubting the claim that this was entirely the work of the eighth earl in 1450, anticipating trouble from James II; it probably belongs instead to a late fifteenth-century phase of royal custody following the forfeiture of the castle in 1455.[27]

Another major acquisition that lay closer to the Douglases' home base in Clydesdale was the lordship of Bothwell, which was acquired through marriage in 1362 by Archibald, later third earl. This lordship was centred upon a huge, albeit slighted, thirteenth-century castle which, until their forfeiture in 1455, the Douglases proceeded to modify and develop, most notably at the eastern end where an upper-floor chapel and a two-storeyed great hall range (measuring some 21 m by 12 m overall) were inserted.[28] The scale and detailing of these operations fell not far short of contemporary royal works, exotic features such as the arcuated machicolations crowning the south-eastern, so-called 'Douglas Tower', possibly betraying the French tastes of the fourth earl who became duke of Touraine and died in 1424 fighting in France.

Bothwell, Threave and other major strongholds were associated with the 'Black' Douglases, who descended through an illegitimate line from the uncle of the first earl of Douglas. A rival branch, who actively assisted in the downfall of their kindred, was formed by the 'Red' Douglases, earls of Angus, who descended from an illegitimate son of the first earl and Margaret Stewart, countess of Angus. They created problems of their own for the crown, particularly in relation to two of their major strongholds, Tantallon and Hermitage.

In use by 1374, Tantallon in its original form was almost certainly a product of the first earl of Douglas. What is especially relevant in the present context is not so much its distinctive military architecture,[29] but the fact that in 1491 and 1528 successive Douglas earls of Angus defied their monarchs to the extent that on each occasion the castle was besieged by royal forces attended by the king in person.[30] Treasonable dealings with England were at the root of both episodes, which were apparently resolved by diplomatic rather than military means. James IV quickly re-established amicable relations with the fifth earl in 1491, but the outcome in 1528 was not so friendly, for having failed to take Tantallon in a twenty-day siege, James V eventually sent the sixth earl into exile in England, placed the castle under direct royal control and strengthened it, having witnessed its military value.

Hermitage Castle, which the Douglases had progressively enlarged since 1371 (evidently, to judge from the surviving remains, largely for domestic, not military purposes), was at the centre of the dispute in 1491 when James IV learnt of Angus's secret agreement to exchange the lands, lordship and castle for holdings in England. James persuaded Angus to exchange them instead for equivalent rights in Scotland; the choice eventually fell on Bothwell and in 1492 Patrick Hepburn, first earl of Bothwell, was entrusted with Hermitage in Angus's place. Direct royal control did not seem to have been an option on this occasion but royal annexation of the lordship and castle and banishment of its owners finally occurred in 1540 following the treachery of the third earl of Bothwell and his secret dealings with England.[31]

In the new regime under James IV another estate redistributed to the first earl of Bothwell was that of Crichton in Midlothian, where a large courtyard castle had grown up around a late fourteenth-century tower. The development of the castle may have consciously followed royal example (e.g. Linlithgow Palace), and certainly corresponded with the fortunes of its Crichton family owners in royal service, especially of Sir William Crichton, later Lord Crichton, master of the household under James I and chancellor and leading political figure during the minority of James II. Either he or his son, who was chamberlain to James II, was responsible for the significant addition of a hall-gatehouse range and associated services. But William's grandson fell foul of James III and, charged among other things with 'stuffing' his castle with men and provisions in order to hold it against the king, was forfeited in February 1484.[32]

Another family made by royal service and broken by royal displeasure was that of the Boyds of Kilmarnock who rose to prominence during the minority of James III. Created a lord of parliament by James II, Robert, Lord Boyd, secured control of the young James III in July 1466, and using his royal authority virtually ran the government of the kingdom for the next three years, a period which included the marriage negotiations with Denmark.[33] The scale of the Boyds' principal establishment at Dean Castle, though slightly altered and restored, remains a good measure of their days of power and glory: a large, early fifteenth-century tower and a detached great hall range which marks the zenith of the Boyd fortunes in the middle decades of the fifteenth century. But their ambitions came to an abrupt end in 1469 when James began his personal rule, the discredited and forfeited Boyds being forced to retire into exile in Bruges.

The architecture of power politics is also discernible among the castles and palaces of ecclesiastical magnates. The principal element in the palace of the medieval bishops of Moray at Spynie, for example, is a great six-storeyed tower, commonly referred to as 'Davie's Tower' after its original builder Bishop David Stewart (1462-76); it is the fourth tower in Scotland in terms of area[34] but possibly the greatest in overall capacity. On the north side of the palace, close to the one-time loch, are the remains of a great banqueting hall, the familiar adjunct of a lay establishment, whilst the distribution and character of the gun-ports throughout the palace dispel any doubts that late medieval bishops' notions of security were any different from those of other members of the nobility.[35]

III

The surviving remains of royal architecture dating from before the fifteenth century show little evidence of superiority in size or quality over non-royal structures, and it is arguable that such distinguishing marks become generally obvious and unquestionable only with the works of James IV. The buildings of the nobility, on the other hand, display little evidence of any external constraints imposed upon their numbers, siting, size or character. There are few written indications of negative royal control over castle-building, one of the few recorded instances being in 1528 when James V prohibited the building of fortifications near the English Border without permission of the king and council.[36] It was mainly the use of a castle and the conduct of its owner that were called into question, the greatest sanction normally being forfeiture and banishment. Phases of castle destruction, like political executions,[37] were the exception rather than the rule, and were confined mainly to the reign of James II, the first Scottish ruler to make extensive use of gunpowder ordnance.[38]

His campaign against the Douglases was marked by destructive violence of an unusual intensity. Abercorn, probably the most strongly forfeited of all the Douglas castles, did not survive his one-month siege in 1455, although slightly more survives of the Hamilton stronghold of Inveravon which James reportedly 'kest down' in the same campaign.[39] Further destruction may have been wrought at Douglas and Avondale Castles, but the siege of Threave was settled without recorded damage. Indeed, royal possession of the new weapons, symbolised by the great bombards such as Mons Meg (manufactured for the Duke of Burgundy in 1449 and given to James II in 1457)[40] was for a time of deterrent value, merely the threat of force being sufficient to focus minds and settle issues. Most of Meg's recorded activity was in the reign of James IV, its principal domestic duty occurring in 1489 when it was trundled into action against the castles of Crookston, Duchal and Dumbarton which were held by the earl of Lennox, Lord Lyle and their supporters.

Judging from the amount of land forfeited to the crown between 1424 and 1542,[41] tension, conflict, feuding and forfeiture abounded, but episodes of threatened or actual destruction were exceptional. Historians have shown that it was largely a matter of the crown *and* the nobility, not of the crown *versus* the nobility, and that, compared to the pattern of centralisation and mistrust observable in other kingdoms, the Stewart monarchy was remarkable for the degree of delegation and trust that it placed in its nobility.[42] The architectural evidence points towards a similar conclusion.

A positive royal attitude towards the maintenance and use of private castles is expressed in James I's enactment of 1426 ordering landowners north of the Mounth (the Grampian Mountains) to build, repair and 'reforme' the castles, fortalices and manor-places on their lands, and to 'duell in thame be thaim self or be ane of thare frendis for the gracious governall of thair landis be gude polising and to expende the froyte of the landis in the cuntre quhare the landis lyis'.[43] They were thus enjoined to combine administrative and political control with the economic and social benefits generated by estate improvement, an aim defined in later royal documents as an 'increase of policy' within the kingdom.

The requirements of national defence also encouraged interdependence and co-operation. In 1481, for example, the Scottish parliament, faced with the prospect of war with England, recited the arrangements that the king was to make with regard to his own castles, and listed a number of non-royal castles on the sea coast and near the Anglo-Scottish Border, commanding each lord to strengthen them with victuals, men and artillery, and to alter and repair them where necessary.[44] Mutual interests 'in tyme of were and all the trublous tyme' prompted a similar enactment in 1535 relating to the provision of fortified enclosures in the Border areas by landowners of £100 annual rental.[45]

However, relationships were not formed only in emergencies. Regular administrative links were maintained through the keepership of royal castles, the office of keeper, captain or constable being entrusted to local magnates in whose families it often became hereditary. Within their provinces the regional authority of such families thus became synonymous with royal power. A classic promotion of this kind was that of the Gordons, a family of relatively humble Berwickshire origin who became earls of Huntly and strong royal supporters in the north and north-east. They were granted the custody of royal strongpoints such as Inverness and Inverlochy, whilst they continued to develop and embellish their own castles, most notably their power-base at Strathbogie which was renamed Huntly.[46] In the west, from the mid-fifteenth century onwards, it was mainly the Campbells, earls of Argyll, who served as captains of royal castles,[47] including those that came to the crown through forfeiture. Meanwhile, the Campbells consolidated their own patrimony within their western seaboard empire, moving their principal residence to Inveraray and building there a large L-shaped tower which served them from the late fifteenth century down to the 1740s.[48]

Political rewards or expediency even involved outright grants of royal castles, not just their custody. In 1346, for example, David II granted to William, earl of Sutherland, lands and power to build a castle upon 'rupem nostram' ('our rock') at Dunnottar;[49] in 1390 Lochleven Castle, a major royal stronghold as late as 1368, was granted to Henry Douglas;[50] and in 1470, after only ten years in royal possession, Ravenscraig Castle (Fife) was included among the subjects ceded to Earl William of Orkney in exchange for the earl's castle of Kirkwall and all his right in the earldom.[51] The Sinclairs appear to have made positive use of their new acquisition, for although Ravenscraig is considered to be a homogeneous royal artillery fortification of 1460-3, much of the tall western tower probably dates from about 1500. Urquhart Castle was under royal control for much of the fourteenth and fifteenth centuries, but in 1509, as part of a general scheme to strengthen royal authority in the Highlands and Islands, James IV granted the lordship to John Grant, evidently in return for good service against the Lord of the Isles, requiring him, among other things, to repair or build at the castle 'turrim cum antemurale sive propugnaculo ex lapidibus et calce pro custodia ab invasione furum et malefactorum' ('a tower, with an outwork or rampart of stone and lime, for protection from the attacks of robbers and malefactors').[52]

In some cases royal authority was delegated to such an extent that the precise status of a castle is now uncertain. The builder of Castle Stalker, for example, despite the prominent display of a royal armorial and the strength of persistent tradition, was probably not James V himself but Alan Stewart of Appin. However, his family strongly supported royal efforts to subjugate the west, and loyalty to their distant kinsmen was rewarded by grants of lands and offices, especially in 1538 and 1542, the period when this refined tower is likely to have been erected.

The number of known licences granting permission to build fortifications or to fortify dwellings stands at about thirty, which remains a minute proportion of all towers and castles erected in late medieval Scotland.[53] As has been suggested,[54] such documents may have been a matter of proper legal conveyance in particular circumstances, but their significance may have been essentially political rather than legal, providing confirmation of administrative or political ties that were already strong.

Sir William Urquhart, a typical grantee, was of a trusted family that had served as hereditary sheriffs of Cromarty since the middle of the fourteenth century, and in 1470 he was granted special permission to build a tower on the motte of Cromarty and to equip it with suitable defences.[55] In a licence issued in 1454 to another royal agent, William, thane of Cawdor, James II made special provision that Cawdor Castle 'nobis heredibus et successoribus nostris semper promptum existat et paratum et . . . nos heredes et successores nostri semper habeamus liberum introitum et egressum sine difficultate aut obstaculo' ('be always open and ready to us, our heirs and successors, and that we and our heirs and successors have always free entry and exit without difficulty or obstacle'),[56] a condition that almost certainly reflects James's concern over Douglas defiance at nearby Lochindorb and Darnaway rather than suspicion of the loyal thanes. Another old-established family that remained high in royal esteem was that of the Dundases of Dundas who were prominent among lowland beneficiaries of similar licences. They were granted special royal permission in 1424 to build a tower or fortalice with various defensive features 'ad huiusmodi fortalicium iuxta modum regni Scotie consuetis' ('as is usual in a fortalice of this kind according to the manner of the kingdom of Scotland'), and in 1491 James IV granted John Dundas licence to build a castle on Inchgarvie, an island in the River Forth.[57]

The charter that accompanied the 1491 licence and conveyed the island of Inchgarvie to Dundas explained that the castle was intended to remedy the problems caused by English and Danish pirates, and that payments for the maintenance of the castle fabric, garrison and munitions were to be levied on vessels seeking safety and help.[58] The fortification was still being completed 'in all possible haist' by John Dundas's daughter-in-law in early 1514.[59] The state of national emergency in the aftermath of Flodden probably explains why the bills were paid by the royal Treasurer, for Dundas's Inchgarvie, like Sir Andrew Wood's Largo, also of 1491, was essentially a private contract for public defence 'ob piratarum et invasorum resistentiam et expulsionem, qui regnum et ligeos per mare sepius invaserant' ('for resistance against and repulsion of pirates and raiders who have often attacked from the sea our kingdom and subjects').[60]

From the early sixteenth century, however, it was the process of feuing, not the immediate needs of national defence, that produced most royal authorisations for building. Although not unknown before the middle of the fifteenth century, feu-holding of crown lands, which brought short-term financial advantages to the crown, became much more widespread after 1503. Most of the numerous feu-charters from this period specified an obligation to erect buildings and make improvements, a typical grant in feu-ferme in 1510 requiring the construction of 'sufficientem mansionem de lapide et calce cum aula, camera, orreo, bostari, stabello, columbario, pomeriis, ortis, apium custodibus dictis *le be-hivis*, cum cepibus et plantatione quercuum' ('an adequate house of stone and lime, with hall, chamber, granary, byre, stable, dovecot, orchards, gardens and bee-hives with hedges and a plantation of oaks').[61] But the initial capital payment probably restricted the feuar's abilities to carry out such works without delay. At Denmilne in northern Fife, for example, the Balfour family first became feuars of the royal mill in 1509 but, judging from the architecture of the surviving tower, the obligation to undertake building does not appear to have taken effect until at least thirty years after the confirmation of the grant in 1541.[62]

The feuing of crown and church lands contributed significantly to the proliferation of tower building in the sixteenth century, when the practice spread to most grades of landholding society and when entry into the stone tower 'bracket' continued to be a mark of wealth, status and pride, not a matter of defying the king or one's neighbours.[63] The larger castles and towers continued to demonstrate gross imbalances in the structure and economy of late medieval society, but to claim that such buildings *in themselves* reflect turbulence among the nobility, or a state of tension between the nobility and crown is an argument that has serious weaknesses. In their interpretation of the evidence, modern commentators have too often imposed a military gloss upon these buildings and have overlooked the ambiguities.[64] Appearances can be deceptive, as the case of mighty Borthwick Castle shows.

William Borthwick, who was granted special licence in 1430 to construct a castle in a place commonly called the Mote of Lochorwart, had undertaken a good deal for his king in the previous decade. Traditions of royal service were maintained in later generations, and William's son, who probably completed the castle in the middle of the fifteenth century, became a lord of parliament. The Borthwick licence, like others, can thus be interpreted as confirmation of political trust, and, also like others, its provisions included 'in summitate ornamentis defensivis' ('defensive ornaments at the wall-head').[65] Even in the fifteenth century, it seems, battlements and turrets were as much a symbol of lordship and authority as a practical means of defence.

NOTES

1. Jennifer M Brown, ed., *Scottish Society in the Fifteenth Century* (London, 1977); idem (Jenny Wormald), 'Taming the Magnates?' in Gordon Menzies, ed., *The Scottish Nation* (London, 1972), 46-59, reprinted in Keith J Stringer, ed., *Essays on the Nobility of Medieval Scotland* (Edinburgh, 1985), 270-80; idem, *Lords and Men in Scotland: Bonds of Manrent, 1442-1603* (Edinburgh, 1985); Alexander Grant, *Independence and Nationhood, Scotland 1306-1469* (London, 1984); idem, 'Crown and Nobility in Late Medieval Britain' in Roger A Mason, ed., *Scotland and England, 1286-1815* (Edinburgh, 1987), 34-59; and Norman A T Macdougall, *James III, A Political Study* (Edinburgh, 1982). The references to architectural descriptions cited in this essay are supplementary to those contained in standard works such as David MacGibbon and Thomas Ross, *The Castellated and Domestic Architecture of Scotland* (5 vols, Edinburgh, 1887-92), and the *Inventories* of the Royal Commission on the Ancient and Historical Monuments of Scotland (Edinburgh, 1911-   ).

2. G W S Barrow, 'The earliest Stewarts and their lands', *The Stewarts*, 10, part 2 (1956), 162-78, reprinted in idem, *The Kingdom of the Scots* (London, 1973), 337-61.

3. W Douglas Simpson, 'Dundonald Castle', *Colls. of Ayrshire Archaeological and Natural History Soc.*, 2nd series, 1 (1947-9), 42-51.

4. W Douglas Simpson, 'The royal castle of Kindrochit in Mar', *Proceedings of Society of Antiquaries of Scotland* (hereafter *PSAS*), 57 (1923), 75-97, and 'The excavation of Kindrochit Castle, Aberdeenshire', *Antiquaries Journal*, 8 (1928), 69-75; John M Gilbert, *Hunting and Hunting Reserves in Medieval Scotland* (Edinburgh, 1979), 36, 61, 80 and 225.

5. W Douglas Simpson, 'The architectural history of Rothesay Castle', *Trans. of Glasgow Archaeological Soc.*, new series, 9, part 3 (1939), 152-83, and 10 (1941), 78-9.

6. *Exchequer Rolls of Scotland* (23 vols, 1878-1908), iv, pp. cxxxvi-ix and refs cited; A A M Duncan, *James I* (Glasgow, 1976), 11, 16; Grant, *Independence and Nationhood*, 164, 188.

7. John G Dunbar, 'Some aspects of the planning of Scottish royal palaces in the sixteenth century', *Architectural History*, 27 (1984), 15-24.

8. For the architectural sculpture see Christopher Wilson in Colin McWilliam, ed., *The Buildings of Scotland, Lothian* (Harmondsworth, 1978), 291-301.

9. *Accounts of the Masters of Works* (Edinburgh, 1957-   ), i, passim.

10. John G Dunbar, 'The palace of Holyroodhouse during the first half of the sixteenth century', *Archaeological Journal*, 120 (1963), 242-54.

11. Dana Bentley-Cranch, 'An early sixteenth-century architectural source for the palace of Falkland', *Review of Scottish Culture*, 2 (1986), 85-95.

12. See e.g. John G Dunbar, *The Stirling Heads* (Edinburgh, 1975).

13. Geoffrey Stell, 'Late medieval defences in Scotland', in David H Caldwell, ed., *Scottish Weapons and Fortifications 1100-1800* (Edinburgh, 1981) (hereafter Caldwell, *Scot. Weapons*), 21-54 at 41-5.

14. Cambridge, Corpus Christi College, MS 171, f. 265 (reproduced in G W S Barrow, *Robert Bruce* (London, 1965 edn), frontispiece).

15. Leslie Alcock, 'A multi-disciplinary chronology for Alt Clut, Castle Rock, Dumbarton', *PSAS*, 107 (1975-6), 103-13.

16. *Cartularium Comitatus de Levenax* (Maitland Club, 1833), 1-2; Joseph Irving, *The Book of Dumbartonshire* (Edinburgh and London, 1879), i, 58-9.

17. I M M MacPhail, *Dumbarton Castle* (Edinburgh, 1979), 32-4; R L Mackie, *King James IV of Scotland* (Edinburgh, 1958), 54-5.

18. H M Colvin, ed., *History of the King's Works*, ii (London, 1963), 563-71.

19. Iain MacIvor, 'Artillery and major places of strength in the Lothians and the east Border', in Caldwell, *Scot. Weapons*, 94-152; see also Macdougall, *James III*, passim.

20. MacIvor, op. cit., 128-32.

21. In 1465 the king's council ordered that the castle be demolished and that the burgh of Linlithgow be permitted to make use of the stone and lime for their harbour works at Blackness *(Registrum Magni Sigilli*, 11 vols, 1882-1914 (hereafter *RMS)*, ii, no. 857).

22. Iain MacIvor, *Blackness Castle* (Edinburgh, 1982), 5.

23. W Douglas Simpson, 'Doune Castle', *PSAS*, 72 (1937-8), 73-83.

24. E.g., R S Mylne, *The Master Masons to the Crown of Scotland* (Edinburgh, 1893), 60-1.

25. Sir J Balfour Paul, ed., *The Scots Peerage* (9 vols, 1904-14) (hereafter *SP*), iii, 132-85; and for Douglas, earl of Angus, ibid., i, 170-213.

26. George L Good and Christopher J Tabraham, 'Excavations at Threave Castle, Galloway, 1974-78', *Medieval Archaeology*, 25 (1981), 90-140.

27. Cf. Stell, 'Late medieval defences', op. cit., 46-8, and Christopher J Tabraham and George L Good, 'The artillery fortification at Threave Castle, Galloway' in Caldwell, *Scot. Weapons*, 55-72. The history of Newark Castle, another Douglas tower, which came to serve as a royal hunting-lodge for the forest of Ettrick, roughly parallels that of Threave. The revenues of both of these and other former Douglas possessions were made over in 1473 to Margaret of Denmark in lieu of the third of the revenues of the kingdom originally assigned to her in dower. Royal keepership of Threave eventually became hereditarily vested in the Lords Maxwell, whilst the Lords Hume were granted custody of Newark.

28. W Douglas Simpson, 'The architectural history of Bothwell Castle', *PSAS*, 59 (1924-5), 165-93; 'Bothwell Castle reconsidered', *Trans. of Glasgow Archaeological Soc.*, new series, 11 (1947), 97-116; 'The donjons of Conisborough and Bothwell', *Archaeologia Aeliana*, 4th series, 32 (1954), 100-15.

29. W Douglas Simpson, 'Tantallon Castle', *Trans. of E.Lothian Antiquarian Soc.*, 7 (1958), 18-26; MacIvor, 'Artillery . . . in the Lothians', op. cit., 122-4, 132-3.

30. *Accounts of Lord High Treasurer of Scotland* (13 vols, 1877-1978), i, 180, 181; R K Hannay, ed., *Acts of Lords of Council in Public Affairs, 1501-54* (Edinburgh, 1932), 285; R Lindesay of Pitscottie, *Historie of Scotland* (Scottish Text Society, 3 vols, 1899-1911), i, 330-3 (cited by Mackie, *James IV*, 65, and MacIvor, op. cit., 122-4).

31. Sir William Fraser, *Scotts of Buccleuch* (2 vols, Edinburgh, 1878), ii, 361; *Accounts of . . . Treasurer,* as above, vii, 289.

32. Macdougall, *James III,* 198-9.

33. Ibid., 170-87.

34. *PSAS,* 57 (1922-3), 92.

35. W Douglas Simpson, *The Palace of the Bishops of Moray at Spynie* (Elgin, 1927). The wide-mouthed gun-ports were probably inserted by Bishop Patrick Hepburn (1538-73).

36. Peter McNeill, ed., *The Practicks of Sir James Balfour of Pittendreich* (Stair Society, 2 vols, 1962-3), ii, 595.

37. Grant, 'Crown and Nobility', op. cit., 36, 52.

38. Margaret Toynbee, 'King James II of Scotland: Artillery and Fortification', *The Stewarts,* 11 (1962), 157-62; Stell, 'Late medieval defences', op. cit., 39-40.

39. T Thomson, ed., *The Auchinleck Chronicle* (Edinburgh, 1819), 12. For the siege of Abercorn see ibid., 54; G Buchanan, *History of Scotland* (4 vols, Glasgow, 1827), ii, 159; J Pinkerton, *History of Scotland* (London, 1879), i, 486-8.

40. Claude Gaier, 'The origin of Mons Meg', *Journal of the Arms and Armour Society,* 5 (1965-7), 425-31, 450-2.

41. Athol Murray, 'Crown Lands 1424-1542', in Peter McNeill and Ranald Nicholson, eds, *Historical Atlas of Scotland c.400-c. 1600* (St Andrews, 1975), 72-3 and 185 (Map 83).

42. Wormald, 'Taming the Magnates?', op, cit., 275-6; Grant, op. cit., 'Crown and Nobility'.

43. *Acts of the Parliaments of Scotland* (12 vols, 1814-75) (hereafter *APS),* ii, 13.

44. Ibid., 133.

45. Ibid., 346.

46. Wormald, 'Taming the Magnates?', op. cit., 276; *SP,* iv, 506-62; *RMS,* 11, nos. 2950, 3286, 3379; *Registrum Secreti Sigilli* (8 vols, 1908- , i, nos. 1668, 2279; W Douglas Simpson, 'The architectural history of Huntly Castle', *PSAS,* 56 (1921-2), 134-63, 'Further notes on Huntly Castle', ibid., 67 (1932-3), 137-60; and Thomas Innes of Learney, 'Heraldic decoration on the castles of Huntly and Balvenie', ibid., 69 (1934-5), 387-95.

47. E.g. Tarbert Castle appears to have functioned as a royal castle from the 1220s, and in 1504 the office of captain of the house and fortalice *when it shall be built* (the tower and associated enclosure-wall) was, together with accompanying lands and revenues in Kintyre and Knapdale, conferred by James IV on Archibald Campbell, second earl of Argyll *(Historical MSS Commission, 4th Report* (Appendix), 485, no.239). See also *RMS,* iii, nos. 345, 2306, 2812; *SP,* i, 318-93; and John G Dunbar and A A M Duncan, 'Tarbert Castle: a contribution to the history of Argyll', *Scot.Historical Review, 1* (1971), 1-17.

48. Ian G Lindsay and Mary Cosh, *Inveraray and the Dukes of Argyll* (Edinburgh, 1973), 25-7.

49. *RMS,* i, Appendix 1, no. 122; Sir William Fraser, *Sutherland Book* (3 vols, Edinburgh, 1892), iii, 15-16, no. 15; W Douglas Simpson, *Dunnottar Castle: Historical and Descriptive* (Aberdeen, 8th edn, 1962); and Sally M Foster, Stephen T Driscoll, Leslie Alcock, *Excavations at Urquhart and Dunnottar Castles 1983 and 1984: Interim Reports* (Glasgow, 1985). The earliest standing remains, those of the frontal tower, are attributable to the later fourteenth century and to the Keiths, earls Marischal, not the Sutherlands.

50. *RMS,* i, no. 796; *APS,* i, 504a.

51. *RMS,* ii, nos. 746-7, 996-1002; Barbara E Crawford, 'The pawning of Orkney and Shetland: a reconsideration of the events of 1460-9', *Scot.Historical Review,* xlviii (1969), 35-53; W Douglas Simpson, *Ravenscraig Castle* (Aberdeen, 1938).

52. *RMS,* ii, no. 3390. See also Sir William Fraser, *The Chiefs of Grant* (3 vols, Edinburgh, 1883), iii, 53; W Douglas Simpson, 'Urquhart Castle', *Trans. of Gaelic Society of Inverness,* 35 (1929-30), 51-82; and idem, 'Glen Urquhart and its castle: a study in environment' in W F Grimes, ed., *Aspects of Archaeology in Britain and abroad: essays presented to O G S Crawford* (London, 1951), 316-31.

53. W Mackay Mackenzie, *The Medieval Castle in Scotland* (London, 1927), 215-29.

Additional references are cited in Stell, 'Late medieval defences', 52,n. 33; see also *RMS*, ii, no. 1959 (Broughty Castle, 1490) ibid., no. 3336 (King Edward Castle, 1509), Scottish Record Office, GD 160/2/4 (Drummond Castle, 1491; the author is grateful to Dr David H Caldwell for this reference), and A J Warden, *Angus or Forfarshire* (Dundee), i (1880), 421-2, and ii (1881), 328, for an unauthenticated licence relating to Airlie Castle *c.* 1431-2. For England see T H Turner and J H Parker, *Domestic Architecture of the Middle Ages*, iii, part ii (Oxford, 1859), 401-22, and discussions by C L H Coulson in *Journal of the British Archaeological Association*, 132 (1979), 73-90, and in *Medieval Archaeology*, 26 (1982), 69-100.

54. Mackenzie, op. cit., 215-23.

55. *Genealogical Collections concerning Families in Scotland* (2 vols, Scottish History Society, 1900), ii, 375; W Mackay Mackenzie, 'Old Cromarty Castle', *PSAS*, 82 (1947-8), 60-8.

56. *Book of the Thanes of Cawdor* (Spalding Club, 1859), 20-1. For Lochindorb and Darnaway see *APS*, ii, 76.

57. *RMS*, ii, no. 1; *Royal Letters . . . from the Family Papers of Dundas of Dundas* (Edinburgh, 1897), lvii-lix *(RMS*, ii, no. 2038; *APS*, ii, 270).

58. *Dundas Papers*, lxi-lxxii.

59. Ibid., lxxiii.

60. *RMS*, ii, no. 2040 *(APS*, ii, 227-8).

61. *RMS*, ii, no. 3407. For the nature and effects of feuing in general see I F Grant, *The Social and Economic Development of Scotland before 1603* (Edinburgh, 1930), 265-86, and Margaret H B Sanderson, *Scottish Rural Society in the Sixteenth Century* (Edinburgh, 1982), 64-168.

62. *Exchequer Rolls*, xiii, 615, 618; *RMS*, iii, nos. 2408, 2460.

63. The vow traditionally attributed to William Forbes of Corse in 1581, for instance, to the effect that he would build himself 'a house, at which thieves will need to knock ere they enter' cannot be traced back before 1842 *(New Statistical Account of Scotland*, xii (Edinburgh, 1845), 1123).

64. Geoffrey Stell, 'The Scottish Medieval Castle: Form, Function and "Evolution" ', in Stringer, *Nobility of Medieval Scotland*, 195-209.

65. *RMS*, ii, no. 157; *SP*, ii, 95-8. The licences for Cawdor *(Cawdor Bk.*, 20-1) and Inchgarvie *(Dundas Papers*, lvii-lix) also refer to 'defensive ornaments'.

7

A NOTE ON SCANDINAVIAN TRADE WITH SCOTLAND IN THE LATER MIDDLE AGES

David Ditchburn

The commercial relations which existed between Scotland and Scandinavia in the later middle ages have received scant attention from historians. The view expressed by the late James Dow — that 'Scottish trade with Sweden was, in effect, a complete novelty in the early years of the sixteenth century' — has been generally accepted without dissent by historians.[1] It is only recently that Dr Thomas Riis has produced the first detailed analysis of the relations (including the commercial contacts) which were maintained between Scotland and Denmark from about 1450.[2] The lack of evidence indicating contacts between the two countries before that date has been commented upon with an implicit air of curiosity, presumably since both Scotland and Denmark bordered the North Sea and both had long since maintained commercial contacts with other countries bordering the North Sea.[3] In Dr Riis's view, however, Scottish-Danish relations only developed as a consequence of, firstly, Scottish trade with the Hanseatic towns and, secondly, the union of the Danish and Norwegian crowns in 1380. With Scottish ships and merchants travelling increasingly frequently to the Baltic, they inevitably on occasions stopped off in Denmark *en route*; and, with the union of the crowns, the claims of the kings of Norway to the payment of an annual sum (in return for the transfer of sovereignty over the Western Isles to Scotland in 1266) passed to the union kings based in Denmark.[4] What, then, of Norway? The political relations between, on the one hand, Scotland and, on the other hand, Norway and subsequently the joint kingdom of Denmark-Norway have been the subject of much discussion.[5] By contrast the commercial relations between the two countries before the later sixteenth century have received virtually no examination.[6] Nevertheless, while bemoaning the lack of evidence of Norwegian-Scottish trade, some Scottish historians have expressed the view that there *must* have been at least some commercial contacts between the two countries. Dr Crawford, for example, has stated that 'it is clear that [the flourishing state of Scottish-Norwegian trade in the sixteenth century] must have been based on growth in the fifteenth century'.[7] There are, then, perhaps two obvious questions which arise from the various views and attitudes expressed about Scottish-Scandinavian trade in the later middle ages. The first is *were* there any commercial relations between Scotland and Scandinavia; and the second is, if there were not, why not? The subject of Scottish-Scandinavian trade in the later middle ages awaits a great deal of further research. This essay will only attempt to provide tentative answers.

Bergen was the most important centre of trade in later medieval Norway. In 1955 archaeologists began to excavate the Tyskebryggen (the German Wharf) in Bergen. The work continued until the 1970s and detailed reports on the excavations are now beginning to be published. During their excavations the archaeologists discovered, among other things, at least 100,000 sherds of pottery.[8] Among these sherds, however, only a minute number have been identified as Scottish. These finds of white gritty ware from southern Scotland have been dated to about the thirteenth century.[9] Specific documentary evidence of trade between Scotland and Scandinavia is similarly meagre. References to Scandinavian shipwrecks in Scotland, which are discussed elsewhere in this volume, may be indicative of trade, through not necessarily of trade between Scotland and Scandinavia.[10] Ships were often shipwrecked due to storms and storms not infrequently drove ships aground miles from their intended destinations.[11] Nevertheless, it may have been the frequency of such incidents and the inability of Norwegian merchants to recover their shipwrecked goods from the Scots which prompted the inclusion of a clause covering such matters in the Treaty of Perth in 1266.[12] This clause, however, like the references to shipwrecks, is not a certain indication of Scottish-Norwegian trade. Neither, for that matter, is it altogether certain that a Norwegian ship, recorded at Berwick about 1286, was there for commercial purposes.[13] For some reason, which is unclear, the ship was impounded by the Scottish authorities. Alv Erlingsson, the jarl of Tornberg, complained to James the Steward, one of the Scottish Guardians, about the incident, adding that Norway had not been weakened to such an extent that it would tolerate such action. Erlingsson was perhaps alluding to the events of 1284-5 when a Wendish fleet had successfully blockaded Norway in retribution for Norwegian attempts to curtail German commercial privileges in Norway.[14] The outcome of Erlingsson's complaint is not, however, known and there is very little indication of Norwegian merchants visiting Scotland or Scottish merchants visiting Norway during the remainder of the thirteenth century or during the period of the Wars of Independence.

The clause relating to shipwrecks which was incorporated in the 1266 Treaty was repeated when the 1266 Treaty was reconfirmed in 1312 by the Treaty of Inverness.[15] Whether this repetition was intended to address a problem which was still current in 1312, or whether, as is perhaps more likely, the repetition was simply *pro forma*, is not known for certain. Whatever the case, the commercial aspects of the 1312 Treaty are negligible when compared with the commercial privileges which Robert I granted to both merchants from the towns of northern Germany and merchants from Holland and Zeeland.[16] Had trade between Scotland and Norway been of importance one might have expected greater emphasis on commercial matters in the 1312 Treaty.

That, however, is not to argue that there was no trade between Scotland and Norway at this juncture. In a corollary to the Treaty of Inverness, also dated at Inverness on 29 October 1312, the ambassadors of both kingdoms came to an agreement to settle various outstanding disputes between their two countries.[17] Among these was a claim by the Scots for amends to certain unnamed merchants of St Andrews who had been imprisoned in Norway and whose goods, to the value of £600, had been detained by the Norwegian king's officials. From other evidence it is clear that merchants from English-held Berwick were also in Norway in 1316, when their ship was arrested.[18] The arrest was in response to an earlier visit paid by Berwick merchants to Widahel, when they had allegedly invited a Norwegian governor and ten young nobles aboard their ship, only to throw boiling water and hot cinders over their guests as a prelude to murdering them. Whether, however, Berwick's trade with Norway was at this point a new venture, mounted by the English burgesses with whom Edward I had resettled the burgh after 1296, following long since established English trade patterns, or whether the English burgesses were following commercial routes employed by their Scottish predecessors is not clear.[19]

During the remainder of the fourteenth century explicit evidence of a Scottish mercantile presence in Norway remains negligible. Robert I's sister, Isabella, had married King Eric II in 1293 and she survived her brother some thirty years. Several Scots travelled to Norway on diplomatic business in the first half of the fourteenth century. The agreement made in 1323 between Andrew Harcla, earl of Carlisle, and Robert I was known of in Norway.[20] The chamberlain's account of January 1338 records that 60s. was given to Robert the Skinner for travelling to Norway with a letter.[21] This entry follows a similar one for a mission to Guelders. In 1336 Edward III of England had requested, *inter alia*, the king of Norway and the count of Guelders to prohibit trade between their domains and Scotland.[22] Perhaps, then, the Scottish missions to Norway and Guelders the following year were a diplomatic counter-offensive by the Scots, designed to plead for the continuation of trade. The chamberlain's account for 1342 reveals that Patrick Graham was sent on royal business to Norway and an envoy from the queen of Norway (perhaps Isabella, by then the dowager queen) is recorded in the same account. Another royal envoy was sent to Orkney in 1372-3.[23] How any of these envoys travelled between Scotland and Norway is not known. It is possible that they journeyed on merchant ships and it is likewise possible that Robert the Skinner, at least, was a merchant. Indeed, it seems probable that ships were sailing reasonably regularly between Aberdeen and Orkney since the earliest surviving Scottish exchequer rolls record that the bishop of Orkney received annual grants of wine and corn from the fermes of Aberdeen.[24]

Evidence of Norwegian merchants visiting Scotland is similarly scanty, but one Norwegian, who received a remission on customs duties, is recorded at Aberdeen in 1341-2.[25] Of course trade between Norway and Scotland need not have been conducted solely by Scottish or Norwegian merchants. Dr Crawford has suggested that the violent incidents involving the Berwick merchants in 1316 — and, indeed, other incidents of friction between English and Norwegian merchants at about this time — were part of 'a general tension between merchants of the countries bordering the North Sea', which was associated with the growing prominence of German merchants in the region.[26] In the thirteenth century the merchants of Lübeck had acquired extensive commercial privileges in Norway for themselves and merchants from the other Wendish towns. It was an attempt to restrict these privileges that had led to the Norwegian debacle of 1284-5.[27] The extent and nature of the German domination of Norwegian trade should not be over-estimated. A considerable amount of the pottery discovered during the archaeological excavations of the Tyskebryggen and in Trondheim hails from England. In the thirteenth and even in the fourteenth century some English merchants continued to visit Norway. Some Norwegian ships can also be traced in England. Nevertheless much Anglo-Norwegian trade by the fourteenth century was conducted by German merchants using German vessels.[28] German ships may also have carried the commodities and conducted much of the trade between Scotland and Norway. Certainly by about 1300 the German community in Bergen was aware of political developments in Scotland. An either crazed or impious woman from Lübeck, resident in Bergen, claimed to be Margaret, the Maid of Norway, who had died in Orkney ten years or so previously.[29] Dr James Dilley has suggested that some of the German merchants who traded in Scotland during the Wars of Independence did so from Norway.[30] On this there is no conclusive proof, but it is certain that some of these German merchants, such as John Witte of Lübeck, also participated in Anglo-Norwegian trade.[31] Indeed, German ships and merchants may have called at a Scottish port throughout the fourteenth century and beyond whilst *en route* between England and Norway.

On 25 October 1383 Robert of Glenesk, a Scottish notary, drew up an agreement in Edinburgh between three men of Sluys and fifteen Hansards following the seizure of five German ships by the men of Sluys.[32] Among the goods captured by the Flemings were fish and fish oil, both typically Norwegian products, though the document does not specifically indicate their origin. This agreement did not settle the dispute. Three of the Hanseatic skippers named in the notarial instrument (Jacob Znedwint, Symon Holeswaker and Marquard Spissen) subsequently testified that their ships had been captured 'in Scotland'. Moreover they added 'dit weren die schepe, de de copman van Berghen mit gude scheped hadden'.[33] Holeswaker, at least, had connections with the Hanseatic *Bergenfahrer* of Boston in England.[34] In 1387, during a series of negotiations between Hanseatic and Flemish representatives, the matter of the five vessels captured in 1383 was raised by the Hanseatic envoys. They advanced the testimony of Heyne Hagemester, a skipper from Rostock, who can probably be identified with Hans Hagemester, skipper of Rostock, whose name appears on the notarial instrument drawn up in Edinburgh five years previously. According to Heyne '. . . ik seghelde van Berghen mit stokvissche. Do wii weren komen under Schotlande, do leghende uns an de Vlaminge de de van Brugge unde van der Slus utghemaked hadden, unde nemen uns beyde ghut unde schip'.[35] The ship of the fifth skipper involved in the 1383 incident, Tideman Block of Colberg, also contained stockfish as well as various hides of unspecified origin. Part of the cargo of the other three ships was sold to the earl of Dunbar and other Scottish lords.[36] All five of the Hanseatic vessels were, then, involved in trade with Bergen and at least Holeswaker's ship, if not all five ships, had connections with Boston. All five ships were, at the very least, sailing close to Scotland when attacked. It is possible that they had called at, or were intending to call at, a Scottish port whilst *en route,* either in order to sell some of their cargo or to pick up supplies.

In addition to their possible trading activities between Norway and Scotland, German merchants also conducted some trade between Scotland and Scania. 'Eastland' (i.e. Baltic) herring was imported to Scotland in 1329.[37] A few references to the irregular import of Scanian herring survive from the later fourteenth century. Scanian herring captured by pirates from a Hanseatic vessel in 1379 and from an Amsterdam vessel in 1392 were subsequently sold in Scotland. In 1402 a ship skippered by Meynekin Melsing of Hamburg, with a cargo of 24 lasts of herring owned by merchants from Hamburg and Lübeck, was attacked by Englishmen while visiting one of the Forth ports. There is also specific evidence of at least one Scottish merchant trading in Scania in the later fourteenth century. In 1381 Finlay Usher, a Scottish merchant, was dispossessed of a cargo of Scanian herring when a Zeeland ship sailing from the Baltic to Flanders was captured by Englishmen.[38]

Scanian herring was sold at the fairs which were held annually around the towns of Scanör and Falsterbo. The fishing season lasted from July until September and the associated fairs commenced in July and terminated in late October or mid-November. From the thirteenth century these fairs attracted an international clientele from all over western Europe, though German merchants were always very numerous visitors. The king of Denmark granted several Hanseatic towns a strip of land, or *Vitte*, on which the fish were prepared, salted and sold. The *Vitte* came to include not just commercial buildings but also churches and cemeteries. Each *Vitte* was supervised by a *Vogt*, appointed by the town in possession of each *Vitte*. Again perceiving a threat to its commercial interests, the Hansa, allied to Sweden, had embarked upon a war with Valdemar IV of Denmark and Haakon VI of Norway in 1367. The Hanseatic victory in the war, confirmed by the Peace of Stralsund in 1370, was used to protect the Hansa's commercial interests.[39] A month after the surrender of Helsingborg Castle by the Danes, the Hanseatic diet advised various foreigners, including Scots, to stay away from Scania. Moreover it ordained specifically that Scotsmen, Englishmen and Welshmen were not to be allowed to salt herring at the fairs.[40] This decree was clearly designed to restrict foreign competition in the fairs. Herring could not be transported over long distances unless it was preserved with salt. Since the most important source of salt in the western Baltic was the salt mines of Lüneburg (a Hanseatic town), the Hansa was quite capable of enforcing its restrictive policies in Scania. The Hanseatic diet meeting at Lübeck in 1377 reissued the 1369 ordinance regarding the salting of herring by Scots and other foreigners. In 1378, at a diet held in Stralsund, the restrictions on foreign activity in Scania were tightened still further. Henceforth the *Vögte* were ordered neither to admit those from Flanders, Brabant, England, Scotland or Wales to their *Vitte* nor to protect them.[41] The frequency of specific references to Scots in these Hanseatic edicts must surely mean that the Scots were active in the Scanian herring trade. Their reaction to the Hanseatic measures is not known, though English merchants reacted with outrage.[42] Yet the presence of Finlay Usher in Scania in 1381 indicates that the Scots were not completely forced out of the Scanian herring trade.

In the fifteenth century Scottish trade with Orkney, which remained under Danish-Norwegian jurisdiction until 1468, was probably still quite frequent. The grants of wine and corn to the bishops of Orkney from the fermes of Aberdeen continued. Some more specific evidence of trade with Orkney also survives. In 1405, for example, a ship sailing from Orkney to Scotland was driven off course by gales and ended up in Norfolk. In 1424 one of the complaints of the Orcadians against the misrule of David Menzies of Weem was that he had allowed five or six ships laden with grain to depart from Orkney for Scotland in a time of dearth.[43]

The number of references to trade between Scotland and the Scandinavian mainland remains, however, sparse. Dr Stevenson noted only three references to Norway and Denmark in the Aberdeen council registers between 1434 and 1499, an insignificant proportion when compared to the total number of references to foreign parts in the registers.[44] Of course, this hardly represents reliable statistical data as to the level of trade between Aberdeen and the Scandinavian mainland. It was only in specific circumstances (usually when some dispute about trade was brought to the council's attention or when it became the focus of a court case) that such references to trade were included in the registers. Morever, there are additional references to Norwegians in the burgh's sasine registers.[45] For the fifteenth century, then, as for earlier centuries, there are no statistical data available to provide an adequate reflection of the volume and value of Scotland's trade with Scandinavia. Once again, therefore, the historian has to make do with a few scattered, chance references.

Some of the trade between Scotland and Scandinavia continued to be conducted in German vessels and by German merchants. Apart from references to German ships trading in Scotland which were blown off course and arrived by accident in Norwegian harbours, some German ships deliberately called at Scandinavian ports: in 1479, for example, Claus Berchman (probably a German) sent eight barrels of wine and twelve sacks of alum from Leith to Elsinore on the ship of Olaff Misner.[46] The rulers of the united Scandinavian kingdoms were also, however, keen to support the activities of non-German merchants in their domains.

The Scottish-Norwegian treaties of 1266 and 1312 were renewed in 1426 at a time when Eric of Pomerania, king of the united kingdoms of Denmark, Norway and Sweden, was at war with the Hansa.[47] The commerical clauses of the 1426 treaty, as Dr Riis has noted, were more extensive than those included in the earlier treaties.[48] This can probably be explained by the friction between Eric and the Hansa. Eric welcomed English and Dutch merchants to his domains as well as Scottish merchants.[49] He was apparently, therefore, attempting to curtail the Hanseatic predominance in the trade of all three of his kingdoms. In 1468 James III married Margaret of Denmark. The 1468 marriage treaty was, in fact, more than just a marriage treaty.[50] It amounted to a full diplomatic and military alliance. Although nothing was included in the treaty about trading connections between the two parties, it seems logical that merchants from Scotland would *ipso facto* be welcomed in the union kingdoms and *vice versa*. The alliance was renewed and ratified following negotiations between 1491 and 1494 and the renewed alliance now formally included provision to safeguard bilateral commercial intercourse.[51]

The extent to which merchants availed themselves of the inducements to trade afforded by the fifteenth-century treaties is less certain. Norwegian merchants can only rarely be traced in Scottish sources. In 1430-1 the customars of Edinburgh bought swine, lampreys and other victuals on behalf of the king from some Norwegian merchants.[52] This is the only certain reference to Norwegian merchants in the fifteenth century exchequer rolls, though others, as has been noted, can certainly be traced at Aberdeen.[53] On 31 January 1467, the Scottish parliament, meeting in Edinburgh, prohibited trade with Bruges, but provided for the continuance of trade with Middelburg, La Rochelle, Bordeaux, France (*sic*) and Norway. Dr Stevenson is surely correct in suggesting that these places were specifically mentioned in the statute because ships were known to be preparing to depart (from Leith?) for these destinations. The omission of both Baltic and English destinations would otherwise seem most odd.[54] Some Norwegian commodities of trade are also referred to in Scottish sources. Norwegian hawks, for example, were presented to James IV on 3 May 1497, and timber is recorded at Aberdeen in 1498.[55] Danish merchants, too, can only be traced rarely in fifteenth-century Scottish sources. A Danish merchant is recorded in the exchequer rolls in 1468-9 and Lutkyn Mere, a Danish pirate, was in Scotland in 1489. Some of the Danish envoys who, in the later fifteenth century, are recorded with increased frequency in Scottish sources, may also have participated in trade. Zeland Pursuivant was granted the custom on ninety dozen woollen cloths exported from Edinburgh in 1496-7. Danish ships are recorded at Ayr and Leith in 1488.[56] References to Sweden are even more jejune. There is, however, a reference to thirteen barrels of Osmond iron, which was almost certainly of Swedish origin, at Edinburgh in 1425-6. These were escheated to the crown from a foreigner who had hanged himself. This foreigner was almost certainly not a Swede, but rather Reinhold von dem Walde, the factor of four Hanseatic merchants from Danzig, who, from other evidence, is known to have committed suicide in Edinburgh at about this time.[57] It is likely that other iron imported to Scotland was of Swedish origin, particularly that which was purchased from Prussian merchants: iron was one of the most important commodities which was shipped from Sweden to Danzig.[58]

There is rather more evidence of Scottish merchants taking advantage of the impetus to commercial relations provided by the fifteenth-century Scottish-Scandinavian treaties. All Scottish ships sailing to and from the ports of the eastern Baltic ought, from the fifteenth century, to have called at Elsinore in order to pay the Sound toll.[59] Some Scots had also settled in Danish towns such as Aalborg, Copenhagen and Elsinore.[60] Likewise, there is some indication by the later fifteenth century, at least, of Scottish merchants visiting Norway. In 1491, for example, James Drummond of Perth appeared before the lord auditors concerning goods pertaining to four other Scots which he 'recouerit in Norway'. Moreover, as in Denmark, some Scots had settled in Norway: John Reid is recorded as a burgess of Bergen by 1488.[61] For Sweden, again, there is less evidence. The Swedish crown was united with that of Norway and Denmark in 1396 and technically, therefore, the inducements provided by the fifteenth-century treaties to Scottish merchants to trade in Scandinavia also applied to Sweden. Moreover, if Scottish ships and merchants bound for the Baltic were calling at Danish ports, there was no physical impediment to them calling at Swedish ports, or, at least, in the area around modern Gothenburg. That, too, was conveniently sited on the shipping routes to Danzig. The Swedes, however, were often in revolt against the crown. Since, after James III's marriage to Margaret of Denmark, Scotland was closely allied to Denmark, the Swedes might have regarded the Scots with some suspicion. Indeed, there is some evidence to support such a hypothesis. In 1473 the Swedish council of state wrote to the authorities of Danzig concerning the arrest of two Danzig ships in the vicinity of Alvsborg Castle (presumably at or near the port of Lödöse). One had been released, but the other remained under arrest because it was suspected that Scots, 'that is, enemies of Sweden', were aboard this ship.[62]

From the sixteenth century evidence begins to survive to allow a detailed quantitative assessment of Scotland's overseas trade. The evidence is very patchy, but for some ports and for some years some 'particular' customs accounts survive. Early surviving accounts from Dysart, Haddington, Linlithgow and Stirling include no discernible Scandinavian references.[63] The picture at the larger ports is similar: Aberdeen accounts survive for 1499-1500, 1523-4 and 1531-2.[64] There is not a single discernible reference to Danes, Norwegians or Swedes, or to trade with Denmark, Norway or Sweden, in these accounts. Accounts from Dundee are extant for 1526-7, c. 1550, 1550-1, 1554-5 and 1555-6. The only reference to Scandinavia in these accounts is to two Norwegian merchants who paid duty on two separate consignments of cloth in 1526-7.[65] Even at Edinburgh, the most important centre of overseas trade, there are only a few references to Scandinavia. In 1510-11 one ship left Leith for Copenhagen. Two more departed for Copenhagen in 1512-13. No ship in either of these accounts is recorded as departing for Norway or Sweden. The number of ships bound for Copenhagen may appear small. Indeed, the number is small when compared to the ships leaving for Vere and Dieppe. Nevertheless, in 1510-11 no ships are recorded as departing for any other Baltic port and in 1512-13 the only other Baltic references are to three ships heading to Stralsund and two bound for Danzig. The cargoes of all three ships leaving for Copenhagen were similar. That of 1511 included cloth and salt; those of 1512-13 cloth, salt, coal and a pack of lambskins.[66] There are further references to three ships trading with Denmark in an account of 1528, but again no ship is recorded as bound for Norway or Sweden. The cargoes of these ships were also composed principally of salt, though they also included some hides and lead.[67] Other surviving accounts for Edinburgh from the early sixteenth century, however, include no references at all to trade with Scandinavia.[68]

While the 'particular' customs accounts give the first detailed evidence of trade passing through certain ports, they do not provide a complete picture of Scottish trade, even for those ports and years for which they survive. Several of the surviving accounts only include information about the duty paid by particular merchants on specified commodities. Not all of the accounts include information about vessel movements. The impression given by the accounts is that the bulk of Scottish trade was conducted by Scottish merchants, but it cannot be certain that the customars explicitly identified in their accounts all the foreign merchants paying dues.

Moreover, the customars were only interested in those goods on which customs were levied. Only from 1597 did the collection of duties on imports become widespread. Before then timber, for example, was not liable for customs payments.

On 7 October 1550, the provost, bailies and council of Dundee ordered 'all Estrange schips resorting to the port and peir of this bourgche . . . to present thair Entres on the next morne before provost or baillies in opine court'.[69] From then ships which arrived at Dundee were recorded in the burgh and head court books. To compare these entries with the surviving 'particular' customs accounts from the same period is instructive. In the latter there are few references to Scandinavia. In the former, by contrast, references to Scandinavia are comparatively numerous. Between 1550 and 1555 at least ten ships with Danish masters or skippers arrived in Dundee, all of their vessels laden with timber. During the same period at least eight ships arrived with Norwegian skippers, all of them laden with timber. Other ships, also laden entirely with timber, are recorded, though it is not clear from where their skippers originated. Contacts were, however, clearly also maintained between Dundee and Sweden, for there are references in the burgh and head court books not only to Swedish timber and Osmund iron but also to the port of Nylöse.[70]

It is difficult to identify the Scandinavian ports from which the ships arrived in Dundee. Although some skippers are described as 'of' a specific place, skippers did not necessarily sail from their home ports. Besides, many of the references in the Dundee burgh and head court books are simply to Norway, in general, without reference to a specific place. For what it is worth, however, the Dundee books include references to Tönsberg, Trondheim, Ackershusen, 'Salisbourgch' and above all Bergen.[70a] The home ports of Danish skippers recorded before 1555 include Copenhagen, Landskrone, Varberg, Malmö and Lolland. The arrival of the timber ships from Scandinavia was concentrated in the summer months between May and September. The pattern of the timber trade in the mid-sixteenth century was thus very similar to that which existed in the later sixteenth and seventeenth centuries.[71] The timber from Scandinavia recorded at Dundee varied in type, shape and size. Some was oak, some was fir. Some, such as the 24 fir 'treis' on the ship of Martin Peirss of Malmö apparently arrived unprocessed; but Peirss's cargo also included 'leichtaris', 'rauchtreis', boards and girthstings (suitable for making barrel-hoops).[71a]

Since the surviving Scottish 'particular' accounts of the early sixteenth century make little mention of Scandinavian trade, and since local records of ship arrivals do not survive before 1550, it is difficult to ascertain when the timber trade became important. Moreover, the gaps in the Scottish source material cannot be made good by references to Scandinavian sources. The Sound toll registers do not begin to give details of cargoes passing the Sound before 1557 and Scandinavian customs accounts rarely survive for the first half of the sixteenth century. The first account for Lödöse, for example, dates from 1546, when 16 ships left the Swedish port for Scotland and 11 arrived from Scotland.[72] In the general absence of such statistics other sources such as the records of the Scottish government and the records of the Scottish burghs must again be made use of. The extant volume of these Scottish sources is much greater for the early sixteenth century than for the fifteenth century. And the number of references to Scandinavian trade is that much higher.

Hawks were still occasionally acquired by the king from Norway. John Caldwallis received £22 from the Treasurer in 1542 for his expenses in fetching hawks from Norway, while John Muir was paid £11 'to gyd the said Johnne in Norroway'.[73] On occasions victuals, especially grain, were sought in Denmark, as were horses.[74] Some of the iron recorded in the Treasurer's accounts may have come from Sweden (either directly or via the German towns), though much also arrived from Spain and France. The references to commodities such as these are, however, far outweighed by the number of references to timber. In 1501 the Treasurer purchased five 'jestis' from some Norwegian merchants. In 1512 the skipper Thomas Bannatyne was sent to Norway in a ship hired by the King to 'bring hame gret tymmer'. In July 1517, Andrew Cullan, a burgess of Aberdeen, bought timber from a Norwegian ship which arrived at the town.[75] Countless other examples could be given and not only of Norwegian timber. In 1503 the Treasurer purchased 208 Swedish boards from Andro Hanson.[76] A considerable amount of the timber purchased by the crown was probably used for the construction of ships. Norwegian timber was apparently used in the construction of James IV's ship, the 'Michell'. James IV also sought timber suited for the masts of ships from Norway.[77] But Scandinavian timber was also used during construction work, carried out, for example, at Holyrood in the 1530s.[78] In addition to this evidence of flourishing trading connections, considerably more Scottish settlers can be identified in both Denmark and Norway. By the 1520s there were serious disturbances between the newer Scottish settlers in Bergen and the long since established German community.[79]

There are, then, many more extant references to trade between Scotland and Scandinavia from the early sixteenth century than there are for the two previous centuries. One possibility in this is simply that the record material is that much better for the later period. That is certainly true, but it is perhaps too simplistic an explanation. The existence and development of trade between any two areas depends on a number of factors. Geographical proximity is obviously an important consideration. Trade depends upon viable communications, though the latter does not necessarily give rise to the former. Political factors are also important. In an atmosphere of hostility trade is unlikely to flourish, though it is worth recording that during the Wars of Independence Scots certainly acquired some supplies from England. By contrast, good political relations do not necessarily give rise to trade, since ultimately all trade is based upon the existence of complementary markets.

If the first of these criteria (that of communications) is applied to Scotland and Scandinavia, it is clear that there were few geographical impediments to trade. Norway is, of course, the closest of Scandinavian countries to Scotland and until 1468 one of its appanages (Orkney) was closer to Scotland than to mainland Norway. The vast bulk of medieval Scotland's overseas trade was funnelled through the east-coast ports. The largest of medieval Norway's trading communities were situated in the coastal regions of either western Norway (such as Bergen) or southern Norway (such as Oslo and Tönsberg). In other words, the principal trading communities of Scotland and Norway were easily accessible to each other by sea. Applied, on the other hand, to Scotland and Denmark and Sweden, the communications criterion at first sight produces less favourable results. The principal foci of Danish trade were not situated on western Jutland, but rather in the Sound region. Since until 1658 Scania, Halland and Blekinge were normally part of Denmark, Swedish access to the Kattegat was limited to the region surrounding Lödöse (latterly Nylöse). The most important ports of medieval Sweden (such as Söderköping, Norrköping, Kalmar and especially Stockholm) were in the eastern, Baltic-facing side of the country. Nevertheless, the sea route through the Sound (the *Umlandfahrt*) was increasingly used by ships from the fourteenth century, thereby avoiding the laborious task of unloading cargoes at Lübeck, transporting them overland to Hamburg and reloading them for onward shipment (or *vice versa*). By the 1380s Prussian ships and merchants are recorded in Scotland while Scots were travelling to Prussia.[80] The sea route between Prussia and Scotland took the traveller very close to Lödöse and the Danish trading centres in the Sound region. A stop-off at one of these ports involved no major route deviation. This, of course, is Dr Riis's contention, but it should be noted that such possibilities existed at least seventy years before about 1450, when Dr Riis begins his survey of Scottish-Danish relations. Indeed, the *terminus a quo* might be taken back to an even earlier date. Evidence that Scots were visiting the Wendish towns in the early fourteenth century is, at best, inconclusive, but Roger Bishop, a merchant from English-held Berwick, was certainly in Stralsund by 1312.[81]

If there was little in the way of geographical impediments to trade, there were perhaps slightly more in the way of political obstacles. The refusal of the Scots to pay the 'annual' led to some friction with Norway between 1291 and 1312 and, before James III's marriage, with Christian I. The closeness of the Scottish-Danish alliance after 1468 led some Swedes to regard the Scots as their enemies. And during rhe reign of James V, the exiled Christian II of Denmark won considerable sympathy and support in Scotland against his supplanter, Frederick I.[82] On the other hand, these political problems should not be exaggerated. The treaties of 1266, 1312, 1426, 1468 and 1492-4 demonstrate that Scotland's relations with both Denmark and Norway were usually quite friendly, and sometimes even close.

It is the third criterion (that of complementary markets) which best explains the pattern of trade between Scotland and Scandinavia. The Hansards, of course, dominated much of medieval Scandinavia's trade; but to some extent that is a red herring, for the Hansards too were quite capable of supplying any market which existed for Scottish goods to Scandinavia and any market for Scandinavian merchandise in Scotland. Recently a considerable amount of research has been devoted to the study of the Scottish customs accounts which are included in the series of *Exchequer Rolls* and which date from the early fourteenth century.[83] The study of these accounts has enabled historians to compile reasonably full statistics on the level of customable Scottish exports.[84] Wool, fells and hides were customed throughout the middle ages. In the fifteenth century new duties were collected on several commodities, including cloth, skins, salmon, cod, herring, salt and coal. No statistical evidence survives for exports which were not customable, though the level of these was probably not high: if it had been, the crown would probably have imposed a duty on them. Statistical evidence for imports before the late sixteenth century is scant, though it is clear from a variety of sources that Scotland imported various comestibles (such as wine and, not infrequently, grain); various raw materials (such as iron and timber); and various manufactured products (such as the better quality cloths of Flanders).

There are no customs statistics extant from Scandinavia before the sixteenth century. Agricultural products were, however, an important export from all three Scandinavian countries throughout the middle ages. Butter, horses and cattle came from Denmark and the fifteenth-century Danzig customs accounts reveal that regular consignments of herring arrived in Danzig from Aalborg.[85] It was, however, Scania which was most renowned for its herring, though there are indications of a slight downward trend in the amount of herring handled in the Scanian fairs from the fifteenth century.[86] Sweden was an important area of cattle breeding. Meat and horses were regularly sent to Danzig from Swedish ports. Butter, too, was exported, though probably not to the same extent as from Denmark. In addition, however, the Swedes also exported furs and sylvan products. Iron, usually described as 'Yser' or 'Osmund', passed through the ports of southern Sweden and Stockholm. Copper, too, came from the district of Falun. From the twelfth century, at least, the principal export of Bergen was stockfish. In addition some fish oil and smaller amounts of salmon, skins and butter were also exported. In the more southerly ports of Oslo and Tönsberg skins and furs were rather more important. Norwegian falcons were highly valued and used for hawking. Some timber was exported from Norway in the thirteenth century — it is recorded at Grimsby in 1230 — but it is unlikely that timber exports were substantial until the later fifteenth century.[87] Substantial numbers of Norwegian farms were abandoned after the Black Death and the ensuing population decline, and, in time, many of these lands became overgrown with trees. The technology of sawmilling, which greatly facilitated the cutting of timber, was, however, only introduced to Sweden from Germany in the 1460s. It did not become common in Norway until the sixteenth century.[88] Moreover, until this period, much of the timber market in western Europe including Scotland was supplied from the ports of the eastern Baltic. Indeed, even in the mid-sixteenth century many ships arriving at Dundee from Hanseatic towns continued to be laden with large amounts of timber.[89]

Since none of the Scandinavian countries was an important centre of textile production, cloth was imported by all three kingdoms. Wine and salt, too, were imported in quantity. Norway in particular in the later middle ages was an important importer of grain (especially wheat and rye), malt and beer. Denmark required iron and, in the early 1490s, exports from Danzig to Copenhagen and Aalborg included significant amounts of timber and sylvan by-products, such as pitch and tar.

If the imports and exports of Scotland and Scandinavia are compared there are a number of similarities. Both imported commodities, such as wine, from southern Europe and the commercial entrepôts of the Low Countries. The Scandinavian countries all imported salt. Though Scotland exported a limited amount of salt, better quality salt was also imported. Similarly, while Scandinavia imported cloth, Scotland both exported some low quality cloth and imported better quality foreign textiles. Norway and Scotland both imported grain. Scotland and Denmark both imported iron, timber and timber by-products. Since Scandinavia was not an important centre of textile production, Scottish wool would be unlikely to figure prominently in Scottish-Scandinavian trade. Skins and hides were exported from both Scotland and Scandinavia. Fish is somewhat more problematic. In the thirteenth century Scottish cod was apparently well known in Flanders. The herring industry, too, seems to have been important.[90] Some cod and herring was exported in the fifteenth century though the amount of dues collected from the exports of these items was never large. In the intervening period of the mid and later fourteenth century, however, some Scandinavian fish certainly found a market in Scotland.[91] Timber was certainly imported to Scotland in the later middle ages, but it was only once sawmilling was established in Norway that Scottish sources begin to include a substantial number of references to Norwegian timber.

Much research remains to be done on the subject of trade between Scotland and Scandinavia in the later middle ages. The Norwegian angle in particular deserves far greater investigation. The results of this preliminary study, however, suggest that there were at least occasional commercial contacts between Scotland and Scandinavia in the later middle ages. In the fourteenth century some fish, iron and, from the early sixteenth century, increasing amounts of timber were shipped westward. A market existed in Scandinavia for salt, coal and cloth, but the amount of salt and coal especially which was exported from Scotland was small. Despite the ease of communication between Scotland and the generally friendly political relations between Scotland and Norway-Denmark, trade was impeded by the paucity of exchangable merchandise. Indeed, to some extent the commercial clauses of the various Scottish-Norwegian-Danish treaties reflect this. The references to commerce in the 1266 and 1312 treaties are minimal. The more extensive references to commerce in the 1426 and 1494 treaties were an inducement to develop trade and to challenge the dominance of the Hansa. They were not apparently a reflection of a flourishing extant trade. Timber, not the treaties, explains the increasing number of references to Scottish-Scandinavian trade in the early sixteenth century.

NOTES

1. J Dow, 'Scottish trade with Sweden 1512-80', *Scottish Historical Review* (hereafter *SHR*), xlviii (1969), 64.

2. T Riis, 'Scottish-Danish relations in the early sixteenth century' in TC Smout, ed., *Scotland and Europe, 1200-1850* (Edinburgh, 1986), 82-96; T Riis, *Should Auld Acquaintance Be Forgot . . . Scottish-Danish relations c.1450-1707* (2 vols, Odense, 1988) (hereafter Riis, *Acquaintance*), especially vol.i, chaps.i,ii. For Scottish trading activities in Scania see also J Dow, '*Skotter* in sixteenth-century Scania', *SHR*. xliv (1965), 34-51; and for rather briefer comments on later medieval trade between Scotland and Denmark, B E Crawford, 'Scotland's foreign relations: Scandinavia', in J.M. Brown, ed., *Scottish Society in the Fifteenth Century*, (London, 1977) (hereafter Crawford, 'Scandinavia'), 94-6; D Ditchburn, 'Trade with northern Europe, 1297-1540', in M Lynch *et al.*, eds, *The Scottish Medieval Town* (Edinburgh, 1988), 163, 166-7.

3. G W S Barrow, *Robert Bruce and the Community of the Realm of Scotland* (3rd edn, Edinburgh, 1988), 100.

4. Riis, *Acquaintance*, i, 15-20, 39, 53-69.

5. See, for example, Crawford, 'Scandinavia', 85-94, 96-100; B E Crawford, 'The Earls of Orkney-Caithness and their Relations with Norway and Scotland, 1158-1470' (PhD, University of St Andrews, 1971) (hereafter Crawford, Thesis), passim.

6. On Scottish-Norwegian trade in the later sixteenth century, see, for example, S G E Lythe, *The Economy of Scotland in its European Setting, 1550-1625* (Edinburgh, 1960), 142-9; A Lillehammer, 'The Scottish-Norwegian timber trade in the Stavanger area in the sixteenth and seventeenth centuries', in TC Smout, ed, *Scotland and Europe 1200-1850*, 97-111. See also A Lillehammer's further study of the timber trade, below, 100-6.

7. Crawford, 'Scandinavia', 94. E Ewan, 'The Burgesses of fourteenth-century Scotland: a social history' (Ph D, University of Edinburgh, 1984), 203, argues for the importance of Scottish-Norwegian trade in the early fourteenth century. Dr Torrie is more cautious, stating that 'it must be certain however, that commercial contact between Norway, Sweden, Denmark and Scotland . . . in the earlier fifteenth century was *slight*' (my italics) (E P D Torrie, 'The Gild of Dunfermline in the Fifteenth Century' (Ph D, University of Edinburgh, 1984), 254).

8. H Lüdtke, 'The Bryggen Pottery I', *The Bryggen Papers*, supplementary series, iv (1989), 11.

9. I am grateful to Mr J C Murray for the information about the Scottish finds, which has not yet been published.

10. See above, 20-2.

11. E.g., K Hohlbaum *et al.*, eds, *Hansisches Urkundenbuch* (Halle, etc, 1876-1939) (hereafter *HUB*), ix, no.46.

12. T Thomson and C Innes, eds, *Acts of the Parliaments of Scotland* (Edinburgh, 1814-75) (hereafter *APS*), i, 420-1; *Diplom.Norv.*, viii, no.9.

13. *Regesta Norvegica*, ii (Oslo, 1978), no.444.

14. P Dollinger, *Die Hanse* (3rd edn, Stuttgart, 1981), 72-3.

15. *APS*, i, 461-3; A A M Duncan, ed., *The Acts of Robert I, King of Scots, 1306-29* (Edinburgh, 1988) (*Regesta Regum Scottorum*, hereafter *RRS*, vol.v), no.24.

16. *HUB*, ii, no.379; H J Smit, ed., *Bronnen tot de Geschiedenis van den Handel met Engeland, Schotland en Ierland, Eerste deel, 1150-1485* (2 vols, The Hague, 1928) (hereafter Smit, *Bronnen*), i, nos.302, 310, 311.

17. *APS*, i, 463-4; *RRS*, v, no.25. The date of the incident is not referred to.

18. J Bain *et al.*, eds, *Calendar of Documents relating to Scotland* (Edinburgh, 1881-1987) (hereafter *CDS*), iii, no.500.

19. On Anglo-Norwegian trade in the thirteenth century, see K Helle, 'Anglo-Norwegian Relations in the Reign of Håkon Håkonsson (1217-63)', *Medieval Scandinavia*, i (1968), 101-14.

20. *RRS*, v, no.215.

21. J Stuart *et al.*, eds, *The Exchequer Rolls of Scotland* (Edinburgh, 1878-1908) (hereafter *ER*), i, 450.

22. T Rymer, ed, *Foedera, Conventiones, Litterae et Cuiuscunque Generis Acta Publica* (Record Commission, London, 1816-69), ii, 949-50.

23. *ER*, i, 507, 511; ii, 390. See also Crawford, 'Scandinavia', 87, n. 6, for possible evidence of continued payments of the annual during the fourteenth century; and *APS*, i, 507.

24. *ER*, i, 60, 90, 261, 349, 480, 482, 525, 615; ii, 32, 58, 103, 158, 300, 327, 390, 415, 493, 543, 577, 597; iii, 25, 76, 102, 126, 142, 156, 185, 217, 233, 261.

25. Ibid., 474.

26. Crawford, Thesis, 169.

27. Dollinger, *Die Hanse*, 59-60; J A Gade, *The Hanseatic Control of Norwegian Commerce during the later Middle Ages* (Leiden, 1957), 7-9, 30-57.

28. H Lüdtke, 'The Bryggen Pottery I', *The Bryggen Papers*, supplementary series, iv (1989), 21-5; A Tuck, 'Some evidence for Anglo-Scandinavian relations at the end of the fourteenth century', *Medieval Scandinavia*, v (1972), 76-8; E Carus Wilson, 'The medieval trade of the ports of the Wash', *Medieval Archaeology*, vi-vii (1962-3), 196.

29. J Anderson, 'Notes on some entries in the Icelandic Annals regarding the death of Princes Margaret, "The Maiden of Norway", in A.D. 1290 . . .', *Proceedings of the Society of Antiquaries of Scotland*, x (1873-4), 411, 414-15.

30. J W Dilley, 'German Merchants in Scotland, 1297-1327', *SHR*, xxvii (1948), 142, n.1.

31. *Diplom.Norv.*, xix, nos. 423, 436, 503.

32. W Junghans and K Koppmann, eds, *Die Recesse und andere Akten der Hansetage von 1256-1430* (Leipzig, 1870-97) (hereafter *HR*,A), ii, no. 348.

33. *HUB*, iv, no.891.

34. Ibid., no.791.

35. *HR*, A, iii, no.345 (2,A).

36. Ibid., no.345 (5).

37. *ER*, i, 134-5.

38. *Calendar of Close Rolls* (London, 1892-) (1377-81), 276-7; Smit, *Bronnen*, i, nos.584, 718; K Kunze, ed., *Hanseakten aus England, 1275 bis 1412* (Halle, 1891), nos.329 (1), 337 (1).

39. For further details on the Scanian fairs and the Danish-Hanseatic war, see Dollinger, *Die Hanse*, 96-102, 313-16; D J Bjork, 'The Peace of Stralsund, 1370', *Speculum*, vii (1932), 447-76.

40. *HR*, A, i, nos.510 (11, 5; 11,11). See also no.522(11).

41. Ibid., ii, no.150 (11), 158 (10; 11).

42. *HUB*, iv, no.378; H Palais, 'England's first attempt to break the commercial monopoly of the Hanseatic League, 1377-80', *American Historical Review*, lxiv (1959), 852-65.

43. *ER*, iv-vii, passim. (During the Schism the grant was paid to the bishop of Aberdeen (*ER*, iii, 579; iv, 92, 121, 154, 184).) *CDS*, iv, no.690, v, no.934; J S Clouston, ed., *Records of the Earldom of Orkney, 1299-1614* (Scottish History Society, 1914), 37. For further evidence of trade with Orkney see e.g. *ER*, v, 150, 347.

44. A W K Stevenson, 'Trade Between Scotland and the Low Countries in the Later Middle Ages' (PhD, University of Aberdeen, 1982), 330.

45. City of Aberdeen District Archives, Sasine Register, 1484-1502 (hereafter ADA, SR, i), 650, 750.

46. *HUB*, ix, nos.46, 715, 728.

47. *Diplom.Norv.*, viii, no.276.

48. Riis, *Aquaintance*, i, 15.

49. Dollinger, *Die Hanse*, 381.

50. J Mooney, ed., *Charters and other Records of the City and Royal Burgh of Kirkwall* (Third Spalding Club, 1952), 96-102.

51. Riis, *Aquaintance*, i, 19.

52. *ER*, iv, 542. (The value of the goods was £3 16s.).

53. See above, n. 45.

54. *APS*, ii, 87; A Stevenson, 'Trade with the South, 1070-1513', in *The Scottish Medieval Town*, 199. There does not appear to be any reason for trade with the Baltic to have been interrupted in this year. For evidence of trade with England in 1467 see W R Childs, ed., *The Customs Accounts of Hull, 1453-1490* (Yorkshire Archaeological Society, 1984), 97-120, passim.

55. T Dickson and Sir J Balfour Paul, eds, *Accounts of the Lord High Treasurer of Scotland* (Edinburgh, 1877-1916) (hereafter *TA*), i, 332; ADA, SR, i, 750. For trade between Stavanger and Scotland, see *Diplom.Norv.*, ii, no 978.

56. *ER*, vii, 630; x, 47; xi, 55; *TA*, i, 89-90, 94, 96, 118; *APS*, ii, 214.

57. *ER*, iv, 412-13; *HUB*, vi, no 618.

58. E.g., *ER*, iv, 437; v, 150. For statistics on the iron trade between Sweden and Danzig, see H Samsonowicz, 'Handel zagraniczny Gdanska w drugiej połowie xv wieku', *Przeglad Historyczny*, xvii (1956) (hereafter Samsonowicz, 'Handel'), 311-13.

59. See *HUB*, viii, no. 1245, for an example of a ship which was arrested for trying to avoid the payment of the Elsinore toll by sailing through the Belt.

60. Crawford, 'Scandinavia', 95-6; Riis, *Aquaintance*, i, 15-16, 74-6; ii, 273 (David N); T Jexlev, 'Scottish history in the light of records in the Danish National Archives', *SHR*, xlviii (1969), 103-4.

61. T Thomson, *et al.*, eds, *Acts of the Lords of Council in Civil Causes* (Edinburgh, 1838-) (1478-95), 189; T Thomson, ed., *Acts of the Lords Auditors of Causes and Complaints* (Edinburgh, 1839) (1466-94), 149; *Records of the Earldom of Orkney*, 333; Crawford, 'Scandinavia', 95.

62. *HUB*, x, no. 184. (See also nos.234, 274).

63. Scottish Record Office (hereafter SRO), E71/13/1, E71/16/1-2, E71/20/1-2, E71/27/1-3.

64. SRO, E71/1/1-6.

65. SRO, E71/12/1-6. (For the references to Norwegian merchants E71/12/1, fos.3v, 7.).

66. SRO, E71/29/2-3; D Ditchburn 'Destination of ships departing Leith, 1510-13', *Historical Atlas of Scotland* (2nd edn, forthcoming). Twenty-four ships are recorded as leaving for Vere in the two accounts and twenty-three left for Dieppe.

67. SRO, E71/29/4.

68. SRO, E71/30/1-7.

69. City of Dundee District Archives, Burgh and Head Court Book (hereafter DDA, BHCB), ii, fo.3.

70. For the Danish entries see Riis, *Aquaintance*, i, 69. For Norwegian entries, DDA, BHCB, ii, fos.49v, 76v, 152v, 170v, 246v, 303, 328v, 329. For indications of contact with Sweden, ibid., fos.155, 189.

70a. I have been unable to identify 'Salisbourgch'.

71. T C Smout, *Scottish Trade on the Eve of Union, 1660-1707* (Edinburgh, 1963), 155. Ships arriving at Dundee from Norway between 1580 and 1584 also usually arrived between May and September (AH Miller, ed., *The Compt Buik of David Wedderburne, Merchant of Dundee* (Scottish History Society, 1898), 198-215).

71a. Riis, *Aquaintance*, 69. Other types of imported timber included roof spars, wooden beams and corbels.

72. J Dow, 'Scottish trade with Sweden, 1512-80', *SHR*, xlviii (1969), 67-71. These figures amount to just over 24% of all departures from Lödöse and just over 22% of all arrivals. Timber (spruce, oak, and some lime) and iron formed the bulk of the cargoes bound for Scotland, though some tar, wax, wooden vats and pitchforks are also recorded. Salt and cloth formed the basis of the eastward bound cargoes.

73. *TA*, viii, 84.

74. R K Hannay and R L Mackie, eds, *The Letters of James the Fourth, 1505-13* (Scottish History Society, 1953) (hereafter *James IV Letters*), nos.168, 326; *TA*, i, 96, iii, 416.

75. *TA*, ii, 84; iv, 289; ADA, Council Register, ix, 721-2.

76. *TA*, ii, 273. Other timber was also brought from Hanson and two other skippers, Eb Neilson and Esgir Laurenceson, whose names appear to indicate a Scandinavian origin.

77. R Lindesay of Pitscottie, *The Historie and Cronicles of Scotland*, ed. A J G Mackay, i, (Scottish Text Society, 1899), 251; *James IV Letters*, nos 236, 436.

78. H M Paton *et al.*, eds, *Accounts of the Masters of Works* (Edinburgh 1957-), i, 95-7, 181-2.

79. F Techen, *Die Deutsche Brücke zu Bergen* (Bremen, n.d.), 40-1. For Scottish settlement in Denmark (including Scania) see Riis, *Aquaintance*, i, 74-9, 155-241).

80. D Ditchburn, 'Merchants, Pedlars and Pirates: a history of Scotland's relations with Northern Germany and the Baltic in the later middle ages' (PhD, University of Edinburgh, 1988), 286-9.

81. *CDS*, iii, no 252.

82. R Nicholson, 'The Franco-Scottish and Franco-Norwegian Treaties of 1295', *SHR*, xxxviii (1959), 114-32; Riis, *Aquaintance*, i, 15-32.

83. These should not of course be confused with the 'particular' accounts, dating from the sixteenth century, which give details about the revenue collected from particular merchants and (sometimes) particular ships.

84. A Grant, *Independence and Nationhood: Scotland, 1306-1469* (London, 1984), 236-7; I Guy, 'The Scottish Export Trade, 1460-1599' in Smout, ed., *Scotland and Europe*, 62-81. The forthcoming *Historical Atlas of Scotland* (2nd edn) will include further statistics compiled by M Lynch, A W K Stevenson and D Ditchburn.

85. This, and all subsequent references to imports or exports to or from Danzig, is based on Samsonowicz, 'Handel', 304-13; V Lauffer, 'Danzigs Schiffs- und Waarenverkehr am Ende des xv. Jahrhunderts', *Zeitschrift des Westpreussischen Geschichtsverein*, xxxiii (1894), 1-43. More generally, see also Dollinger, *Die Hanse*, 310-18.

86. Ibid., 315-16.

87. E Gillet, *A History of Grimsby* (London, 1970), 15.

88. M L Parry, *Climatic Change, Agriculture and Settlement* (Folkestone, 1978), 128-33; A Lillehammer, 'The Scottish-Norwegian timber trade in the Stavanger area in the sixteenth and seventeenth centuries' in Smout, ed, *Scotland and Europe*, 99-100.

89. E.g., DDA, BHCB, ii, fos.55v, 67v.

90. Stevenson, 'Trade with the South, 1070-1513', in *The Scottish Medieval Town*, 186.

91. See above, 77.

8

SCOTTISH SOLDIERS IN THE SWEDISH ARMIES IN THE SIXTEENTH AND SEVENTEENTH CENTURIES

Alf Åberg

The earliest Scottish troops in the service of Sweden arrived during the Northern Seven Years' War of 1563-70. An officer named Willem Cahun commanded a squadron of Scottish cavalry, in all 119 men, at the battle of Axtorna in 1565. It seems nearly certain that Cahun was descended from the Scottish Clan Colquhoun, whose arms he bore: the cross of St Andrew.[1] Among the officers listed under his command we find the names Hugh Cahun, Robert Crichton and William Moncrieff.

Fresh troops were raised in Scotland during the war, but the Swedish treasury was empty, and as early as 1566 we hear the first complaints about non-receipt of pay. Twelve officers of William Ruthven's Regiment appealed in writing to King Eric XIV: 'Most Gracious Lord and King, We, Scottish troopers, complain of the great wrong done to us in not paying us for the horses that were killed in the last battles and leaving us without pay for the last three months'. Among the officers we find names such as Stuart, Wallace, Murray, Young, Lockhart and Galloway.[2]

In 1568 Eric XIV was deposed and imprisoned, and his brother John III ascended to the throne. After the Peace of 1570 John intended to disband his foreign regiments, three of which were Scottish, but war then broke out between Sweden and Russia, and instead of demobilising the king was compelled to raise new forces. In June 1573 a large contingent arrived from Scotland (possibly 4,000 men) under the command of Colonel Archibald Ruthven. Complications arose immediately after the arrival of these troops in Sweden. The reason was non-receipt of pay. The Scots believed that their countryman, Hugh Cahun, had embezzled the money, and they refused to make their way to the scene of hostilities until he had been executed. To bring them to reason the king was forced to have Cahun beheaded in Stortorget in Stockholm.

The Scots now sailed to Livonia, where they began to lay siege to the fortress of Wesenberg which was held by the Russians. The troops suffered from hunger and cold, and an attempt to storm the fortress cost the lives of 1,100 Scots, according to Ruthven's report. The Swedish besieging force also included enlisted German soldiers. A fight broke out between the Scots and the Germans on account of some beer which had not been paid for at the canteen. Several hundred Scots were slain, among them a number of officers. Many Scots fled and joined the Russians.[3]

A court-martial in Stockholm blamed the Scots for the unsuccessful campaign. Their leaders, Archibald Ruthven and Gilbert Balfour, were sent as prisoners to the Swedish capital. Balfour was condemned to death and executed in 1576, while

Ruthven died two years later in prison, although the government in Scotland and 23 Scottish officers in Sweden craved pardon for them.[4]

Despite these distressing events, in 1591 there were two units of Scottish cavalry in Swedish service in Estonia; Henrik Leyell with 290 men and William Ruthven with 114. Ruthven's patent for the enlistment has been preserved and declares that he was entitled to enlist Scottish cavalrymen wherever he could find them.

In 1592 John III died and was succeeded by his son Sigismund, who was also king of Poland and a Roman Catholic. War broke out between him and John's brother, Duke Charles. In 1598 Sigismund arrived in Sweden with a Polish army. Many Scots in Sweden joined him, among them Andrew Keith, who was a Swedish baron and court counsellor, and Jacob Nef, the governor of Vastmanland and Dalecarlia. After the king had been defeated and returned to Poland, Keith was driven into exile by Duke Charles, while Nef was slain by the peasants of Dalecarlia. His origins are obscure but on his tombstone we can read: 'Jacob Nef, a Noble Scot of Noble line and birth'.[5]

Other Scots volunteered for service under Charles IX, the new king of Sweden. Hans Stuart was appointed colonel of a regiment which he had raised in Scotland. In 1609 he became inspector of all foreign enlisted troops in Sweden; and in 1611 he led a Swedish legation to Russia. He died in 1618. The Swedish noble family of Stuart still survives.

During the 'Time of Troubles' in Russia at the beginning of the seventeenth century a number of pretenders fought each other for the throne. Charles IX intervened, and in support of Tsar Vassili a Swedish army under the command of Jacob de la Gardie marched into Moscow in 1610. Among the troops there was a regiment of Scottish and English foot-soldiers, 1,200 men strong, under the command of Samuel Cockburn. During the withdrawal the Swedes were attacked by a superior Polish army. The foreign troops who had not received their pay mutinied in the field and went over to the enemy. De la Gardie succeeded in reaching Swedish territory.[6] Samuel Cockburn was one of the few non-Swedish officers who accompanied him. With freshly enlisted troops he later took part in the campaigns in Poland. He died of fever in the field in 1621.

Charles IX died in 1611 and was succeeded by his sixteen-year-old son, Gustavus Adolphus. During his reign the Swedish enlistment of troops in Scotland reached its climax. Tens of thousands of Scottish officers — possibly as many as 30,000 — helped to establish the Swedish 'great power' ascendancy to east and south. The majority fell in battle or died of sickness in the camps. Some returned to Scotland, but many Scottish officers settled in Sweden, and they and their sons introduced new families into the houses of nobility: Douglas, Hamilton, Ramsay, Spens, Sinclair, Forbes, Duwall (Macdougall), to name only some of them.

Among these troops there were probably numerous Irishmen. When the great rebellion in Ireland had been crushed at the beginning of the seventeenth century, the English governor in Dublin tried in various ways to get rid of the rebels. In 1610 he reported that he had executed many of them, but he had also sent away 6,000 men 'of the same belief and profession' to the wars in Sweden.[7] We know nothing of these Irish 'Wild Geese'. They do not seem ever to have reached

Sweden. Perhaps they stayed in Danish service. We know that Swedish enlistments took place in Ireland, but it is very difficult to determine which troops and soldiers were Irish in the Scottish lists in the Military Records Office in Stockholm.

In 1611, when the war with Denmark broke out, there was only one Scottish regiment in Swedish service. This consisted of 350 foot-soldiers under the command of Colonel Robert Rutherford. At that time Denmark commanded the services of 18,000 mercenaries. The Swedish king asked James Spens, a Scottish colonel in Swedish service, to enlist 3,000 men in Scotland, but James I refused permission on the grounds that the king of Denmark was his brother-in-law.

Nevertheless, in the summer of 1612 two companies of Scottish recruits, in all 350 men, embarked in Caithness for Sweden. They were commanded by two captains: George Sinclair and Alexander Ramsay. They landed in the Molde fjord in Norway and marched through the Guldbrandsdal in the direction of Sweden. On 26 August they were ambushed by Norwegian peasants in the Pass of Kringelen, where the narrow road wandered along a steep mountain slope. The peasants overturned piles of timber from the heights on to the troops far below. Most of them were swept into the river where they were drowned. 134 Scots were taken prisoner, but the next day the peasants shot 66 of them. The remainder were sent to Copenhagen where they were made to join a Danish regiment. Sinclair fell, but Ramsay later entered Swedish service.[8]

This unfortunate embarkation did not lead to any considerable reduction in enlistment for Sweden. In the summer of 1624 Gustavus Adolphus could count on eight Scottish regiments, all up to full strength, in his army. Still another regiment arrived the following year and was sent to garrison Riga, 'but only if the Scots have sufficiently warm clothing to withstand the cold', as the king instructed Colonel Ramsay in December 1625.

During the fighting in Finland and Livonia the Scottish troops suffered extremely heavy casualties. The two regiments commanded by Colonel James Duwall had enlisted a total of 2,351 men in 1625, but those fit for combat numbered only 1,216 the following year. 1,052 men fell in the field or in the garrisons and 83 were sick.

The year 1627 witnessed extensive recruitment in Scotland. According to the calculations, 2,400 recruits arrived that year at Kalmar, where they were received by the Count Palatine, John Casimir, at the beginning of July. The figure of 2,400 is, however, unreliable, and it is uncertain whether it represents the number requested or the true active strength of the unit.[9]

In a large private archive — the Reay Papers — at the Scottish Record Office, we can study in detail how enlistment was carried out. These documents give us interesting information concerning the financial transactions between the various headquarters and the Scottish enlistment centre.[10] The documents concern a colonel first in Danish and then in Swedish service: Donald Mackay, first lord of Reay and chief of the Clan Mackay.

In March 1626 Mackay undertook to raise a regiment of Scottish soldiers and together with them enter the service of 'the Winter King', the unfortunate Frederick, Elector Palatine and king of Bohemia. The solemn agreement was made in London between the Scottish Captain David Lermont, who was King

Frederick's emissary, and Lord Ochiltree, Mackay's representative. Mackay was to receive 20 shillings for every man he could raise for the enlistment. Captain Lermont offered to transport the troops to Germany. The archive contains a contract, according to which William Robertson, an Edinburgh shipowner and proprietor of the vessel *Archangel,* offered to transport 300 men from Aberdeen to Glückstadt on the River Elbe for £1,200 Scots.

There do not seem to have been any serious difficulties in getting the lists signed by volunteers. In addition to those from Mackay's own clan-lands far in the north along Strath Naver, he was able to raise more than 1,000 men. On 10 October they set sail from the harbour of Cromarty north of the town of Inverness. Five days later the 2,400 soldiers disembarked on the banks of the Elbe. This must have been a fantastic spectacle for the good burghers of Glückstadt. The officers, the musketeers and the pikemen all wore the kilt, and every company had its own colours in standards and uniforms. Many officers wore gold chains around their necks, and the pipers played their wild tunes morning, noon and night.

Soon controversies broke out between the Highlanders and the Germans. The Reay Papers contain a number of complaints about acts of aggression on the part of the troops against the civilian population. Soon it was time for the Scots to take the field. Tilly, the military commander of the Catholic League, was advancing with his huge forces, and Mackay's regiment fought in the battles in northern Germany where the Protestants tried in vain to stop the numerically superior Imperial army. The casualties were unheard of. Of the 100 officers who were serving the regiment, 36 were reported as killed in the battle.

In March 1628 Mackay and the remnants of his unit entered the service of Christian IV, king of Denmark. About this unfortunate episode in military history, one of the officers of the regiment, subsequently Colonel Robert Monro, wrote a renowned chronicle entitled 'His Expeditions'.[11] The regiment experienced a crushing defeat ȁt Lutter am Baremberge. The surviving veterans and the newly arrived recruits were quartered during the winter of 1628 in various Danish towns. Monro's Company lay in winter quarters in Malmö. From this time there are some dismal reports to be read in the Malmö Court Records. The citizens of Malmö objected to the soldiers being quartered in their homes; and a series of incidents ensued. A Scottish captain was found guilty of rape. In the town church a German soldier, who had been stabbed to death by a Scot in the street, was buried.[12]

In the spring of 1629 King Christian was forced to conclude peace, and his Scottish troops were gathered together to be transported home as soon as the ships were ready to sail. But Mackay's regiment had still not finished marching along the roads of Germany. Monro claims that the Scots had served their Danish master in good faith and honourably, but now they were prepared to choose a new lord, and the greatest of them: Gustavus Adolphus.

A letter from Marienburg dated 17 July 1629 tells us that Mackay entered Swedish service as Colonel of a regiment of 'foreign soldiers'. Vigorous recruitment had restored the regiment to its old strength, and during the winter of 1629 it was quartered in Sweden to be trained in the new arts of war introduced by the king. Mackay and Monro were often the king's guests and also visited their fellow-countrymen in Sweden, among them the renowned artillery designer Alexander Hamilton. Mackay's Regiment was included in the force of 13,000 men which sailed from Stockholm during the summer of 1630 and disembarked on 30 June at Peenemünde on the island of Usedom to make their contribution to world history at the side of the king. The commanding officer of the regiment was now Robert Monro. Together with three other regiments, Mackay's Regiment now served in the Scottish brigade, which, on account of its colours, was known as 'The Green Brigade'. The brigade commander was the Scottish Colonel John Hepburn.

Mackay had been entrusted with other duties. In the summer of 1630 the king sent him to Scotland to raise new troops. To start with, he raised a new regiment, but after some time he became the senior representative for enlistment propaganda in the British Isles. In March 1631 the king sent him a crushing message: half his regiment — 600 soldiers with all their officers — had been massacred by Tilly's forces in Brandenburg. Fresh troops were urgently required, and Mackay was tireless in his efforts to produce new recruits. He came to an agreement with John Monro that a regiment should be raised in the Highlands, and with an Irishman, George Crosby, that troops should be enlisted in 'the Emerald Isle'. Raising troops cost money, and Mackay was obliged to pay large sums to the new regimental commanders. He received payments for his outlays from the king's emissary in London, Eric Larsson von der Linde, who obtained the necessary funds by selling Swedish copper.

Meanwhile Mackay's Regiment followed the Swedish king. The regiment became a kind of military academy for the Scottish officers who wished to serve in the Swedish army. Monro's chronicle follows the fate of the regiment, and throughout there sounds a Scottish national tone. Thus in description of the battle of Breitenfeld: 'We were in a dark cloud, not seeing the half of our actions, much less discerning either the way of our enemies or yet the rest of our Brigade. Whereupon, having a drummer with me, I caused him to beat the Scots march, till it cleared up, which recollected our friends unto us, so that the Brigade coming together, such as were alive missed their dead and hurt Comrads'.[13]

In 1633 — after the battle of Lützen and the death of Gustavus Adolphus — Monro travelled to Scotland to enlist recruits. He returned to Germany only to experience the catastrophe of Nördlingen in 1634. Of the regiment there now remained only one company. The king's death was a severe blow to Mackay. He was never fully repaid for his outlay for the enlistment of in all 10,000 men. From the contracts in the Archive it is evident that he was forced to sell one area after another in the Highlands. Finally, he had to give up his inherited lands around Strath Naver. Once more he entered Danish service and died at Bergen in Norway of a heart attack at the age of fifty-nine in 1649, a few days after he had learned that his King Charles I had been beheaded in London. The surviving company of his regiment came back after the Restoration and formed the nucleus of the Lothian Regiment.[14]

Several Scottish officers attained high position in Gustavus Adolphus's army. The 'Nestor' among them was Alexander Leslie, who entered Swedish service as early as 1605. In 1623 he became the first commanding officer of a Swedish regiment, the Närke-Värmland Regiment, and followed the king with the regiment to Germany. In 1638 he returned to Scotland as a Swedish general. In Scotland he became Lord-General and commander of the Scottish forces. During the confusing civil war on one occasion in 1651 he was placed in the Tower of London, but at the request of Queen Christina he was released and subsequently lived in retirement on his estate of Balgonie, where he died in 1661.[15]

A few years after Leslie another renowned Scot, Patrick Ruthven, entered Swedish service. Like Leslie, he took part in various wars and he also became the commanding officer of a Swedish regiment, the Kalmar Regiment. He followed Gustavus Adolphus to Germany and in 1632 he received the rank of general. On account of his age — he was sixty — he was appointed commander of Ulm, but after the king's death he found his way, once more, to the field of battle. In a critical moment he won a decisive victory over the Saxons at Dönitz. Patrick Ruthven — or Pater Rotwein, as he was called — was a typical mercenary, a hard drinker with a head of iron, swift with the sword, as in repartee, carefree and full of the joy of living. He was often host at the banquets held by the king in the field. In 1636 he returned to England to fight in the civil war on the side of Charles I. He followed the king's son into exile in France, where he lived in poverty. He succeeded in being awarded a pension by Queen Christina before his death in 1652.[16]

In 1630 the Scottish Marquis James Hamilton conducted extensive enlistment campaigns for the Swedish army in the British Isles. He raised an expeditionary force consisting of four full-strength regiments, in all 6,000 men, of whom 1,000 were Scots. In July 1631 the corps sailed from Yarmouth with a fleet of 40 ships. After a voyage of 14 days the corps disembarked at the estuary of the River Oder. The troops looked magnificent, and their gleaming new breastplates contrasted strongly with the rusty worn armour of their comrades who had served the king for years, declared an observer.

But the encampment was wretched in the war-torn country. Sickness swept through the ranks, and after only a fortnight 2,000 of the troops were already sick or dead. The corps continued to be decimated, and on 1 February 1632 Hamilton reported that 'the English Army' had shrunk from 6,000 to 700 men. The same year Hamilton returned to England. He joined Charles I and was active for his cause in Scotland. After the battle of Preston he was taken prisoner by Cromwell, condemned to death and executed some weeks after the king's death in 1649.[17]

In 1631 Gustavus Adolphus had 20 Scottish colonels and their regiments under his command. Enlistment proceeded in all parts of Scotland. In one and the same regiment we can find some 20 captains, second-lieutenants and corporals with the same name. Many recruits came from the Lowlands and from the Border region in the south. Other soldiers were from the towns.

A large proportion of the recruits came from the Highlands. If we wish to determine from which clans the men came, the lists at the Military Records Office in Stockholm are a good source, but they are not completely reliable. Many of the lists have been destroyed in the course of the years, and what remains from this period consists only of fragments of long series. Secondly, the Scottish names are often incorrectly spelt or are Swedicised. We have long known that Duwall is the name on the list standing for Macdougall, Robert MacCloue is surely derived from Macleod, and David MacFerling from the Clan MacFarlane. But are the officers with the name Makeleer descended from the Clan Maclean, and how many officers named Roos come from the Clan Ross or Rose? There are problems which in each case are worthy of serious consideration, and we cannot yet be sure of the answers. To the best of my knowledge no detailed study of the Scottish officers on the Swedish lists has yet been undertaken. The information which I shall present here is based on a study of a register of all the officers' names to be found in the army lists.

About 500 officers and civil/military officials have Scottish clan names in these lists from the seventeenth century. These are derived from 44 of the approximately 80 Highland clans, but the distribution within the clans varies greatly. There are clans with only one representative and others with 40. The clans best represented are the Clans Forbes, Lindsay, Douglas, Stuart, Gordon, Drummond, Leslie and Monro. In these cases we can almost speak of an emigration.

Of the 500 officers, no less than 390 came from the clans in the eastern Highlands, and of these most came from the clans who lived closest to the Highland line in the east from Inverness via Aberdeen to Edinburgh. In these regions there has always been a strong *Drang nach Osten*. From here and from the towns of the coast also came the majority of the civilian immigrants to Sweden: merchants, captains of industry and university graduates.

Some 50 officers had their origins in the most northerly regions, where contacts with the Scandinavian countries have always been lively and many place-names are of Norse origin. Here the greatest contributors were the Clans Monro, Sinclair and Mackay. The poverty-stricken clans of the west Highlands sent only a little more than 50 officers. One explanation may be that these districts were isolated. There the clan system still survived and kept the local inhabitants bound to the district.

Why did the Scottish officers wish to join the Swedish army and why did so many offer to help the Swedes in the matter of enlistment? Religious reasons have been put forward. It has been pointed out that the Presbyterian faith encouraged the young men of Scotland to involve themselves in the Protestant cause. Information from the army lists does not appear to confirm a development along these lines. Among the clans in the north-east which supplied the majority of the officers, Episcopalians and Roman Catholics were more numerous than in other parts of the country. John Hepburn, who became Commander of the Green Brigade, was himself a Catholic, yet did not hesitate to serve under Gustavus Adolphus, the 'Champion of Protestantism'.

Possibly other motivations are more important. The officers sought the chance of training in the army of a great power, and during the reign of Gustavus Adolphus the Swedish army became a military academy for officers from all over the world. The Scots deeply admired the Swedish king, whom many came to know personally, and they surely agreed with Robert Monro's words: 'The Captain of Kings and the King of Captains, Gustavus the invincible, the most valiant Captain of the World'.

Many of these officers were appointed to Swedish units, and we may wonder how they managed the language and made themselves understood by the soldiers and their Swedish brother officers. In the field they acquired a scanty knowledge of German. Patrick Ruthven wrote many letters in ungrammatical German to the Chancellor Axel Oxenstierna, but they are terse and graphic. In the various regiments the Scots maintained a close comradeship under all circumstances. They were conscious of their nationality and were certainly prepared to heed Robert Monro's warning: 'Let us always keep together wherever we are and let us always remember our fallen comrades'.

Another and possibly even stronger motivation for the officers to seek foreign service was the possibility, with Swedish help, of acquiring land of their own. Many achieved this ambition and settled in their new country. Advancement in the national Swedish army meant for the most part the acquisition of land in Sweden or Finland and thereby a chance of improved living conditions.

We do not know what the officers promised the recruits when they sounded the drums in the Scottish glens, but in all likelihood they promised them gold and loot and perhaps also land of their own in the foreign country. A more detailed account of what happened in connection with recruiting is given in a letter in the Forbes Collection in the Scottish Record Office in Edinburgh. This constituted an agreement between Alexander Forbes, an officer in Swedish service, and his cousin Arthur Forbes, in the summer of 1631. For the sum of 1,500 Swedish 'rixdaler' Arthur Forbes undertook to recruit 500 soldiers in good health and of reasonable height. The troops would be transported in the early autumn from Glasgow to the German battlefields, where they would join Alexander Forbes's regiment.[18]

The recruiting staff in Scotland seem sometimes to have resorted to severe measures in their activities. In 1612 two officers in Edinburgh were accused of press-ganging the sons of decent folk and forcing them on board the ships destined for Sweden against their will. In the rural districts there was such a fear of the press-gang that the peasants did not dare to go out into their fields. It was also reported at the same time that the soldiers on board the ships were treated like prisoners and slaves.[19]

The rank and file did not find much contentment in the Swedish armies. Many died of diseases before they even had time to take part in the fighting. They were loyal to their officers, in Sweden as in Scotland, as long as they received their pay and decent treatment, but when they were neglected by their superiors they did not hesitate to change sides. So, in fact, did all the mercenary troops in the Germany of the Thirty Years' War, and the Scots merely followed their example.

We often hear the soldiers complain, usually through their officers, but sometimes in letters, with the aid of a scribe. Life is hard and the rations are poor — they had expected a different fate. 'For we have during these many years suffered so much for the Crown of Sweden that we would never think of offence except when driven to it by extreme necessity. Since your Majesty's departure we have received now a couple of marks, now half a daler, nay sometimes only half a mark, and thus we have led a miserable life, so much so that very many have on the very streets exchanged life for death', as the Scottish soldiers of Samuel Cockburn's Regiment complained in a letter in Latin during the siege of Narva in 1615.[20] Behind this letter we find a worn-out company of Scots. Some years previously they had descended from the green hills of Sutherland and embarked on ships at Inverness. They had tried their luck and they had seen what it was worth. The kilts they wore were little more than rags, and the way home was far too long.

Twenty years later William Forbes, a colonel in Swedish service and the chief of the Clan, wrote some words in his book during a pause in the German campaign. His words reveal something of the spirit of the Scots in the Swedish army. 'Three of my brothers have lost their lives in the service of the Crown', he wrote. 'I had likewise to witness many of my dearest blood relations and friends fall for the honour of their adopted country, holding mostly higher commands and having gained for themselves an honourable name by their faithful and long services.' He concludes with a verse in German: 'die so viel Gutt verschossen und so viel tapferes Blut vergossen, doch biss dato kein recompens genossen'. (They have fired away so much of their property, spilt so much brave blood, but have up to date received no recompense.)[21]

Many could have made similar observations. Those who were successful formed a small minority, and when it was a matter of the rank and file they had even less chance of securing a brighter future. At the end of the 1630s the Scottish officers began to return home to the Civil War between king and parliament. The situation was now totally the reverse. James King, a general in the Swedish Army, made his way to England, where he was commissioned by Charles I to enlist men on the Continent. When Alexander Leslie landed at Leith in 1638 to take command of the Covenanters, he was welcomed by 36 brother officers from the German War.

Many other Scottish officers remained in Swedish service after the Peace of 1648. They married, acquired estates and farms and became naturalised Swedes. Some were raised to the nobility without being of true baronial lineage in their own country, but Queen Christina showed great benevolence to all of them and also helped the widows and orphans of fallen officers.

Before the new war against Poland in 1655 recruiting took place in Scotland under Colonel William Cranston, who succeeded in raising 1,800 men. But only a small part of this force arrived in Poland. The rest are said to have run aground in their ships off Danzig, where the Scots were taken prisoner and afterwards entered the service of the city.

Some of the Swedish Scots served during the war. Of these, Robert Douglas was promoted to field marshal and commander-in-chief in Livonia. He built the manor of Stjärnorp in Östergötland. One of his descendants, Archibald Douglas, commanded the Swedish army during the Second World War and later wrote a biography of his ancestor.[22]

These families continued to serve in the Swedish army under Charles XII. Many Scots from Sweden took part in the battle of Poltava in 1709, and in the list of Swedish officers, who spent thirteen years of their lives as prisoners-of-war in Siberia, we find some 50 Scottish names — Spens, Sinclair, Ramsay, Douglas, Duncan, Stuart, Ogilvie and others. In this way Scottish families followed and served Sweden during her period as a 'great power', from the very beginning until the bitter end.

NOTES

1. Axtorna: see 'En studie i organisation och taktik', *Bulletin of the Swedish Military Records Office*, iv (1926), 68.
2. Th A Fischer, *The Scots in Sweden* (Edinburgh, 1907) (hereafter Fischer), 50.
3. J Berg and B Lagercrantz, *Scots in Sweden* (Stockholm, 1962), 10.
4. F Ödberg, *Om stämplingerna mot Konung Johan III åren 1572-75* (Stockholm, 1897).
5. Fischer, 18.
6. H Almquist, *Sverige och Ryssland 1595-1611* (Uppsala, 1907), 142.
7. J Jordan, 'Wild Geese in the North', *An Cosantoir: the Irish Defence Journal*, xiv (1955).
8. A Larsen, *Kalmarkrigen* (Copenhagen, 1869), 238ff.
9. Fischer, 66.
10. *A Guide to the Materials for Swedish Historical Research in Great Britain* (*Bulletin of the Swedish Military Records Office*, v, 1958), 225.
11. R Monro, *His Expedition* (London, 1637).
12. J Dow, *Skotter in 1500-talets Skåne* (Ale, 1964), 20.
13. Monro, op.cit., 66.
14. J Mackay, *An Old Scots Brigade* (Edinburgh, 1885).
15. W Fraser, *The Melvilles, Earls of Melville, and the Leslies, Earls of Leven* (3 vols, Edinburgh, 1890).
16. F Rudelius, *Kalmar regementes personhistoria 1623-1923*, i, (1952), 1ff.
17. Birger Steckzén, *1:ste hertig av Hamilton* (Svenskt och brittiskt, 1959), 63ff.
18. *Guide* (as above, n.10), 223.
19. Fischer, 57.
20. Fischer, 85.
21. Fischer, 127.
22. A Douglas, *Robert Douglas* (Stockholm, 1957).

9

BOARDS, BEAMS AND BARREL-HOOPS: CONTACTS BETWEEN SCOTLAND AND THE STAVANGER AREA IN THE SEVENTEENTH CENTURY

Arnvid Lillehammer

I

On 8 August 1641 (it was a Sunday), a skipper called William Walker of Aberdeen sailed his ship called *Jonas* (15 lasts or *lester* or about 30 tons) into the Boknafjord basin at the south-west corner of Norway. He passed the Customs House at Nedstrand approximately 40 km north of Stavanger and ended up in a small harbour called Tednalandsvagen a few kilometres further west. In the next few days he loaded timber there: 220 boards, 60 narrow beams of pinewood 12 ells long, 360 so-called 'Scottish' pinewood beams, 180 pieces of birch and 4 cords of firewood. Nine days later, on Tuesday 17 August, *Jonas* and her skipper William Walker and his crew cleared outwards at the Customs House and set sail across the North Sea to Scotland.

The *Jonas* and her skipper are not presented here at the very beginning of this paper because they are unique. On the contrary, William Walker is mentioned here because he was quite an ordinary kind of guest in the fjords of Ryfylke, north and north-east of Stavanger, in the seventeenth century. He was a Scot; his ship was 15 *lester*; he bought boards, beams and firewood; and he was one among hundreds of foreigners who visited and brought about hustle and bustle in these fjords three to four hundred years ago.

Thus, William Walker from Aberdeen is a suitable introduction to the subject of this paper, which is the contacts between Scotland and the Stavanger area in Norway in the seventeenth century, elucidated by the timber trade, that is the trade in boards, beams, barrel-hoops and firewood. This trade brought Swedish, Danish, German, Frisian, Dutch, French, Spanish, Irish and English in addition to Norwegian and Scottish vessels to these fjords. In spite of this variety of nations taking part in the trade, the activity is very often called the Scottish trade. In the Stavanger area, today's Rogaland fylke, this trade is still called 'The Scottish Trade' (*Skottehandelen*) in oral tradition. And in particular, the seventeenth century is still called 'The Scottish Period' (*Skottetida*).

The background to this trade was the increasing consumption of wood in western Europe in early modern times. Norway had easily accessible timber to offer the rest of north-western Europe. Ryfylke by Stavanger was a district covered with woods at

100

that time, and more than 130 sawmills in the district made it possible to offer processed wood, that is, boards and beams.[1]

II

It is possible to say something about this activity due to some very informative sources. Most important are the local Customs Books, starting in 1601, which are kept in the Norwegian National Archives (Riksarkivet) in Oslo. The contents of these books undergo some alterations during the century under study, and from a Scottish point of view the books from the first half of the century give the most interesting and detailed information. Apart from five years, the Customs Books are complete from 1602-03 to 1623-4.[2] (A tax-year started at 1 May and ended on 30 April in the next year). In these books very detailed information is given about the ships: the tonnage, their type, their arrival and departure, names of skippers and their origin, the quantification of the commodity, the names of the sellers, what they had to pay in customs and excise and now and then what goods they brought with them to pay for the timber.

In 1630 the fjords got their own Customs House at Nedstrand. From then on and up to 1646-7 the Customs Books[3] are complete and almost identical to the older ones, with two exceptions. We lose one kind of information: the names of the farmers and others selling timber are not given any longer. Instead a new piece of information is given: the name of the vessel, like the *Jonas* in the example that introduced this paper. The Customs Books from the second half of the seventeenth century do not contain as many details as the older books, but are still important since they give us summaries which make it possible to measure year by year the volume of the trade.[4] But the names of the farmers, the skippers and the vessels disappear, unfortunately enough.

Among other sources throwing light on this trade, I will mention just one: the tax-lists regarding the sawmills.[5] The intensity of the sawmilling seems to be closely connected with the fluctuations of the timber trade.

III

According to the Customs Books the first Scottish vessels used to appear in the fjords of Ryfylke in March-April, and the last Scottish vessels used to leave in September. After 1630 the ships first passed the Customs House at Nedstrand, sailed from there into the fjord of destination, anchored up for a couple of weeks, then returned to the Customs House at Nedstrand again before they sailed for the North Sea and home to Scotland, as William Walker did in August 1641. It is fortunately also possible to follow the individual skippers on their trading journeys. And since this paper was originally delivered in Aberdeen, I would like to use that burgh as an example.

The visits from Aberdeen to Ryfylke vary from a few years without any visits at all, to seven vessels in 1642-3. I know of 47 calls from Aberdeen between 1603 and

1646. Some of the vessels crossed the North Sea more than once each year. Let us have a look at the year 1642. In that year three of the calls to Ryfylke were by the skipper who was my starting-point: William Walker in his ship of 15 lester. After having left Ryfylke on 17 August 1641, he was back at a port called Ilsvag on 8 June the year after, 1642, where he stayed for nine days, to 17 June, loading timber. He was then away from the Stavanger area for about a month, but on 19 July he was back again in a port called Straumen. This time he stayed for 12 days before he left on 31 July. For the third time that particular year he returned to Rogaland on 1 September, to Tednalandsvagen where we met him the year before. He left for the last time that year, 1642, on 8 September, after just one week.

The other Aberdonian skippers visiting Ryfylke in 1642-3 were John Andersson (the elder or the younger — I do not know which), George Abercrombie, Patrick Findlay and Thomas Serris, the last one representing a merchant, John Strachen.

It is interesting to note that all these names, except that of Thomas Serris, are found in the Aberdeen Shore Work Accounts, 1596-1670.[6] For instance, we find William Walker coming from Norway to Aberdeen in 1642, and it is said that he left for Flanders in September. That must be immediately after he returned from the Stavanger area for the third time. This makes it probable that some Scottish skippers, even in their small vessels, made trilateral journeys towards the middle of the century. About another skipper from these years it is recorded that he brought 'Scottish goods and goods from Holland, which later are exported to Scotland'. This means that the Scottish vessels sailed from the burghs along the eastern coast of Scotland, to the north-western corner of the continent, traded there, and on their way back sailed to Ryfylke in order to exchange some Dutch goods for Norwegian timber before returning home to Scotland.

IV

The wood was as a rule processed before it was exported. Very seldom one finds whole trees, that is, logs, in the lists. Four types of goods dominate the Scottish trade: boards, beams, barrel-hoops and firewood.

Table 1: Exported Firewood (in cords of wood)

	Scots	%	Others	%	Total
1602-03	244½	42.1	336½	57.9	581
1605-06	69	20.7	264½	79.3	333½
1620-21	235	25.7	680	74.3	915
1631-32	188	18.7	815½	81.3	1003½
1641-42	323	51.3	307	48.7	630

The most important and valuable items were the boards, but beams (from 6 to 12 ells long) formed a large part of the trade, while the hoops were in fact the most numerous items. The firewood, of birch, had the least prominent place in these export operations: Table 1 shows that the firewood exported in Scottish ships often accounted for only a quarter of the total amount of firewood exported each year. But in the trade in barrel-hoops the Scots were strongly represented, sometimes handling more than 50 per cent of the export (see Table 2). Does this indicate a large production of barrels in Scotland at this time in connection with fisheries? Or does it tell us about trade in grain?

Table 2: Exported Barrel-hoops (in dozens)

	Scots	%	Others	%	Total
1602-03	9910	75.5	3220	24.5	13130
1605-06	7030	53.5	6110	46.5	13140
1620-21	35120	61.9	21610	38.1	56730
1631-32	21105	83.9	4050	16.1	25155
1641-42	2035	80.3	500	19.7	2535

Regarding the boards, the highest percentage, when it comes to Scottish vessels, is reached in 1635-6 and 1641-2 with about 43 per cent of the total amount exported directly from the fjords of Ryfylke. As shown in Table 3, the Scots did not dominate the export of boards as we might have expected from the number of Scottish ships.

Table 3: Exported Boards (in dozens)

	Scots	%	Others	%	Total
1602-03	1334½	36.9	2278	63.1	3612½
1605-06	605	16.6	3043	83.4	3648
1620-21	927	23.8	2960	76.2	3887
1631-32	523	15.5	2860	84.5	3383
1641-42	6176	43.1	8159	56.9	14335

It was the Dutch, the Frisian and the German vessels that left the fjords with most of the sawn boards. Even though the Dutch and the Frisians after 1635 almost disappear from the records, the Germans, the English and the Danish/Norwegian ships, thanks to their larger tonnage of 40, 50, 60 and even more *lester*, managed to intercept most of the increasing production. If we take the year 1641-2 as an example, a year when the Scots completely dominated the timber trade in numbers, out of a total export of about 170,000 boards, only 74,000 or 43.5 per cent of these boards went by Scottish vessels.

However, the most important kind of timber for the Scots trading in Ryfylke consisted of beams. Up to around 1630, beams 9 and 12 ells long dominated the export. Yet the longest beams were comparatively few in number: one year most of

Table 4: Exported Beams 12 Ells Long (in dozens)

	Scots	%	Others	%	Total
1602-03	56	41.0	80½	59.0	136½
1605-06	9¼	12.8	62⅙	87.2	71⁵⁄₁₂
1620-21	138⅓	59.3	95	40.7	233⅓
1631-32	80½	30.4	184	69.6	264½
1641-42	172	88.7	22	11.3	194

Table 5: Exported Beams 9 Ells Long (in dozens)

	Scots	%	Others	%	Total
1602-03	128½	88.9	16	11.1	144½
1605-06	282½	71.3	113¾	28.7	396¼
1620-21	706	76.9	212	23.1	918
1631-32	550	59.6	373	40.4	923
1641-42	2123½	90.9	212½	9.1	2336

them went to Scotland, another year to some other country. Beams of 9 ells length were on the other hand a typical Scottish commodity. In the early 1630s the length of the beams changed. From then onwards most beams were 6 or 8 ells long. At the same time the contemporary written sources call the beams 'skottebjelker', that is, Scottish beams. This shows that beams first and foremost were connected with the Scots. In 1641-2, which is a year with an export of about 28,000 beams, almost 91 per cent left Ryfylke in Scottish vessels, as shown by Tables 4 and 5.

V

The connection between Scotland and the Stavanger area did not only express itself in direct trade between Scottish skippers and local farmers: the timber trade also led Scottish immigrants to settle permanently in the area.

A man called Gilbert Black, selling timber in the years 1615-18 to Scots and others from Sauda parish, including farmers, must be a Scottish immigrant. It is highly probable that he is identical with a certain Gilbert Skotte, i.e. Scot, mentioned in 1610-14. Gilbert does not seem to have become a farmer in his new country, but earned his living as a servant either to some of the farmers in Sauda, or at one or other of the many sawmills in use at that time on the Sauda fjord.

Other Scots settled as farmers. One of them was Thomas Bruce, who leased a farm called Topnes in Nedstrand (not far from the Customs House) in 1616 and lived there as a tenant farmer for many years. Another one was Jakob, i.e. James, on the farm of Finnvik in the Vindafjord. He seems to have settled in the Stavanger area in the 1580s, living at first on one of the islands in the Boknafjord basin, but just before 1602 settling as a farmer in Finnvik. He is now and then called 'Jakob Skotte på Finnvik', that is, James Scot at Finnvik. His descendants lived as farmers there for at least two generations after him.

In 1611 we meet David Skotte as a servant on the farm of Imsland, and in 1625 Sander Skotte was fined 2 *daler* because he had been to bed with a young girl from Kjolvik. Sander promised to marry the girl and is probably the Sander Sawmiller whom we meet in the parish of Jelsa some years later around 1630.

The countryside was not alone in attracting Scots. Quite a few of them also settled in the town of Stavanger; and some of them used Fife as a family name, indicating their origin. The first of this family that we know of in the Stavanger area is John Andersson Feiff, a Scottish skipper. His son George Johnson or Jørgen Jonsen Feiff, as he was called in Norway, settled in Stavanger, earned his living just like his father as a skipper, and traded in timber and grain. He married a woman by the name of 'Giønnette' (Jannet?) Williamsdaughter Key, probably also of Scottish origin. As a widow Jannet married a man called Robert Feiff. The third generation, Jon Jørgensen Feiff, was born in Stavanger in 1634. He owned a ship and lived as a merchant in Stavanger in addition to being a jeweller or goldsmith there for many years. And these Feiffs were not the only Scots settling in the town of Stavanger. I consider that more genealogical work would bring to light quite a few more citizens of Stavanger with a Scottish background. Until now not much research has been systematically done on that particular aspect of the Scottish trade.[7]

VI

The strong trade connections between the east coast of Scotland and south-western Norway are readily explainable in economic terms: in Scotland there was a great need for easily accessible timber; Ryfylke was a district with a deficiency in grain. Scottish textiles, shoes, bar iron, beams, soap and other items form part of the import trade; but the most important commodity brought to the Stavanger area on board Scottish vessels was certainly cereals. Information about the import of these to Ryfylke is not as comprehensive as that about the export of timber. But the records are rich enough to give us a fairly clear picture of the import trade as a whole and of the differences between Scottish and other imports.[8] Overall, it is clear that a 'symbiotic relationship' existed between the burgesses and skippers from the east coast of Scotland and the farmers east and north-east of Stavanger in Norway. The Scots had cereals to offer, either locally grown, or acquired in the Baltic trade thanks to their fleet of small vessels. The Norwegians had just the kind of timber that the Scots wanted, particularly beams and barrel-hoops.

Yet this direct trade between skipper and farmer ended in 1717 due to the changing relationship between the town of Stavanger and the district around it. In the 1680s the Customs House at Nedstrand was shut down, and in 1717 a royal resolution ensured the privileges of Stavanger and forbade the Scots to trade in the fjords: all timber had to go through Stavanger and its Customs House. From that year the number of Scottish vessels in Rogaland dropped remarkably: the Scottish trade was brought to an end.

NOTES

1. Further details and discussion of the subject can be found in Arnvid Lillehammer, 'The Scottish-Norwegian timber trade in the Stavanger area in the sixteenth and seventeenth centuries', in TC Smout, ed., *Scotland and Europe, 1200-1850* (Edinburgh, 1986).

2. In Lensregnskapene for Stavanger len 1601-24 (Riksarkivet in Oslo).

3. In Tollregnskaper for Ryfylke fogderi 1630-46 (Riksarkivet in Oslo).

4. In Tollregnskaper for Ryfylke fogderi 1660-85 (Riksarkivet in Oslo). The statistics from the different Customs Books must of course be used with caution and only looked upon as trends. The absolute figures stated must be too low. After 1685 the figures are found in Bytollen for Stavanger (Riksarkivet in Oslo).

5. In Lensrekneskapene for Stavanger len 1601-60 and Amtsregnskapene for Stavanger amt 1661-1717 (Riksarkivet in Oslo).

6. Louise B Taylor, ed., *Aberdeen Shore Work Accounts, 1596-1670* (Aberdeen, 1972).

7. The information above about Scottish immigrants is generally based on Axel Kielland, *Stavanger Borgebog, 1436-1850* (Stavanger, 1935), and Johannes Elgvin, *En by i kamp. Stavanger bys historie, 1536. 1814* (Stavanger, 1955).

8. For further details of the import trade, see Lillehammer, 'The Scottish-Norwegian timber trade', as above, n.1.

10

GOTHENBURG IN STUART WAR STRATEGY 1649-1760

Göran Behre

The city of Gothenburg on the west coast of Sweden was founded in 1621; its population grew during the seventeenth and eighteenth centuries to about 12,000. It lies at the mouth of the Göta river and was from early times an important trading post. Thus when the Swedish East India Company was founded in 1731, the Company established Gothenburg as its Swedish port. Another feature of the city was a military presence, as the position of Gothenburg had great strategic value. As a result it became one of the most fortified cities in Europe.

Gothenburg immediately attracted Scottish immigrants who came as traders. Many Scots arrived as refugees after the Jacobite risings and wars in the seventeenth and eighteenth centuries. With fair winds Gothenburg could be reached from Scotland in two or three days.[1] Gothenburg very soon became a key city in the military plans of the Stuarts and Jacobites in their times of crisis and rebellion. The aim of the present study is to give a brief account of those plans.

I *The Years of Montrose, 1649-50*

During the spring and summer of 1649 there were repeated talks at The Hague between the exiled King Charles II and representatives from Scotland. The subject of these talks was the Scottish crown. One of Charles's most faithful supporters was James Graham, marquis of Montrose. To end the discussions and to reinstate Charles as king of Scotland once and for all, Montrose worked out a plan for an armed invasion. Charles hesitated, but accepted in June 1649. The plan was, briefly, to assemble men, ships, guns and ammunition in Gothenburg and from this town invade Scotland.[2]

Both before and after Charles's acceptance of Montrose's plan experienced Scottish warriors from the Thirty Years War came to Sweden as emissaries from the Stuart headquarters. Patrick Ruthven, earl of Forth and Brentford, arrived in January 1649. Another emissary was James King, Lord Eythin, well known among the Swedes for his achievements at the battle of Wittstock in 1639. Their task was to tie Sweden more tightly to the Stuarts. That was easy because Queen Christina herself regarded the execution of Charles I as a blood-stained violation of a kingdom.[3]

Thus weapons from Sweden were almost immediately put at the disposal of Charles II. In November 1649 Gothenburg became — according to Montrose's plan — the Stuart headquarters in Sweden and the base for the invasion of Scotland. Montrose himself arrived in Gothenburg on 12 November 1649 and on 21

November Charles issued the following order to his new envoy in Sweden, Robert Meade:

> You shall take Gothenburg in your way where now remains a considerable quantity of Arms, Ammunition and Cannon, which by the care and order of Our right trusty and right beloved Cousin and Councillor the Earl of Brentford have been conveyed and transported from several parts unto the said port of Gothenburg for Our use and are now remaining in the hands of John Macklier, a Scottish Merchant, who has disbursed several sums of money for the charge of bringing the said Arms, Ammunition and Cannon to that place.[4]

The instruction is interesting in many respects. It points out that the Stuart emissaries had succeeded in getting Swedish support and in building up a supply of weapons in Gothenburg. The instruction also shows that the Stuart cause had got the support of Scots living in Gothenburg. James Maclean, or in Swedish, Johan Macklier was one of the richest merchants in Sweden at the time and highly respected all over the country.[5] Finally the instruction shows the importance of Gothenburg to Stuart military planning.

Once in Gothenburg Montrose discreetly settled down in Maclean's house and the two men co-operated closely. Maclean became a kind of unofficial intermediary between Queen Christina and Montrose. The Swedish government supported the operation but did not want to show this. Montrose co-operated, however, with the governor-general of western Sweden, the famous military commander from the Thirty Years War, Count Lennart Torstensson, and with the commander of the Gothenburg Navy Squadron, Admiral Mårten Anckarhielm.[6]

In Gothenburg Montrose worked out a proclamation to the Scottish people and copies of this circulated in Edinburgh as early as December 1649. The standards of Montrose's troops were also designed and sewn in Gothenburg. His own was of white damask with a lion leaping between two cliffs and the inscription 'Nil Medium' — no compromise.[7] The Stuart invasion force gathered in Gothenburg during November and December 1649. Montrose could muster about 800 men and seven ships. One of the ships was a Swedish frigate that had been bought by Lord Eythin. By order of the Swedish government Mårten Anckarhielm, the naval commander at Gothenburg, helped Montrose in arming the frigate. Guns and ammunition were stored in Gothenburg, the food supplies at Marstrand north of Gothenburg and on Danish territory. This took place with the approval of the Danish authorities.[8]

The Orkneys were planned to be the first target because of strong royalist feelings that were to be found there. From the Orkneys Montrose planned an attack on the Scottish mainland. The operation was delayed because Montrose waited — in vain — for orders from Charles II about his plans once the invasion had taken place. Finally, Montrose could not wait any longer but departed from Gothenburg. At the end of March 1650 he reached Kirkwall. The rest of the Montrose story is well known.[9]

As had been shown, Queen Christina supported the Montrose expedition. The Swedish attitude towards Cromwell's England changed, however, as Queen Christina's plans to abdicate ripened. In 1653 Cromwell sent an ambassador,

Bulstrode Whitelocke, to Sweden. In November 1653 Whitelocke arrived in Gothenburg where he stayed about a fortnight. There he met socially several of the men who had been involved in the Montrose expedition, among them James Maclean.[10]

II *Change of Heart, 1688-90*

The approach to Cromwell's England did not alienate Sweden from its main ally, France. But some twenty years later the Swedish government changed its diplomatic tactics. A strong naval power was considered an indispensable ally for Sweden in order to defend its seaways. The choice was between England and Holland. Sweden chose Holland which was ruled by William of Orange and, thus, in 1681 a formal treaty was signed.[11]

The foreign policy of western Europe at this time was dominated by the power struggle between Louis XIV and William of Orange. William's strategy at the end of the 1680s was to defeat Louis XIV and to invade England. In order to succeed with the invasion of England it was absolutely vital for William not to deplete his own country's troops. Thus he turned to Sweden for help. Already in 1683 a Dutch naval force had arrived in Gothenburg with the purpose of recruiting Swedish troops for William's armies. The mission did not succeed. The situation changed, however, a few years later when in 1686 William made a deal with Sweden: she promised to assist with 6,000 men. The deal was formally signed in September 1688. One thousand men were to be sent from Gothenburg to William's army, the rest were to come from Sweden's German provinces. At the end of October 1688 the Gothenburg contingent was ready, but stayed in the town until December, when it travelled to join William's forces. The German contingent followed in February 1689.[12]

William landed in England in November 1688. Thus the Gothenburg contingent did not take part in the landing itself. But the Swedish auxiliaries could be regarded as one of the conditions precedent to the operation. During the summer of 1690 William's forces fought the decisive battle at the Boyne against James II's army of Irishmen with French auxiliaries. Whether the Gothenburg force or other Swedish troops fought alongside William's other troops at the Boyne — as has been mentioned by some historians — is, however, doubtful, but later that year Swedish troops fought with William at the battle of Fleury in Belgium and took a heavy beating.[13]

But military strategy was one thing and the treatment of royal families another. The Stuart succession in England and Scotland became before long a matter of interest for the king of Sweden.[14]

III *Much Ado About Nothing, 1715-19*

At the same time as Sweden's fortunes were declining in the Great Nordic War, the Jacobites were dealt what to many of them proved to be traumatic blows. The union between England and Scotland was one, the accession to the throne of George of

Hanover was another. These events inspired Jacobite activities all over Europe. During 1715 and the following years the Jacobites made repeated attempts to procure Swedish military support for the Stuart cause, and Gothenburg became a focus of interest for their strategy.[15]

The first attempt took place at the beginning of 1715. The Jacobites contacted Count Carl Gyllenborg, the Swedish envoy in London (since 1704). In January and February 1715 several discussions were held between them. The proposition was that Charles XII should give orders for 5,000-6,000 men to sail from Gothenburg to Scotland as soon as possible. A quick attack would be a total surprise to the Hanoverians. Once in Scotland the body of troops would be reinforced by Scots. The Jacobites were to pay all the costs. The Jacobites had to wait long for the Swedish reply and therefore gradually lost heart, and their demands shrank: 3,000-4,000 men in the invasion force from Gothenburg would, they thought, surely be enough, but weapons for another 10,000 men would be needed.[16]

In July 1715 Sweden turned down this proposal.[17] By this time a different scenario was apparent. Probably on Bolingbroke's initiative, in June 1715 plans were made for a joint French-Spanish-Swedish expedition to overthrow George I. For that purpose, several conferences were held in June and July 1715 at the castle of Marly in France. Among the more important participants were the duke of Berwick, Torcy, who for many years had worked for Louis XIV in foreign affairs, and Eric Sparre, the Swedish ambassador to Paris. Their plans were ready on 7 July 1715 and shortly afterwards Eric Sparre sent a report to Charles XII, describing the general outline of the Stuart strategy.[18]

Gothenburg and the Swedish west coast were of great importance. An invasion force was to gather in Gothenburg and one of Charles XII's field marshals was to be appointed a commander-in-chief; and the Gothenburg naval squadron was to act as convoy and protect the transport ships. Surprise was necessary. The main target was to be Newcastle. The Gothenburg invasion force would consist of infantry, but on arrival in Newcastle it was proposed to form a cavalry force, recruited from sympathetic Englishmen.[19]

Newcastle is of interest as the target for the planned attack. It had been discussed as a strategic location by Torcy in conferences with James III in 1705-7. One of Torcy's agents, Brigadier Nathaniel Hooke, then wrote concerning a descent in Scotland:

> It will be easy enough to seize Newcastle. London depends so heavily on
> the coal from this town for its heating that if it were deprived of it for six
> weeks the capital would be reduced to great straits.[20]

It is interesting to note that Sparre in his dispatch urged that as many Scots and Englishmen as possible of those who were in the service of Sweden's armies should join the invasion force. Sparre suggested that the officer in charge should be selected from these men and he named Hugo Hamilton, major-general in the Swedish army and of Scottish lineage. Hamilton was at that time provincial vice-governor of Gothenburg.[21]

Charles XII received Sparre's dispatch during intense military pressures. He was fighting a decisive battle at Stralsund and needed all his Carolines himself. His answer to the proposals was negative but the tone of his answer to the Pretender was positive.[22]

In September 1715 the situation changed once more. At the beginning of September John Erskine, eleventh earl of Mar, raised the Stuart standard at Braemar. The rising surprised even those who had taken part in the discussions about support for the Jacobites. In October George I as Elector of Hanover occupied the Swedish province of Bremen. The Jacobite hope for Swedish support rose: the Swedish king would — they presumed — react on the occupation of Bremen. New military plans were drawn up. These 'new plans' were almost identical with those that Sparre had described in July. The primary target for the Gothenburg invasion force this time, however, was Edinburgh, the main military stronghold of Scotland.[23] The reason for this was that Mar had apparently failed to capture it.

The events during the Jacobite rising of 1715 are well known. The rising was a failure, and the question of a relief expedition from Gothenburg was superseded by the problem of where the Pretender was to reside. Louis XIV had died on 1 September. For reasons of a new diplomacy France did not wish to be host country to the Stuart headquarters, and the Jacobites turned to Sweden. An alternative would be Gothenburg, they thought, 'séjour qui donnerait à l'Angleterre un prodigieux ombrage'. In June 1716, Charles XII replied that he did not want to have the Pretender's headquarters within his country.[24]

In 1716 Charles XII appointed Freiherr Georg Heinrich von Görtz as his personal adviser. Görtz's diplomacy was characterised by action and a lack of prejudice and his objectives were to split Sweden's enemies by separate peace treaties. As a means to put pressure on England-Hanover he would use the Jacobites. Thus with Görtz Swedish diplomacy became more active in the negotiations with the Jacobites. The leading Swedish diplomats in these negotiations were Görtz himself and the Swedish envoys in Paris and London, Eric Sparre and Carl Gyllenborg.[25] At various meetings during 1716 the three Swedish diplomats met representatives of the Jacobites and discussed a Swedish military contribution to the Stuart cause. Their scheming can very briefly be described in the following way. Sweden needed money to continue the war, the Jacobites needed troops to invade Scotland. The Swedes had troops and the Jacobites money.

In every one of these discussions Gothenburg was mentioned as the point of departure for the invasion forces. The talks concerned primarily the size and composition of these forces, which varied from 10,000 men (discussions with Gyllenborg in September 1716) or 8,000 infantry and 2,000 cavalry (discussions with Sparre in October 1716). Arms were to be brought for another 6,000 to 30,000 men — that number too varied in the discussions.[26] In January 1717 the Jacobites told Görtz that they wanted the Pretender himself to go to Gothenburg to command the invading force.[27]

The Swedish-Jacobite negotiations, however, were halted for several months when the British government, which had followed the pro-Jacobite plottings between Gyllenborg and Görtz, arrested Gyllenborg in London in January 1717.

About a month later Görtz was also arrested in Holland after Hanoverian pressures on the Republic. Both were released after a couple of months, but London succeeded in putting at least a temporary stop to their negotiations.[28]

The last act was yet to be played. In the autumn of 1718 Charles XII assembled an army that totalled about 40,000 men and launched a big military campaign against Denmark. The Swedish troops advanced through south-eastern Norway from Gothenburg, and towards Trondheim from northern Sweden. At the same time a strongly re-armed Gothenburg naval squadron appeared in the North Sea.[29] Charles XII's combined attacks against Christiania and Trondheim gave birth to speculations about a bigger strategic operation against Scotland from both towns.[30]

Until the very end negotiations were carried on between Sweden and the Jacobites. In the final stage Cardinal Alberoni, the leader of Spanish foreign policy, played an important role. His final diplomatic objective was to alter the results of the Spanish War of Succession. In these plans a Swedish descent on Scotland was considered more or less a key to success. In the autumn of 1718 Alberoni sent one of his most trusted Jacobite agents to Sweden. His name was Peter Lawless and his orders were to persuade Charles XII to attack England and Scotland. On Alberoni's request another agent was sent from the Jacobite headquarters in Rome to Charles XII. His orders were to propose that the Swedish king send 2,000 men to Scotland with arms for another 5,000.[31] But it all ended on 30 November 1718 when Charles XII was killed outside Fredriksten fortress in south-eastern Norway.

Negotiations had gone on for several years between Sweden and the Jacobites when Charles XII died. Had the king seriously thought of invading Scotland? The answer, in spite of many learned hypotheses, is that we do not know. The fact, however, that Charles XII and his representatives such as Görtz continued the different talks and negotiations with the Jacobites for so long indicates that the king wanted them to go on. But to what purpose is uncertain. It could be that Charles regarded them only as elements of psychological warfare against George I and thus only one of several links in the peace talk processes. If so, the Stuart military plans were merely parts of a diplomatic conversation for the Swedish king.

The Jacobites on the other hand saw Charles XII as one of their last trump cards. For many of them he was also the hero king from the north. One of the Jacobite songs runs as follows:

> Here's a health to the valiant Swede.
> He's not a king whom man hath made,
> May no oppressors him invade.
> Then let his health go round.[32]

IV *Masons and Merchants, 1745-6*

During the interlude from 1719 to 1745 Jacobite activities took partly new forms, often of a mystic and speculative character. One of these was freemasonry, where Jacobite influence was strong.[33]

Two groups at least initiated the 1745 Rising. Those were the French government and Jacobite merchants, some of them freemasons. One of the latter group was the Irishman Daniel d'Heguerty 'who had founded masonic lodges of a Jacobite kind all over France'.[34] Shortly after Prince Charles Edward's departure for Scotland d'Heguerty suggested to the French government that France should help the Prince by enlisting troops in Sweden. In September 1745 the Irish Commander of the Irish-French Picquets, Colonel Daniel O'Brien, contacted Sweden's minister in Paris, Carl Fredrik Scheffer, about this possibility.[35] Scheffer had lived in France frequently since the 1730s and had been Swedish minister since 1743. He had come into close contact with the freemasons. In 1737 he entered a lodge in Paris and became acquainted with the well-known Jacobite mason Charles Radcliffe, earl of Derwentwater. By him Scheffer was granted the authority to institute new masonic lodges.[36] The discussions between O'Brien and Scheffer led to a military plan with Gothenburg as the strategic focus. The plan was very soon accepted by the French government.

The O'Brien-Scheffer plan was roughly as follows. About 200 Swedish officers were to be enlisted for the French-Swedish regiment, *le Royal Suedois*, each officer being accompanied by four men, a total number of about 1,000 men. All the officers and men were to gather at Gothenburg. After being equipped there they were, officially, to be despatched to Dunkirk, but in reality to Scotland. Once there, they were to be assigned for combatant service in the Jacobite army. A little later Louis XV ordered the transfer of 200,000 *livres* to Sweden for expenses connected with the Gothenburg expedition. William Stuart, Lord Blantyre, called Leslie, and serving in *le Royal Suedois*, was appointed as commander.[37]

The French ambassador at Stockholm, the marquis de Lanmary, was as early as October 1745 initiated into the plans for an invasion of Scotland from Gothenburg. His first task was to get the sanction of the Swedish government or — at least — its silent consent. This task was not an easy one, for the Swedish government was then split into two factions, one pro-French (the Hats) and one pro-English (the Caps). After long and heated discussions the pro-French faction carried the day with some minor adjustments. Each officer was allowed to bring only two men with him and the Gothenburg expeditionary force was not regarded as part of *le Royal Suedois* but as an independent corps, called the French Corps. The new force was also given heraldic devices of its own: blue and white banners carrying the St Andrew's cross with yellow lilies in each corner.[38] By the decision of the Swedish government a new phase in Jacobite military planning was completed.

It is interesting to note that this phase too was put through with the help of freemasons. The first Swedish lodge was founded in Stockholm in 1735 by Count Axel Wrede Sparre. He was the son of the Swedish ambassador in Paris, Eric Sparre, who played an important part in the negotiations between Sweden and the Jacobites in the time of Charles XII. A second lodge was founded in Stockholm in 1743 by the well-known Jacobite James Francis Edward Keith, brother of George Keith, ninth Earl Marshal. James Keith then stayed in Stockholm as a general in the service of Russia. Four of the Hat members of the Swedish government were masons, the two most important members of the government being among them. The chancellor, the former minister in London, Count Carl Gyllenborg, had entered James Keith's lodge while the general still remained in Sweden in 1743. The deputy chancellor, Count Carl Gustaf Tessin, had become a member of the first lodge in 1735. Outside the government, but belonging to the party's inner circle, another two important Hats (later senators) were freemasons.[39]

From Christmas 1745 the Swedish officers and men who had enlisted in the French Corps started to gather at Gothenburg. From the very beginning two of the powerful directors of the Swedish East India Company helped in planning and organising. These were the Scot Colin Campbell and the Gothenburgian Niklas Sahlgren. Thus by their help the French Corps could take over one of the Swedish East India Company's ships for the transport of men and arms to Scotland.[40] The furnishing of the French Corps with weapons became an international intrigue involving merchants from different countries. D'Heguerty contacted his business associates in Amsterdam, the firm Grou and Libault, which also had contacts with Niklas Sahlgren. The French state secretary for maritime affairs, Maurepas, provided a ship from the French East India Company for the conveyance of the weapons. Somewhere in the background there were other Swedish merchants who dealt with arms.[41]

The itinerary for the French Corps was settled in Gothenburg. The details were given to Leslie by another Scot in Gothenburg, James Maule of Glithe, in Kincardineshire. Maule was a captain in the service of the Swedish East India Company. The ships were to proceed from Gothenburg across the North Sea to the Moray Firth. Depending on the circumstances at the arrival, the descent was to take place either at the Cromarty Firth or at Inverness.[42] Leslie — also a Scot — had a very high opinion of James Maule. Above all, however, Leslie wanted and received advice and moral support from another Scot in Gothenburg, namely, Colin Campbell. Thus Leslie once wrote to the French ambassador in Stockholm that Campbell was 'a man of honour, who could not dream of doing anything that was dishonest or shady'.[43]

The whole plan to give Swedish support to Prince Charles Edward came to nothing. One decisive cause of the failure was the extraordinarily cold winter in Gothenburg: the transport ships were shut in by the ice. The course of events in Scotland was the other and most decisive cause. While the ships were trapped in Gothenburg developments in Scotland took a disastrous turn for the Prince. The French corps was formally dissolved during the summer of 1746. Most of its officers were offered admission to *le Royal Suedois* in Paris and almost all accepted.[44]

V *Fantasy Game, 1759-60*

A roll-call of *le Royal Suedois* in France in 1754 contains more than sixty names of officers who in 1745-6 had enlisted in the French corps in Gothenburg. Two years later several of them took an active part in the Seven Years War.[45]

In November 1758 the Duc de Choiseul emerged as the leader of French politics and the war effort. He had a strategic vision 'un grand plan' for winning the war.

That vision inluded a major invasion of England and/or Scotland. A combined French-Swedish-Russian force was to invade Scotland, with Sweden and Russia participating with 12,000 men each. The Swedish contingent was to assemble in Gothenburg, the Russian in Stettin. The Russians would be transported from Stettin to Gothenburg on board Swedish vessels. The Swedish force was to join the Russian one outside Gothenburg and together they were to head for Scotland. It was anticipated that a Stuart rising would support the invasion.[46]

Such a plan had to have the co-operation of the Stuarts and, once again, Jacobite hopes re-awakened. Prince Charles Edward was called to a meeting with Choiseul in February 1759. The meeting was not a success. 'The unfortunate Prince arrived very late carried by one of his followers and in a state of drunkenness which augured ill for his ability to lead a great enterprise.' Choiseul also had suspicions that the Prince was surrounded by Hanoverian spies.[47] Prince Charles Edward became a figurehead but no more. But Choiseul's strategy gave new hopes to the old Jacobite guard from Gothenburg and the French corps of 1745. Both Heguerty and Leslie reappeared on the scene and took an active part in the military discussions.[48]

In July 1759 Choiseul drafted a more detailed memorandum. The invasion was to be a big pincer attack against Portsmouth and Glasgow, starting from Le Havre and Brest. All in all, 48,000 men and 337 ships were to be involved. Choiseul counted on Swedish naval support, and the natural gathering-point for the Swedish ships was Gothenburg. A rather remarkable technical point was that the large invasion fleet was to be protected by twelve Swedish flat-bottomed cargo-boats or barges. These were to serve as floating cannon batteries. Later, even the French minister in charge of the Navy concurred.[49]

The Swedes, however, did not agree at all. The Swedish government — even its pro-French senators — disapproved of 'le grand plan' and probably regarded the scheme as a daydream.[50] The end of it all, and of Choiseul's strategic visions, came through the naval battle of Quiberon Bay in November 1759, a decisive defeat for the French navy. Thus, the last phase of Gothenburg's involvement in Stuart military planning was concluded.

NOTES

1. Gothenburg general history: Helge Almqvist, *Göteborgs historia: Grundläggningen och de första hundra åren* (2 vols, Gothenburg, 1929-35); Hugo Fröding, *Berättelser ur Göteborgs historia under enväldestiden, frihetstiden, gustavianska tiden* (3 vols, Gothenburg, 1908-22). Swedish East India Company in Gothenburg: Tore Frängsmyr, *Ostindiska kompaniet* (Höganäs, 1976); Sven T Kjellberg, *Svenska Ostindiska Compagnierna* (Malmö, 1974). Scots in Gothenburg: Göran Behre, 'Scots in "Little London": Scots settlers and cultural development in Gothenburg in the eighteenth century', *Northern Scotland* 7 (1987), 133-50.

2. Montrose in Gothenburg: Birger Steckzén, *Svenskt och brittiskt* (hereafter Steckzén) (Uppsala, 1959); James N M Maclean, 'Montrose's preparation for the invasion of Scotland, and royalist missions to Sweden, 1649-51', (hereafter Maclean), in Ragnhild Hatton and M S Anderson, eds, *Studies in Diplomatic History* (London, 1970).

3. Steckzén, 150-4; Maclean 7-14.

4. Quotation from Maclean, 15-16.

5. James Maclean or Johan Macklier: see Maclean, 8, 51, and Fröding (as above, n.1), 243ff. James Maclean was the youngest brother of Sir Lachlan Maclean of Dowart.

6. Steckzén, 155-6; Maclean, 15, 17. Maclean points out that both James Maclean and Montrose loathed the Marquess of Argyll.

7. Steckzén, 158.

8. Steckzén and Maclean differ on the number of ships in Montrose's fleet. As Maclean has investigated more sources, his view has been followed. Maclean has also found the exact number of arms allocated to Montrose in Gothenburg (Steckzén, 159-60; Maclean, 20, 24).

9. Steckzén, 159-60; Maclean, 24.

10. Georg Landberg, *Den svenska utrikespolitikens historia I:3 1648-97* (Stockholm, 1953), 71; Fröding, (as above, n.1), 274ff; Maclean, 30.

11. Jerker Rosén, *Svensk historia I: Tiden före 1718* (Stockholm, 1962), 666-8, and references.

12. Landberg, (as above, n.10), 228, 238; Ludvig Stavenow, 'Sveriges politik vid tiden för Altonakongressen, 1686-9', *Historisk Tidskrift* (1895), 296-320. The Gothenburg contingency: ibid., 299. The troops' sojourn in Gothenburg, their organisation and transport to William of Orange's armies: Göteborgs Landsarkiv (Regional Archives of Gothenburg), Landshövdingens i Göteborgs och Bohus Län Skrivelser till Kungl. Maj:t (Letters from the Provincial Governor of Göteborg and Bohus Län to the Crown), 8 Aug., 4, 26, 30 Oct., 3, 17, 19 and 29 Nov., 1688.

13. V G Kiernan, 'Foreign mercenaries and absolute monarchy', in Trevor Aston, ed., *Crisis in Europe 1560-1660: Essays from Past and Present* (London, 1965), 136, and Bruce Lenman, *The Jacobite Risings in Britain* (hereafter Lenman) (London, 1980), 28, mention Swedish auxiliaries alongside William's other troops at the Boyne. There could, however, be a confusion between the names of two regiments, one Danish (Jylland's regiment) and one Swedish (Nyland's regiment). The Danish regiment took part in the battle but there is no evidence in the sources that the Swedish regiment did. I thank Professor Alf Åberg, Stockholm, for this information.

14. See also Claude Nordmann, 'Louis XIV and the Jacobites' (hereafter Nordmann, 'Louis XIV'), in Ragnhild Hatton, ed., *Louis XIV and Europe* (London, 1976), 87.

15. The literature concerning Sweden and the Jacobites during this period is rich. The following books and articles are some of the more important. Th Westrin, 'Friherre Georg Heinrich von Görtz' bref ur fängelset i Arnhem 1717', (hereafter Westrin), *Historisk Tidskrift* (1898); Per Sörensson, *Sverige och Frankrike 1715-18: Ett bidrag till kännedomen om Sveriges utrikespolitik efter Carl XII:s återkomst från Turkiet* (hereafter Sörensson), Del 1 (Lund, 1909); Stig Jägerskiöld, *Sverige och Europa 1716-18: Studier i Carl XII's och Görtz utrikespolitik* (Ekenäs, 1937); John J Murray, 'Sweden and the Jacobites in 1716', *Huntington Library Quarterly*, viii (1944-5); Claude J Nordmann, *La crise du Nord au début du XVIIIe Siècle* (hereafter Nordmann, *Crise*), (Paris, 1961); Ragnhild Hatton, *Charles XII of Sweden* (hereafter Hatton), (London, 1968; Swedish edition, 1985); Nordmann, 'Louis XIV'; Lenman; John Simpson, 'Arresting a diplomat, 1717', *History Today* (Jan.1985). As can be seen above the Swedish works are mainly quite old while continuous studies up to recent times have been done by other European scholars. On Sweden's foreign policy in general, see Göran Behre, Lars Olof Larsson, Eva Österberg, *Sveriges historia 1521-1809* (Stockholm, 1985), and its references.

16. Westrin, 90-2; Sörensson, 130.

17. Westrin, 93; Sörensson, 130.

18. Westrin, 94-5; Sörensson, 132; Nordmann, *Crise*, 39-42; Nordmann, 'Louis XIV', 99-101.

19. Sparre's dispatch of 7 July, 1715, is printed in Nordmann, *Crise*, 249-50.

20. Quotation from Nordmann, 'Louis XIV', 93.

21. Almqvist, ii, 161, 165.

22. Westrin, 95; Sörensson, 135-6; Nordmann, *Crise*, 41-2. Charles XII in Stralsund: Hatton, 397ff.

23. Sörensson, 140-9.

24. Sörensson, 154-6; Nordmann, *Crise*, 53ff. (quotation ibid.).

25. Görtz and Sweden's foreign policy: Jägerskiöld (as above, n.15); Jerker Rosén, *Den svenska utrikespolitikens historia*, II, 1 (1697-1721) (Stockholm, 1952); Nordmann, *Crise*; Hatton. All these books have extensive references.

26. Sörensson, 159ff.

27. Sörensson, 167.

28. Gyllenborg's and Görtz arrests: see references in n.15.

29. Charles XII's Western Army, 1717-18, numbered about 40,000 men: 21,000 infantry, 13,000 cavalry and the rest transport. The Northern Army numbered 7,500 men (Hatton, 474-5). The Gothenburg naval squadron consisted of frigates and galleys. Gothenburg was also the central point for the Gothenburg privateers who co-operated with the Crown. They tried especially to hit English merchantmen (Almqvist, as above, n.1), ii, 222ff.; Wilhelm Berg, *Samlingar till Göteborgs historia 2* (Gothenburg, 1887), 32ff.).

30. Hatton, 474, 492-4. On 28 Nov., 1728, Bogislaus von Schwerin wrote a letter to the Swedish Chancery (Kanslikollegium) about Charles XII's plans for an invasion of Scotland. The letter has been published in *Historisk Tidskrift* (1895), 341-2. Schwerin's impression was that Charles XII contemplated a descent from Trondheim on Scotland if the Northern Army succeeded in capturing that town. (See also Hatton, 493.)

31. Jägerskiöld (as above, n.15), 436ff.; Nordmann, *Crise*, 182ff.; Lenman, 189. The so-called 'Madagascar affair' is sometimes regarded as the last phase of the Swedish-Jacobite negotiations. Sweden was supposed to create a kind of trade company by lending its flag to Madagascar entrepreneurs, more or less pirates. Lenman writes (188): 'The Jacobite dimension seems to have derived from the fact that one of the pirate captains who came to Europe to negotiate with the Swedish authorities was a former officer in the Royal Navy, of Jacobite sympathies'. The 'affair' came to nothing. The suggested home port for the ships was Gothenburg (see also A Francis Steuart, 'Sweden and the Jacobites, 1719-20', *Scottish Historical Review*, xxiii (1926), 119-22.

32. Quotation from Steuart, 119.

33. Freemasonry in the 1720s: see A Lantoine, *Histoire de la franc-maçonnerie française* (Paris, 1925), and R Priouret, *La franc-maçonnerie sous le lys* (Paris, 1935).

34. Lenman, 241, and references.

35. Sweden and the rising of 1745: Claude J Nordmann, 'Jakobiterna och svenska hovet, 1745-46' (hereafter Nordmann, 'Jakobiterna'), *Historisk Tidskrift* (1959), 408-17; Göran Behre, 'Sweden and the rising of 1745', *Scottish Historical Review*, li (1972), 148-71 (hereafter Behre, 'Sweden'), and Göran Behre, *Göteborg, Skottland och Vackre Prinsen* (hereafter Behre, *Göteborg*), (Gothenburg, 1982). Behre and Nordmann have extensive references. Alf Åberg, *Klanernas krig* (Halmstad, 1963), gives an account in Swedish of the whole rising.

36. K L H Thulstrup, *Anteckningar till svenska frimureriets historia* (2 vols, Stockholm, 1892-8). Scheffer became an active and important Swedish mason; on early Swedish freemasonry see references in Göran Behre, 'Scots in "Little London" ', (as above, n.1), n.30.

37. Discussions and planning in France: see Nordmann, 'Jakobiterna', 409-12; Behre, 'Sweden', 149-150; Behre, *Göteborg*, 20-2.

38. Behre, 'Sweden', 150-5; Behre, *Göteborg*, 22-7; Nordmann, 'Jakobiterna', 415, n.37; Åberg, (as above, n.35), 70.

39. On early Swedish freemasonry and freemasons see references in Behre, as above, n.36. On James Keith as mason in Sweden see especially Thulstrup, (as above, n.36), i, 14-15.

40. Behre, 'Sweden', 154-8; Behre, *Göteborg*, 28-31.

41. Ibid., 35-6; Nordmann, 'Jakobiterna', 416. Sahlgren's contacts with Grou and Liboult in Justitieprotokoll, 6 June, 1748 (Göteborgs Stadsarkiv (Record Office, Gothenburg)). On Sahlgren's arms affairs see Leslie to Lanmary 2/13 Apr., 1746, C P Suède 212 in Archives du Ministère des Affaires Etrangères, Paris.

42. James Maule had been since 1731 in the service of the Swedish East India Company. He lived with his family in Gothenburg and had good social contacts with important Gothenburgians. His son James Maule, jr, also entered the service of the Swedish East India Company.

43. Behre, *Göteborg*, 50-1.

44. Ibid., 53ff.

45. Ibid., 55.

46. Gunnar Carlqvist, *Carl Fredrik Scheffer och Sveriges politiska förbindelser med Denmark åren 1752-65* (Lund, 1920), 217-19; Lars Trulsson, *Ulrik Schefer som hattpolitiker* (Lund, 1947), 334-6; Claude Nordmann, 'Choiseul and the last Jacobite attempt of 1759', in Evelyn Cruickshanks, ed, *Ideology and Conspiracy: aspects of Jacobitism, 1689-1759* (Edinburgh, 1982), 205.

47. Nordmann, (as above, n.46), 203 (quotation ibid.).

48. Ibid., 204.

49. Ibid., 206-7.

50. Swedish-French negotiations concerning Choiseul's 'grand plan' have been exhaustively discussed by Carlqvist, (as above, n.46), 219ff., and Trulsson, (as above, n.46), 337ff. See also Nordmann, (as above, n.46), 208-9.

11

SOME EIGHTEENTH-CENTURY INTELLECTUAL CONTACTS BETWEEN SCOTLAND AND SCANDINAVIA

John Simpson

The Scot as migrant to continental Europe and beyond has become a fairly familiar figure in Scottish historical writing. The intellectual interaction of Scotland and the wider world is necessarily a more diffuse theme and, no doubt for that reason, one not so often directly addressed. Yet it was a theme present in the minds of those scholars who pioneered the study of the Scottish migrant. T A Fischer, writing at the beginning of this century on the Scots in Germany, closed with the reflection that 'no nation ever stood on its own merits alone. There has been during long centuries a continual fructification, a continual giving and taking of what is best in a nation, a continual fusion in peaceful rivalry'.[1] My paper may serve to suggest, if scarcely to demonstrate in any depth, that such a process of fructification was indeed a feature of Scottish-Scandinavian intellectual contacts in the eighteenth century.

A convenient starting point is 1739, with the foundation of the Kungl. Svenska Vetenskaps Akademie (Royal Swedish Scientific Academy). Considerable impetus towards this foundation came from England, in the person of Mårten Triewald (1691-1747), who had spent ten years there and returned to Sweden filled with admiration for Newtonianism and for the Royal Society of London.[2] It would not appear that the Scottish merchant community resident in Gothenburg, though significant in Swedish economic life, were involved to any great extent in the early years of the Academy. The only one of its early members with a Scottish name, so far as I have been able to discover, was Colonel Thomas Cunninghame,[3] descended from one of the families of the seventeenth-century Scottish diaspora. Cunninghame's grandfather had been provost of Crail, and Cunninghame's father had emigrated to Sweden as long ago as 1659.

There was a Scot, however, who was about to make a notable, indeed an eccentric, appearance in Swedish intellectual and political life. This was Alexander Blackwell, son of one principal of Marischal College, Aberdeen, and brother of another.[4] Alexander was, according to most accounts, the black sheep of the family. He was born in Aberdeen, probably around 1709, as the Swedish historian Anders Fryxell suggested over a century ago;[5] and he proceeded by way of Aberdeen Grammar School to Marischal College, where he matriculated in 1722. That he left there without completing his course might suggest some waywardness in his nature, since his father, Thomas Blackwell senior, was principal of Marischal at the time. Alexander himself claimed to have gone on to Leyden, to study medicine under the great Hermann Boerhaave (1688-1738). I am not sure that we should necessarily discount this claim, as has often been done. Eighteenth-century universities offered a chance to acquire knowledge, but also an opportunity to seek out influential friends and patrons: once students felt they had had some success in both directions, they frequently did not remain long enough to obtain a formal qualification. Alexander Blackwell may have gone to Leyden as soon as he possibly could, fired with genuine zeal for medical or scientific knowledge. But the profession of medicine was still in process of defining itself in the early eighteenth century, while the profession of science was still less well defined. If Blackwell, as may be the case, did indeed become estranged from his family, and had no alternative source of patronage ready to hand, this would explain why he was to be found, in the 1730s, practising neither medicine nor science, but operating in the London book trade. He began as a proofreader for someone else, and then set up business for himself; this venture was financed by money provided by his wife Elizabeth, the daughter of an Aberdeen merchant.

Again, however, he found himself excluded from a charmed circle, that of the London booksellers. He seems to have been forced out of business and into the debtors' prison, where he remained for two years. He was rescued by his wife, who turned herself into a botanical painter and engraver, with the encouragement of Sir Hans Sloane (1660-1753) and of the curator of the Physic Garden at Chelsea. When her two-volume work, *A Curious Herbal*, was published in 1737, it met with the approval of the Colleges of Physicians and of Surgeons, and restored the Blackwells' finances. The book contained five hundred illustrations of plants useful in medicine, and since it was apparently Alexander Blackwell who supplied them with their correct botanical names, it is not to disparage Elizabeth's contribution to suggest that her husband was perhaps more than the charlatan and adventurer that he is usually held to have been.

Alexander now began to offer his services as a consultant on agricultural improvement, and in particular went to work for the duke of Chandos at his estate of Canons (in Little Stanmore) in Middlesex. Chandos had acquired considerable riches as government minister responsible for the troops overseas, and he was very willing to disburse these riches. Some of his money went to St Andrews University, of which he had become chancellor in 1724,[6] but no less than £20,000 of it went on Canons, where George Frederick Handel was employed for two years in composing anthems for the chapel. Blackwell, however, soon left the employment of this promising benefactor, and left as it seems under somewhat of a cloud. But strained relations between people of ability and their patrons are a commonplace of cultural and intellectual history.

In 1741 Blackwell published an agricultural textbook, *A new Method of Improving cold, wet and barren Lands*,[7] where he refers specifically to improved farming methods in Scotland. He states that the topic he proposes to deal with is by intention a narrow one, since most writers on agriculture are tempted to deal with too much, and are thus led to plagiarise the work of others, so that 'this makes the Farmers look on most of these modern authors as Arabs'. There then follows an explanatory footnote on why Spaniards did not think highly of Arabs. Certainly this was a period when improvement was much in vogue among agricultural theorists, in Scotland as elsewhere. Robert Maxwell of Arkland, secretary of the Society of Improvers in Edinburgh, was calling for the foundation of university chairs of Agriculture, and warning that the holders of such chairs should not '(as is too commonly practiced in other Arts) . . . read pompous and superficial Lectures, out of Virgil's Georgics, Pliny, Varro, Columella, or any other Authors, ancient and modern; but surely a practical Farmer should be chosen, who could teach Rules established upon rational Experiments tried in our own country . . .'[8]

But this pioneering generation did not find it easy to be consistently and successfully practical and modern. Maxwell would scarcely have approved the liberal use made by Blackwell of quotations from Virgil and Columella. Maxwell, on the other hand, bankrupted himself through his efforts at practical farming in the late 1740s, whereupon he boldly set himself up as a full-time agricultural consultant to others. And Blackwell's work is undeniably and impressively specific on various matters. He reproduces, for instance, a diagram taken from another, unnamed, author, of a clamp for burning out clay: this clamp, he argues, would not be efficient, and he then supplies his own alternative diagram of an efficient clamp. He would appear at least to deserve a more thorough examination of his work than I — or, so far as I know, anyone else — has so far given it: an examination to determine its practicality, and also, in the context of his remarks about plagiarism and of his own subsequent reputation, to determine its degree of originality.

And so it was probably as an author, and certainly with the recommendation of Carl Magnus Wasenberg (d. 1743), Swedish ambassador in London, and a member of the Swedish Scientific Academy, that Blackwell went to Sweden in 1742. He spent some time living with the industrialist Jonas Alströmer (1685-1761), and advising him on improvements in arable farming and livestock breeding. In 1744, on the basis of very optimistic forecasts he made of the possibility of agricultural improvement in Sweden, he was given considerable financial privileges by King Frederick; and in the following year there was bestowed on him the royal estate of Ållestad in Västergötland, where it was intended that he should experiment. But when he published on Swedish improvement, he was accused of plagiarism by L J Kullin, and of merely translating, or causing to be translated on his behalf, other people's writings in English. Linnaeus had a poor opinion of Blackwell as an agricultural theorist, and ascribed to him the belief that, if sand were blended with topsoil, the resultant mixture would itself turn into topsoil in three years.

In Stockholm, where Blackwell gained an entrée by courtesy of Jonas Alströmer, he established his credentials as a doctor, and became a permanent physician to the king. Quite a catalogue of Swedish insults attended his efforts in this direction too, but after this lapse of time it is hard to know quite how to evaluate them. There is, for instance, the charge that, to cover up his professional deficiencies, he always waited to hear what his patients said of their condition, and then agreed with them. But present-day doctors occasionally at least give the impression of doing this, and it might conceivably arise from politeness or diffidence rather than incompetence!

It may have been a sense of insecurity that led Blackwell to dabble in Swedish politics. His intrigues, of which Göran Behre has written a most interesting account,[9] led to his arrest, trial for treason and execution in 1747, just the year before his brother, Thomas Blackwell junior, was to become principal of Marischal College. Alexander's downfall was a sudden one, since his wife, of whom nothing is subsequently known, was apparently just about to join him in Sweden at the time of his arrest. Colin Campbell, one of the directors of the Swedish East India Company, was related to Blackwell, and described him as given to 'a very indiscrete licence of tongue . . . against persons in power and their measures'. It is hard to believe that Blackwell's intrigues were simply the work of one unbalanced individual, though some historians have assumed exactly that. His troubles seem to have begun when he threw out suggestions that he was in a position, in the aftermath of the Forty-Five rebellion, to make available to the British government some worthwhile secrets of the Jacobite exiles. Göran Behre's admirably clear and cautious account of the whole episode seems to establish, firstly, that there had indeed been some fairly murky connections between the Jacobites and highly-placed people in Sweden; and secondly, that we cannot now uncover exactly what had been going on. Perhaps that was the very result that the Swedish government intended. They give every appearance of having hounded Blackwell to his death, with a leading part played by the chancellor, Carl Gustaf Tessin (1695-1770). Tessin's predecessor, Carl Gyllenborg (1679-1746), to take just one prominent Swede, may well have had powerful reasons for preferring the Stewart monarchs to the Hanoverian ones, reasons dating back to his own arrest as a suspected Jacobite plotter when serving as Swedish ambassador in London in 1717.[10]

It is for the manner of his death that Alexander Blackwell is remembered. Even at the time, his own family in Scotland seem not to have thought it worthwhile to seek to counter a great deal of disinformation that was spread around about him. It may be that, as an agricultural theorist, Blackwell played a more positive role in Scottish-Scandinavian intellectual relations than has hitherto been recognised.

The next Scot to be mentioned was someone whose career was more conventional, and whose contribution, while it remains to be fully investigated, is already clear. This was John Hope,[11] born in 1725, the son of an Edinburgh surgeon. Unlike Blackwell, Hope pursued his studies, at the University of Edinburgh, to a successful conclusion, with the result that he was elected a member of the Edinburgh Medical Society in 1745. Unlike Blackwell, Hope can be with certainty said to have pursued further study abroad, in his case at Paris, where he was taught botany by Bernard de Jussieu (1699-1777). Throughout the 1750s Hope practised medicine in Edinburgh; but he must have maintained his botanical studies because, in 1761 and on the death of his old teacher Charles Alston, Hope was made superintendent of the Royal Botanic Gardens by the crown, and professor of Botany and of Materia Medica by Edinburgh University. In practical terms, Hope did a great deal to build up the Botanic Gardens: in theoretical terms, he was among the first scholars in Britain to accept the new taxonomy of plants (the so-called 'sexual system') of the great Swede Carl von Linné (1707-78), better known of course as Linnaeus.

In 1765 Hope opened a correspondence with Linnaeus. It was an act of hero-worship — Hope's first letter is addressed to 'the renowned Carl von Linné, prince of botanists', and his second to 'the ornament of his country, Carl von Linné'. But it was also a business correspondence. Eighteenth-century botanists wrote letters so as to exchange plants and seeds, and with his first letter to Linnaeus Hope sent a gift of seeds from Quebec, 'on the instructions of a society set up by certain gentlemen for the importation of exotic seeds into our island'.

Hope wrote to Dublin to try to get a plant Linnaeus had requested. Hope also sent a plant from Norway — perhaps the Swedes could not bring themselves to ask the Norwegians direct for a specimen — and one from the East Indies. Along with these he sent a cocoon in a phial, asking the genus and species of the insect and also how to eradicate it, since it was preying upon his garden. And on a later occasion he enclosed a letter to Linnaeus from the Scots judge James Burnett, Lord Monboddo (1714-99). Possibly Monboddo wished to enlist the support of Linnaeus for his hypothesis, shrewd though much ridiculed at the time, that *homo sapiens* is one of the monkey family. After the death of Linnaeus, Hope continued the correspondence with his son, though he now sometimes did not make the effort to write in Latin, as he had always done with his hero. And in the last extant letter from the series, dated December 1782, Hope was looking forward to welcoming the younger Linnaeus to Scotland.

The elder Linnaeus had died in 1778. The following year Hope erected a monument to his memory, which moved with the Botanic Gardens in the nineteenth century to Inverleith, where it may still be seen. It consists of an elegant classical urn on a pedestal; the design was that of Robert Adam, and the work was executed by James Craig, according to whose ground-plan the New Town of Edinburgh was being laid out at this time. Hope himself, one of the greatest of Scottish botanists, died of a sudden illness in November 1786.

If Linnaeus was the hero of John Hope, then Hope was a hero to his pupil Andrew Duncan,[12] to whom I come next. In 1779 Duncan reported how 'at Edinburgh, Dr Hope, Professor of Botany, on opening his course of lectures for the present summer, delivered a discourse in honour of [Linnaeus], this great master of the science which he [Hope] has there cultivated with so much assiduity and success. And at the same time, in presence of the students, he laid the foundation-stone of a monument to be erected to his memory in the botanical garden in that place'.

From Linnaeus, to Hope, to Hope's pupils like Andrew Duncan and like William Roxburgh, who became botanist to the East India Company at Calcutta, we can see a kind of apostolic succession, the academic physicians and biologists in process of defining themselves as a profession, complete with its appropriate rituals. If only Alexander Blackwell could have understood or accepted the way in which these things are achieved, he might have avoided a violent death and been remembered very differently today.

Andrew Duncan (1744-1828) served the University of Edinburgh for thirty years in its chair of the Institutes of Medicine. His chief claim to fame is as a pioneer in the sympathetic study and treatment of mental illness; and a clinic at the Royal Edinburgh Hospital bears his name for this reason. But in the context of this paper he is significant as, in 1773, the main progenitor of a pioneer medical periodical, *Medical and Philosophical Commentaries*. Library catalogues describe it as published in London, but this is misleading to the extent that in fact it was printed on behalf of three publishers, John Murray in London, Ewing of Dublin, and Kincaid and Creech of Edinburgh. Its first number sounded a characteristic eighteenth-century note of optimism: 'medicine has long been cultivated with curiosity and attention, but is still capable of further improvement. Attentive observation, and the collection of useful facts, are the means by which this end may be most readily attended.'[13]

Just as the botanists collected seeds on an international basis, so Duncan's group of Edinburgh scholars of medicine proposed to collect their 'useful facts' internationally. From the start the *Commentaries* reviewed books and reported case histories from several European countries. Just like eighteenth-century literary reviews, the *Commentaries* described books rather than submitting them to critical analysis. By this means, said Duncan's preface to the first volume, 'those who have not leisure for extensive study, may early become acquainted with everything proposed as a discovery in medicine, and with the principal arguments by which it is supported; while those who have, will thus be enabled to select such authors as they themselves judge best deserve attention'.

The *Commentaries* appeared annually, and constituted the most regularly published medical periodical of its day. This enhanced the value of its European coverage for British readers and, as far as I can ascertain, the value of its British coverage for continental readers. Swedish contacts were maintained, and the fifth volume of the *Commentaries* hailed the publication of the *Pharmacopoea Svecica*. 'We have little doubt', it stated, 'in giving it as our opinion, that it is to be considered as, perhaps, the best Pharmacopoea yet extant'. The 'perhaps' presumably stems from the fact that the Edinburgh College of Physicians had also brought out a Pharmacopoeia.[14]

Danish connections were also important. In volume four, the *Commentaries* described the first volume of its Danish equivalent, the *Collectanea* of the Medical Society of Copenhagen.[15] Special mention was made of Johann Clemens Tode (1736-1806), regius professor of Medicine at Copenhagen, royal physician and, as secretary to the Danish society, Andrew Duncan's opposite number. No doubt through Tode's good offices, Duncan was in 1776 elected a member of the Danish society. So too was William Cullen (1710-90), a professor in the Edinburgh medical school whose most lasting contribution was, however, to chemistry. Tode was very like his Edinburgh contemporaries in being a zealous teacher as well as a scholar: indeed, he laid claim to having presided at no fewer than twenty-six doctoral disputations.

One of the leading Danish physicians, when viewed from the perspective of Edinburgh, was Hans Wilhelm Gulbrand (1744-1809).[16] When Gulbrand qualified in 1772, he was the first student to undergo a disputation in public. He makes two appearances in the sixth volume of the *Edinburgh Commentaries*, first when his book *De Sanguifluxu Uterino* (Concerning Menstrual Fluid) was reviewed. Then there was a notice of his contribution to the second volume of the Danish society's *Collectanea*. Here he described the case of a man of twenty-six, 'of a sanguine temperament [who] was suddenly seized with a pain, and paralytic affection of the left arm; which came to such a degree of inveteracy as entirely to destroy both sense and motion, not only of the arm, but also of the hand and fingers'. All remedies and all other physicians having failed, Gulbrand was brought on to the case. He elicited from the patient a confession that previously he had been suffering from gonorrhoea. This had been treated with some 'miracle' cure which had removed the symptoms at the cost of paralysing the patient's arm. Gulbrand at once administered mercury, along with some sarsparilla, rhubarb, senna and burdock — a concoction that illustrates well the operation of the close eighteenth-century links between the physicians and the botanists. 'And in a short time the patient was restored to perfect health', apart, that is, from the return of the symptoms of gonorrhoea.

Eighteenth-century optimism fed on the manifest advances made in the physical and medical sciences, and similar hopes were expressed for the future of the social sciences, or, as they would have then been styled, the 'moral sciences'. More than one Scottish philosopher of the period aspired to be the 'moral Newton', to trace laws that governed human conduct and operated as regularly and predictably as the laws of physics.

One notable worker in this field was Adam Smith (1723-90). The works of Smith and Karl Marx share the characteristic that in the long term they have been cited in support of a bewildering variety of doctrines, some of which at least the original writers would surely have repudiated. But they also share the characteristic that in the short term they attracted very little attention, and, to an extent that seems almost incredible to us now, fell upon stony ground. That this is true of Smith has been argued with compelling force by Richard F Teichgraeber III.[17] The only full and rigorous analysis of the *Wealth of Nations* to be published during Smith's lifetime was a respectful but firm refutation by Thomas Pownall, MP (1722-1805). And in 1790 the *Times* obituarist no doubt felt he had said the last word on Smith when he accused him, 'being in a commercial town', of yielding to the temptation to change 'the Chair of Moral Philosophy into a professorship of trade and finance'. To Smith's extreme free market disciples of today that might seem like high praise, but clearly it was not intended as such at the time. Smith was certainly known as an author to quite a few of his contemporaries, but it was as the author of the *Theory of the Moral Sentiments* of 1759, and not of the *Wealth of Nations*.

One writer, adapting Emerson's aphorism about the battle of Concord, called the *Wealth of Nations* 'an intellectual shot heard round the world in 1776'. In fact the impact seems to have been fairly muffled. Nor is Alexander Pope's phrase, 'what oft was thought, but ne'er so well expressed', really applicable. Smith may indeed have expressed himself well; and within a generation or two a simplified version of his doctrines may indeed have become fashionable. But this was less because of Smith's advocacy of these doctrines than because of economic changes that Smith had been prescient enough to foresee in part. And Smith's thoughts had not been thought so often before: otherwise more people would have recognised them when they were published. It may in fact be argued that, in 1776, Britain with its nascent factory-based textile industry had an immediate and short-term need of a policy of economic protectionism.

Teichgraeber's trenchant account, however, is mainly concerned with Smith's reception in the English-speaking world. In this context, it is all the more remarkable that Smith had a comparatively large short-term impact in Denmark, though admittedly much less in Sweden. Danish was one of the first languages into which the *Wealth of Nations* was translated. There was an instant translation of the work into French in 1776, but this translation was never published. And the first published French translation, which appeared in 1779-80, was apparently a poor one.[18] There was also an Italian translation, which in Spain was banned by the Inquisition because of 'the coarseness of its style and the looseness of its morals'. And so the Danish translation of Smith, published also in 1779-80, ranks among the first.[19] It was by Frants Draebye (1740-1814), who had been in Britain in the mid-1770s as tutor to the sons of a Norwegian merchant, James Collett, and who at the time of the translation was head of the Norwegian secretariat of the Economic and Trade Department. A significant fact suggested by the reviews of this translation is that Smith was being read in Denmark even before the translation appeared, by readers intrigued enough by the work's reputation to be prepared to tackle it in English. The idea of a Danish translation, so that the work could reach a wider Danish readership, possibly came from Peter Anker (1744-1832), also the son of a Norwegian merchant, who had met Smith in Glasgow as early as 1762, and who later became Danish consul general in Britain. Draebye was enterprising enough to add Pownall's reply to Smith as an appendix to his translation, and apparently was anxious to know what revisions Smith might make in a second edition. Smith wrote to his publisher in October 1780, asking him to let Anker and Draebye have complimentary copies of the second edition. Smith added, with the characteristic modesty that helps explain why his book did not make more initial compact: 'I am afraid I am not only your best, but almost your only customer for this second Edition'.

It appears, then, that the state of Danish public opinion was one potentially very receptive to Smith's brand of economic liberalism. The brief period of hectic and violent reform under the quasi-dictator Johann Struensee (1737-1772) had produced almost a decade of extreme conservative political reaction thereafter. But now the Danes were again becoming attracted to the possibility of at least moderate reform. Since, however, the central topic in the economic debate of the 1780s was to be land reform, Smith's ideas could be perceived as a stimulus without seeming to pose a threat to established vested interests. One of the leading participants in this debate was August Hennings (1746-1826), a civil servant who published two books, *Materialen zur Statistik der Dänischen Staaten* (1784-91), which was anonymous but known to be by him, and *Über die wahren Quellen des Nationalwohlstandes* (1785). The German language had considerable cachet in eighteenth-century Denmark, though this was on the wane because of the reaction against the German-born Struensee, and in consequence of the rise of Danish national romanticism. Hennings took his stand as a disciple of Smith, an economic liberal, while at the same time properly insisting that allowance must always be made for the distinctive characteristics of Denmark's economy.[20]

As for Sweden, we have the weighty testimony of Eli Hecksher to the effect that Smith's impact was 'negligible'.[21] A remarkable writer, Anders Chydenius (1729-

1803), a clergyman from Österbotten in Finland, had written some very radical pamphlets in the mid-1760s. He attacked all entrenched economic privilege, believing that the goal of economic policy should be the benefit of the masses. To a great extent this fitted the mood of the 1765 session of the Swedish Riksdag, where he was present, and where the Cap party brought the long political reign of the Hats to an end. The policy of the Hats had produced an inflationary situation, but the Cap programme — the ending of economic curbs and of state subsidies, and a drastic pruning of government spending — produced deflation and slump, and the Caps were discredited. The result was a climate of opinion not at all receptive to Smith's ideas. In any case, it appears that Chydenius and the other Swedish economists did not read texts in English.[22] Smith's ideas were to reach Sweden second- and third-hand; but, as Hecksher points out, the only extensive Swedish translation of the *Wealth of Nations* appeared as late as 1909-11.

Still, Smith did have his Swedish admirers by the 1790s. The group of Uppsala students known as the Junta revered Smith as a 'philosophe', much as they admired Rousseau.[23] But as they grew older, they moved to the right. Men like Benjamin Höijer (1767-1812), who became an Uppsala professor in 1809, and Hans Järta (1774-1847) lived to outgrow their admiration for Smith. Järta, initially an admirer of revolutionary France, at length turned conservative, a sort of Swedish Edmund Burke: indeed, he owed his conservatism partly to reading Burke.

This survey closes at the end of the eighteenth century: Scottish-Scandinavian intellectual relations, however, went on. To take a single example, from a rather different field, but one that surely requires high qualities of intellect, we have the Swedish achievement of Thomas Telford (1757-1834).[24] Drawing upon his experience gained in building the Caledonian Canal in Scotland, Telford planned and helped to construct the great Göta Canal, consisting of 55 miles of artificial waterway, and 120 miles of navigation in all. It is satisfactory to record that in Sweden Telford received a knighthood and all the honours and acclaim that, perhaps because of his humble origins, he was denied at home.

I have looked at Scottish activities and influences in Scandinavia rather than the traffic in the reverse direction. That theme merits separate treatment elsewhere. There was, for instance, Johannes Ewald (1743-81), the fine Danish early romantic poet.[25] He was inspired by Macpherson's *Ossian* and Percy's *Reliques*. Sadly, his poor health deterred him from his projected visit to Scotland to collect folk songs. One Scandinavian who did come was an Icelandic scholar in Danish royal service, Grímur Thorkelín (1752-1829). In 1787 he received an LLD from the University of St Andrews, through the good offices of George Dempster of Dunnichen, provost of the burgh and reforming MP. B S Benedikz has suggested that Thorkelín later made use of his Scottish connections when illicitly disposing of a valuable Icelandic manuscript.[26] His discussion is interesting, but I would characterise it as an unsubstantiated libel upon the memory of a great scholar. It was Thorkelín who, among many other achievements, played the crucial rôle in preserving for posterity the text of the Old English poem *Beowulf*.

It has been my enjoyable task to trace Scottish-Scandinavian contacts in the relatively small-scale intellectual world of the eighteenth century. Future historians who attempt the same task with reference to the twentieth century may find more leads than can ever be all chased up. I can think of such contacts in fields as removed from each other as ethnology and geology, as archaeology and dentistry. It is inspiring that T A Fischer's process of giving and taking, of fructification, still goes on. Looking ahead, he wrote: 'The more accurate our knowledge of history and its bye-ways becomes, the more enlightened and just our judgements upon other nations will be and the readier our hands to burn our war-hatchet for ever and to resort for glory to the quiet study, the busy office, the bright studio, rather than to the reek of the slaughter-house'. A good note on which to close.

NOTES

1. T A Fischer, *The Scots in Germany* (Edinburgh, 1902), 235.

2. B J Hovde, *The Scandinavian Countries, 1720-1865* (2 vols, Ithaca, NY, 1948), i, 120 (hereafter Hovde); Bengt Hildebrand, *Kungl. Svenska Vetenskaps Akademien: förhistoria, grundläggning och första organisation* (2 vols, Stockholm, 1939), i, 139-71.

3. For Cunninghame see *Svenskt Biografiskt Lexikon* (hereafter *SBL*).

4. For Blackwell see *Dictionary of National Biography* (hereafter *DNB*); *SBL*.

5. Anders Fryxell, *Berättelser ur svenska historien*, pt. xxxvii (Stockholm, 1868).

6. R G Cant, *The University of St Andrews: a short history* (Edinburgh, 1970 edn), 87-8.

7. A copy of this apparently rare work is in the British Library, shelf mark 966.d.33; and a photocopy in the National Library of Scotland, shelf mark Mf.15(12[4]).

8. For Maxwell see J A Symon, *Scottish Farming, Past and Present* (Edinburgh, 1959), 110, 302, 309.

9. Göran Behre, 'Sweden and the rising of 1745', *Scottish Historical Review*, li (1972), 148-71.

10. John Simpson, 'Arresting a diplomat, 1717', *History Today*, 35 (1) (1985), 32-6.

11. For Hope see *DNB*; and, especially for his Swedish contacts, A G Morton, *John Hope 1725-1786: Scottish botanist* (Edinburgh, 1986).

12. For Duncan see *DNB*; D Talbot Rice, ed., *The University Portraits* (Edinburgh, 1957), 58-9; Lisa M Rosner, *Andrew Duncan, MD, FRSE* (Edinburgh, 1981).

13. *Medical and Philosophical Commentaries* (6 vols, London, 1773-79), i, 5 (hereafter *Commentaries*). The series continued after 1779 under an amended title.

14. *Commentaries*, v, 62-70.

15. *Commentaries*, iv, 413-19. For Tode see *Dansk Biografisk Leksikon* (herafter *DBL*).

16. *Commentaries*, vi, 21-30, 256-7. For Gulbrand see *DBL*.

17. Richard F Teichgraeber III, ' "Less abused than I had reason to expect": the reception of *The Wealth of Nations* in Britain, 1776-90', *Historical Journal*, xxx (1987), 337-66.

18. D Murray, *French Translations of the 'Wealth of Nations'* (Glasgow, 1905).

19. See E C Mossner and I S Ross, eds, *The Correspondence of Adam Smith* (Oxford, 1987 edn), 247-54.

20. For the background see S Oakley, *The Story of Denmark* (London, 1972), 157-60. For Hennings see *DBL*.

21. Eli Hecksher, *An Economic History of Sweden* (Cambridge, Mass., 1954), 204-7.

22. For the background see S Oakley, *The Story of Sweden* (London, 1966), 144-6. For Chydenius see *SBL* and Tore Frängsmyr, 'The Enlightenment in Sweden' in R Porter and M Teich, eds, *The Enlightenment in National Context* (Cambridge, 1981), 164-75.

23. Hovde, i, 212-19.

24. For Telford see *DNB* and L T C Rolt, *Thomas Telford* (London, 1958).

25. P M Mitchell, *A History of Danish Literature* (Copenhagen, 1957), 93-6.

26. B S Benedikz, 'Grīmur Thorkelín, the University of Saint Andrews, and Codex Scardensis', *Scandinavian Studies*, 42 (1970), 385-93.

12

THE DISTRIBUTION OF PRIVATE WEALTH IN LAND IN SCOTLAND AND SCANDINAVIA IN THE SEVENTEENTH AND EIGHTEENTH CENTURIES

Lee Soltow

How egalitarian were the economies on each side of the North Sea two or three centuries ago? One focus of study allowing empirical measurements and comparisons of equality is that derived from the study of land ownership. We can determine how widely ownership was spread among the agricultural labour force, the proportions of haves and have-nots, and how unequally the land was distributed among the haves. In this paper I shall offer statistical distributions from various times for Scotland and for each of the four Scandinavian countries. These distributions are measures of the extent of economic hierarchies, but only for the well-off and for various classes of the rich.

Shares in *landed wealth* provide measures, or proxies, of socio-economic differences only between minorities of people. I am unable to offer distributions of *income* among all people in a country because the data are not available; for this reason my study is incomplete. In an economic sense, the importance of the nobility — a minority — varied from one country to another. Thus, inequality in Norway was not that of Sweden, or of Denmark, or even of Finland; moreover, it would be possible for Scotland to rank lower or higher in inequality than did one or more of the Scandinavian countries. Differences in landholdings between Scotland's Highlands and Lowlands result in yet another distinction that makes meaningful comparisons difficult.

I *Hypotheses*

An ideal long-term study would include a measure of inequality for each year from 1600 to 1800 for each of the five countries. Suppose the share of total land value owned by the top 1% of the labour force in each year could be determined for a period of 200 years for one country. Its plotting could be compared to similar plottings for the other four countries. Trends — and possibly cycles — in inequality could be noted. Years of famine such as those at the end of the seventeenth century could be noted and we could determine, to a certain extent, those redistributive effects brought about by relative hardship. This grand chart, with its 1,000 points, must remain but a dream. I shall do well enough to provide 10 points that describe the wealth shares held by the rich.

Yet we should develop some hypotheses regarding the general direction of inequality during the two centuries. Adam Smith provides a background in his discussion of the extent of disparities and his beginning notions of inequality levels that arose in conjunction with various stages of economic development. Smith discussed the status of the rich and the reactions of others to persons at the top of the wealth spectrum. While he lashed out against the institution of entailed estates, Smith made no proposals offering the hope of movements toward equality. In fact, he seemed to suggest that inequality would continue to increase as economies developed and private property became a more dominant institution. The initial hunting state, one of relative equality, was followed by a surge that Smith described thus: 'It is in the age of shepherds, in the second period of society, that the inequality of fortune first begins to take place, and introduces among men a degree of authority and subordination which could not possibly exist before it'.[1] Smith suggested that this second state was the one bringing the greatest level of subordination; in succeeding periods there would be fewer servants and menial employees even though the rich had greater wealth. In this way our sage possibly proposed an inverse-U shape for inequality, but in a very rudimentary form.[2] Probably it is safer to say that, as he saw it, the relative inequality of the value of assets increased with time, following a chain of steps in development. Trade produced a surplus arising from the division of labour. Private property was a manifestation of this surplus and it was distributed unevenly, a condition that became increasingly significant. In his essay on *Scotland and Europe, 1200-1850*, Ignatieff states that Smith saw only a direct relationship between inequality and economic growth.

Malthus held a perhaps cyclical theory concerning the conditions of the poor that tangentially affected wealth distribution. In a period of relative abundance, when income shares of the labouring class became favourable relative to those with wealth, marriage and birth rates were stimulated. This stage must be followed by one of great hardship among lower groups.[3] In the Malthus model of oscillations there is little or no hint of any long-run trend toward either relative equality or inequality.

We must turn to Tocqueville, the great student and scholar of inequality in the 1830s and 1840s, to find an overall model of change in the relative status of social, political, and economic classes. His bold hypothesis was of a U-shaped pattern of equality — a view of changes from the eleventh century until the nineteenth century. He held that society was quite egalitarian before the advent of private property since any single individual was able to accumulate very little wealth. The onset of private ownership then caused a downturn in equality to a low or minimum point: thereafter there was continual movement toward equality. The subsequent rise of the middle classes was marked by greater social, political and economic power relative to that of the nobility. He did not propose a date for the minimum point of equality, so we are somewhat at a loss to know whether inequality within our five countries would have been on the fall or on the rise by the seventeenth century. Perhaps the issue is simply whether private property had become a fully entrenched institution.

The whole issue of timing in the ascendancy of private property is a complex one. Enclosures may not have taken place at times of civil strife, or until economic conditions dictated changes in farming practices. Both the extent of church ownership of land, and the extent to which the crown wished to or felt compelled to sell land were important factors. Some may feel that the entire U-shape hypothesis is not appropriate for all five countries, and that we would do better by speculating on a general comparison between Scotland and Norway, for example. Perhaps Smith's 1776 observations signalled the time of the bottom of the U-shape, and his views for the period from 1776 to 1790 were for a period generally at the bottom of the movement in Scotland, but the nadir of equality surely could be different from country to country.

Next, let us turn from speculation about long waves in inequality to cross-sectional comparisons at the end of the eighteenth century. Thomas Malthus provided an alternative perspective concerning inequality movements, in part derived from his tour in Scandinavia in 1799 and his readings about — and later trip to — Scotland. We are interested in the empirical observations reported in the greatly-expanded second edition of his *Essay*, in 1803, and most particularly the chapters on Norway, Sweden and even Scotland. In part, his changed emphasis was on delayed marriages and strict sexual continence before marriage. The notes from his Norwegian travels contain almost no descriptions dealing with poverty and high death rates. He thought that Norwegians ate rather well and that the calves of Norwegian children's legs looked better than those of English children. Norwegian servants and lower classes dressed well, and their wooden houses were satisfactory.[4]

Malthus did worry about the influence of inheritance practices on the distribution of land among children. If the eldest son could not raise the money to buy out the shares of the other sons, he was either forced to sell the farm or divide it among all. 'I do not understand why upon this principle all the farms in Norway have not become exceedingly small.'[5] Yet he did not observe marginal farm operations in his travels from the south-east to as far north as Trondheim. One suspects that he neither actively looked for poverty, nor was exposed to it, since he did not speak Norwegian and he was being entertained by the wealthiest Norwegians.

It was nearly two decades before Malthus broadened his views concerning general inequality. In his *Principles of Political Economy*, he addressed himself to the initial stages of the maldistribution of wealth: ' . . . over almost all Europe a most unequal and vicious division of landed property was established during the feudal times'.[6] He realised that the right of primogeniture and the law of entails in the British Empire placed undue restrictions on achieving an optimum level of inequality from the standpoint of maximizing income per capita. Yet he was unwilling to abandon these institutions except possibly for a certain number of years. To lessen inequality would enhance incomes, wealth and population, thus stimulating demand for food and other products, and stimulating effective demand. 'A very large proprietor, surrounded by very poor peasants, presents a distribution of property most unfavourable to demand.' Too much division of land, as he observed it in France, would lead to a weakening in marital prudence and 'minute divisions of land'.[7]

This line of reasoning means that Malthus was suggesting an optimum level of inequality somewhat less than that in Great Britain, and presumably in Scotland, but greater than in France and probably in Norway.[8] Nevertheless, he found

Norwegians to be cognizant of land-labour ratios. 'Norway is, I believe, almost the only country in Europe where a traveller will hear any apprehensions expressed of a redundant population, and where the danger to the happiness of the lower classes of people, from this cause, is, in some degree seen and understood'.[9] Malthus observed queuing among socio-economic classes. Unmarried servants living in farmers' households waited for the possibility of becoming *husmaend* with or without land — the opportunity of living in their own cottages where they could maintain families.[10]

In his chapter on Scotland in the 1803 volume, Malthus reported that conditions among poor classes had been much improved because of delayed marriages, emigration and the 'union of farms'.[11] From the standpoint of wealth, the first two decreased inequality by curtailing the landless class, while enclosures increased inequality. Malthus was somewhat ambivalent about Scottish inequality. He felt that the country was overpopulated, but not to the extent it had been a century earlier. If only Malthus had travelled in Scotland as he had in Norway in 1799, we could be more certain of his views concerning redundant populations, land-labour ratios, and the distribution of wealth among landowners in these two lands. I can test these propositions only by using data on wealth distributions.[12]

One should note Malthus's report on Sweden: while he left no record of his travels there in 1799, in the 1803 edition he included a chapter on the country.[13] He was struck by the high death rates accounted for in the comprehensive national censuses: he could only conclude that delayed marriage was less of a factor in Sweden than in Norway. Sweden's infertile soil, rocky land of poor quality that had been pressed into cultivation, led him to believe that conditions were bad relative to those in England.[14] He made no mention of wealth inequality except to say that subdivision of land had proceeded to a certain extent after 1748 when restrictions on farm size had been lifted. 'The patience with which the lower classes of people in Sweden bear these severe pressures [periodic famine and epidemics] is perfectly astonishing.' Here, Malthus uncharacteristically lashed out against government and 'the higher classes of society'.[15]

My major data for Scandinavia are for the end of the eighteenth century, so I should not limit myself to the views of Malthus. Mary Godwin found some poverty — less in Norway than in Sweden — during her short residence in Scandinavia in 1796. She portrayed southern Norway as being quite egalitarian, with only two counts in the whole country, and a people with reasonable housing and plentiful food. Farmers owned their own land or were tenants-for-life on land belonging to the church and the crown. The numbers of servants, *husmaend*, and cottagers with gardens seemed quite natural to her. She viewed with favour the Norwegian institution, *Odels* law, that allowed a family to repurchase its farm within a 10-year period after its sale.[16]

For views concerning inequality in Denmark, I turn to Smout's comparison of conditions in Denmark and Scotland where he deals with the manner in which practices and production in agriculture changed in the eighteenth and early nineteenth centuries. He feels that Scottish policy was led mainly by the landowners and only to a lesser degree by their tenants. Denmark, by contrast, experienced dramatic increases in land ownership and equality from 1792 to 1807, largely due to enlightened policies directed by the state. He contends that Norway's changes in agriculture were dominated by owner-occupiers. Perhaps Smout is saying that the change in equality of ownership in land was small in both Scotland and Norway but was radical in Denmark.[17]

II *Norway in 1647*

My approach to understanding wealth and income distributions is based on investigating sets of statistical data. Records for Scandinavian countries are superior for this application; their censuses in the eighteenth century are quite unique. (Perhaps Malthus went there because he felt their demographic data were superior.)

I begin with the earliest data set with which I have worked, the inventory of farm operators, owners and land values made in the year 1647 for all of Norway; some attention also will be given to the distribution of wealth and income classes in cities in the years 1657-1717. This study is the result of my collaboration with Hans Hosar of the Norwegian Local History Institute.

The wealth distribution, estimated from a sample of one-in-twenty persons and supplemented with a complete enumeration of the top 23 owners in 1639, is given in Table 1. The fundamental finding for this early date is that there was substantial

Table 1. *The Distribution of Wealth in Real Estate Among 12,663 Norwegian Owners in 1647.*

Aggregate rental value in lispund tunge (LT)	Number of owners
LT 1,000 and up	23
000-999	680
00- 99	8,240
1- 9	2,620
less than 1	200
	12,663
Mean	38
Gini coefficient of relative inequality, G	0.680
Males 20 and older	120,000

Source: Lee Soltow and Hans Hosar, 'Wealth and Income Distribution in Norway, 1647-1789,' working paper (June 1987). The sample is every twentieth owner listed in Rolf Fladby, *Skattematrikkelen, 1647* (17 vols, Oslo, 1969). The sample size for those with wealth below LT 1,000 was 632, supplemented with a list of 23 persons in 1637 owning landed estates worth more than LT 1,000, as stated in Axel Coldevin, 'Den Norske adel', in *Norske historikere i utvalg*, vii (Oslo, Bergen, Tromsø, 1981), 319.

inequality. This should not be surprising when it is realised that large landowners did exist, but at the other end were some owners of very small parcels. An example of the former is Jens Bjelke who dominated the array, with 13 estates in four counties stretching from the south-east to Trondheim. The crown had been benevolent in granting land to Bjelke's distant ancestors, thus establishing the disparity at an early date. In addition to the inherited estates, Bjelke himself increased the size of his landholdings. In this example we see some semblance of the Tocquevillian model.

The magnitude of shares held by percentile ranges of owners further illustrates the dispersion. The top 1 per cent of wealthholders had 29 per cent of aggregate wealth $(N_W, A_W) = (0.01, 0.29)$, and the top 10 per cent held 59 per cent. We need a summary measure of these shares above all possible percentiles of holders; I choose to use a rather standard measure, the Gini coefficient of relative inequality, G. This coefficient of relative dispersion varies between 0 (if everyone has an equal share of wealth) and 1.0 (if one person has all of the wealth). Its level in 1647 was 0.68, certainly a much higher figure than I would have imagined possible in a country carved into so many non-contiguous areas separated by the sea, fjords and mountains. The level of G in 1647 rather amazingly was greater than it was in the country in either 1913 or 1929; furthermore, it was greater than wealth inequality in Great Britain today.[18]

Did Norwegian inequality change between 1647 and the time of Malthus's visit in 1799? Apparently not, if judged by the data of Table 2. The very top group

Table 2. The Relative Shares of Wealth in Land in Norway in 1647 and Wealth in Real and Personal Estate in the Rural Sector of Norway in 1789 for Persons Having Wealth.

N_W, the top proportion of people	A_W, the proportion of aggregate wealth of the N_W group	
	1647	1789
0.01	0.29	0.22
0.10	0.59	0.56
0.20	0.71	0.70
0.50	0.90	0.90
1.00	1.00	1.00
Number	12,663	69,857
Mean	LT 38	RDL 3,200
Inequality, $G_W > 0$	0.680	0.662

Source: See Table 1 for 1647 sources and Lee Soltow, 'Wealth Distribution in Norway and Denmark in 1789', *Historisk Tidsskrift* (Winter 1981), 225.

dominated wealthholders a little more strongly in 1647, but configurations were similar in the two years. The relative share of the top group in 1789 would have been larger had we included urban wealth. Bernt Anker, host to Malthus in Kristiania, was the second-richest man in Norway, as stated in a 1789 secret wealth declaration.

The distribution of wealth among wealthholders indicates only part of the impact of the dispersion of resources among the population. Consider the proportion owning property (POP), defined as the number of all property owners, divided by the number of adult males aged 20 or 21, or older. This ratio was roughly 12,663/ 120,000, or 10 per cent to 11 per cent for Norway in 1647. These figures indicate that land was not widely distributed. Norway was no Utopia where each man farmed his own land. The number of owners accounted for only one-fourth of the number of farm operators. In part, these low percentages arose because the crown and the church owned half of the inventoried land value. If all land had been held privately, the POP would have been about 20 per cent.

Landowning participation did increase in the following one or two centuries, as shown by the following schedule.[19]

Norway	(1) Number of landowners	(2) Adult males	(3) Adult males in agricultural or rural sector	(4) (1) / (2) or (1) / (3)
Owners of real estate in the rural sector 1647	12,663	120,000	110,000?	0.10-0.11
Owners of real and personal estate in the rural sector 1789	69,857	215,000	196,000	0.33-0.36
Self-owning farmers				
1825	59,464	278,098	255,442	0.21-0.23
1855	91,470	401,499	349,056	0.23-0.26
Owners of real estate in the rural sector 1913	215,852	620,000	450,000	0.39-0.48

The figures indicate an expansion in ownership after 1650, with the POP ratio at least doubling, if not more. The 1789 entries include all real and personal estate — land, tithes, houses or farms, livestock and several other forms of moveable estate.[20] Although the 1789 and 1913 ratios overstate the movement, the data are of interest because they show that not everyone was a landowner in either 1647 or 1789!

Where do we stand with respect to overall heterogeneity in 1647 and 1789? A measure of inequality of wealth among *all* adult males, G_{all}, can be developed from the two measures offered to this point, the inequality coefficient among those with wealth, $G_W{>}_0$ and the participation rate, POP.

$$G_{all} = G_W{>}_0 - POP + (1 - POP)$$
1647: $0.97 = 0.68 - 0.10 + (1 - 0.10)$
1789: $0.89 = 0.66 - 0.33 + (1 - 0.33)$, or possibly as high as:
$0.93 = 0.66 - 0.20 ?+ (1 - 0.20?)$, as suggested above.

The participation rate of 33 per cent surely overstates the decline in inequality; a rate of 20-25 per cent seems appropriate when considering land ownership only. The data strongly suggest that inequality in the rural sector declined by the time Malthus arrived — essentially a confirmation of Tocqueville's assertions. Further analysis of rural data sets for Norway in the nineteenth and twentieth centuries only confirm these findings.

Much could be said about urban distributions in Norway from 1658 to 1712 since a few brilliantly-devised frequency tables from that period have survived, some of which precede Gregory King's for England; they have the further advantage of being more explicit about grouping occupational categories. These data demonstrate substantial inequality so they are not inconsistent with the findings for rural Norway. True, there were sizeable urban groups with relatively low income and no wealth. Even so, one can build a model where inequality in the rural (and possibly in the urban) sector, is decreasing while overall inequality remains constant. This is explained by virtue of the fact that urban inequality is larger than is the rural; furthermore, the populations became at least a little more urban. It is at this point that I would like to leap across the North Sea to observe the extent of landownership in Scotland.

III Scotland in 1656 and 1770

My wealth distribution for Scotland in 1770 is based on Dr Loretta Timperley's *Directory*, supplemented by other data she kindly provided. In this data set each owner's parcels were collated within the country's parishes in 1770. The monetary value of each is based on evaluations made in 1656-67, with essentially no adjustments for improvements made after that date. In a sense, this is a 1656 distribution, since assessed aggregate values for parishes and counties remained essentially the same during the interim period.

I begin with comparisons involving only wealthholders in the two countries, as presented in Table 3. Compared to Norway, the top proportion of wealthholders held greater shares of the total wealth in Scotland and its Gini coefficient of wealth

Table 3. *The Relative Distribution of Wealth in Land in Scotland in 1770 and Norway in 1647 and 1789.*

N_W, the top proportion of people	A_W, the proportion of aggregate wealth of the N_W group		
	Scotland 1770	Norway 1647 rural	Norway 1789 rural
0.001	0.11	0.09	0.08
0.01	0.32	0.29	0.22
0.02	0.41	0.37	0.29
0.05	0.56	0.49	0.42
0.10	0.69	0.59	0.56
0.20	0.82	0.71	0.70
0.50	0.96	0.90	0.90
1.00	1.00	1.00	1.00
Number of persons	7,838	12,663	69,857
Mean	£474	LT 38	RDL 3,200
Inequality, $G_{W>0}$	0.786	0.680	0.662

Source: See Tables 1 and 2 for Norwegian data. L R Timperley, *A Directory of Landownership in Scotland c1770* (Scottish Record Society, New Series 5, Edinburgh, 1976), 18-428; idem., thesis (cited in n. 22), 154-7, 343-76; idem., 'The pattern of landholding in eighteenth-century Scotland', in *The Making of the Scottish Countryside*, ed. M L Parry and T R Slater (London and Montreal, 1980), 150. My data differ slightly in calculation and classification; my total of 7,838 is within the range of 7,804-7,902 suggested in Timperley's thesis, 126.

inequality also was greater. The few dominated the scene more dramatically in the one land than in the other. Among both top groups, the Duke of Buccleuch, who owned properties in six counties and 29 parishes, held 3 per cent of Scotland's wealth; and in Norway, Jens Bjelke owned land in four counties in 1647, accounting for 1.9 per cent of his country's wealth in land. Some might argue that the shares shown in Table 3 really do not differ significantly — that Scotland's inequality was only slightly more severe.

Neither Malthus nor Mary Godwin had been able to note substantive differences in the relative hierarchy among top groups in Norway since they were accustomed to such a structure at home. For example, consider the share of total wealth of the richest man in England, the Duke of Bedford; he held 1800 properties in six counties, accounting for 0.07 per cent of the country's wealth. More appropriately, he owned 8 per cent of the wealth in Bedford County. The relative distribution among wealthholders in England appears to have been about the same as in Scotland. One estimate of the Gini coefficient for England in 1798 is almost exactly the same as that for Scotland in 1770.[21]

Of more fundamental importance to distinctions between Scotland and Norway is the proportion of people owning land. Outstanding in the Scottish distribution is that fact that the participation rate, POP, was only 7,838/370,000, or 2 per cent, considering all adult males in the country, or possibly as high as 4 per cent considering only the 200,000 adult males engaged in agriculture. The 2 per cent to 4 per cent ratios are very far removed from the 10 per cent to 20 per cent range found for Norway in 1647 and in 1789 or later. Stated otherwise, ownership was 5 or 10 times as strong in Norway as in Scotland!

One can argue that a proper accounting for Scotland would show not 7,838 owners, but from 8,000 to as many as 12,000 owners. Dr Timperley admits that certain groups of individuals having joint ownership are not properly represented and that the total number of owners was 'in excess of 8,500'.[22] Other possible inclusions that could raise the total were persons such as wadsetters or owners of debt, or tacksmen holding leases for one or more lives.[23] Yet these possibilities do not lessen the impact of Timperley's figures which state that the few owned so much. Furthermore, the number of landowners remained rather stable in the period from 1770 to 1854. In Scotland as late as 1873 there were only 17,000 persons with one or more acre, while Norway's census of 1825 recorded 59,465 male farmers who were owner-occupiers. It is doubtful whether Scotland's census-takers posed the question of self-ownership among farmers.[24]

IV *Significance of Ownership*

Who in Scotland cared about ownership? Certainly tenants did, since rents amounted to 20 to 40 per cent of the value of farm produce, a margin that could cut deeply into any farmer's surplus.[25] Ownership could make the difference between being able to save and having no savings. The irony is that no prominent Scotsman spoke out against the maldistribution of land. As early as 1758, Robert Wallace dreamed of an egalitarian settlement of new land; yet he discarded his goal of equality because he feared it would cause an excess population. Sir James Steuart desired greater equality, but also feared a multiplication in the population; unequal division of property was the only reasonable scheme. Adam Smith tended to be critical of owners who held land from sea to sea; he felt that great proprietors were inefficient, that small farmers could provide the attention necessary for small gains and small savings. Smith obviously did not suggest redistribution, but he did speak out strongly against strict entails. Lord Kames also fought that institution and he may have been among the first to suggest a progressive income tax. Lord Selkirk's solution to the problem — emigration to America — would have left ownership inequality in Scotland intact. Sir John Sinclair is also disappointing, although he did suggest a scheme whereby cottagers might rent three acres of land. In the 1830s Thomas Chalmers considered redivision but felt it would actually lower production because the new middle class would only attempt to consume at the same level as their superiors and saving actually would decrease.[26]

As far as I can determine, only one Scot spoke out, resoundingly, in castigating 'a most oppressive privilege'. William Ogilvie of the University of Aberdeen said that owners occupied 2 per cent of the land and that 98 per cent of land was farmed by non-owners; furthermore, he proposed a plan whereby those without land might purchase it. His was the only voice in the wilderness. I am unable to explain the reasoning of this iconoclast, this member of the famous Philosophical Society in Aberdeen.[27]

Protests by ordinary individuals against property holders in Scotland in the eighteenth century seem rather minimal. The violence on the part of the tenantry in Ross and Cromarty in 1792, or the Scottish trials of 1793-4 were peripheral manifestations from the standpoint of ownership.[28] There was little evidence of protest in Norway, either in literature or in action, against the extent of ownership. Anger against taxes and the inability to obtain loans found expression in letters to the king in Copenhagen. The Haugian movement at the turn of the century decried the rich and considered the possibility of community property. The armed following of Christian Loftuus in the 1780s was a peasant movement not specifically directed towards the issue of ownership.[29] My purpose here is to focus on the distinction between owners and non-owners, and not between tenants or renters and lower economic groups such as servants, labourers, *husmaend*, crofters, or cotters.[30] The existing distribution of land ownership seems to have been accepted at all levels of society in both Norway and Scotland.

V *Reasons for Differences*

Why was the ownership participation rate in Scotland so low, compared to Norway? Why did Scots in the eighteenth century accept this maldistribution? It is presumptuous of me to attempt to answer these fundamental questions without a thorough review of the cultures and institutions of the two societies. I mention only a few aspects pertaining to them, some of which are quite speculative.

The two countries share certain similarities in terrain, particularly in the north. Yet land in southern Scotland is more fertile and capable of supporting a larger population. The land area of Norway is four times that of Scotland, but its population in 1801 was only half that of Scotland. The sparse population in Norway meant that the plight of any one person was more noticeable. A poor man had easier access to persons of authority and wealth. This argument is not completely consistent since the poor and rich in urban areas often lived in close proximity. Nevertheless, a single individual in a country with a low density of population is a relatively more important person — strengthening egalitarian concepts. Semblances of these arguments are made by Malthus in connection with his observation that Norwegians expressed fears of a redundant population.[31]

In a literate society, where everyone is able to read books, pamphlets, newspapers, broadsides and the like, there is a greater likelihood of ownership of land and other wealth. A literate individual is more cognizant of the means of obtaining property and is more familiar with legal instruments and methods of financing. Was the average Norwegian in the eighteenth century more likely to have been literate than the average Scot? Claims of high rates of literacy in northern Norway were made as early as 1741. Yet the standards of literacy-testing used by Swedish clergymen apparently were not applied in Norway.[32] Nevertheless, Norwegian inheritance procedures demanded written records. If each son and possibly each daughter were to receive a share of a farm, if the oldest son had the right to purchase the farm from the others, if the family had the right to repurchase the farm within ten years after sale, there necessarily had to be an emphasis on written agreements.[33] The 1647 records show that it was not uncommon to find several owners of a single farm. The average number of owners per farm was 1.6.

It is conceivable that ease in emigrating from Scotland, but not from Norway, would have had some bearing on the problems of ownership in the seventeenth and eighteenth centuries. The peasant classes had to be accommodated in Norway — families could not be told to live elsewhere. Lord Selkirk's solution for persons forced from their highland farm areas was that they should emigrate to America, and many did do just that!

An obvious distinction between the two countries is that Scotland experienced the industrial revolution at a much earlier date than did Norway, say after 1780 rather than after 1850. Industrialization provided an outlet for the landless which mitigated against the redundant population that troubled Malthus, cutting the denominator of my calculated participation ratio by a quarter or a half, in the case of Scotland. Nevertheless, the ratio for Scotland remained high. The factors establishing land distribution had been determined before 1800.

Little is gained by stressing the fact that there was a noble class in Scotland but essentially none in Norway. The nobility were a symptom of the maldistribution of wealth rather than a cause. It may be significant that Norway had been dominated by Denmark and thus lacked a hierarchical structure. Yet Finland, long under the control of Sweden, had its own nobility, as attested by the censuses of the two countries from 1750 to 1805.

Decried by Smith and Kames, the institutions of primogeniture and entailed estates describe but do not explain the heightened degree of inequality in Scotland. In Norway, *åsetsrett* gave to the oldest son the right to assume control of the entire farm at a moderate price if he could obtain the financing necessary to compensate his brothers and sisters. In Sweden, an extensive system of entailed estates was developed between 1695 and 1805.[34]

Professor Smout states that the essential difference in property holding in the two countries is a complex issue locked in several hundred years of social and political development. He suggested that the Norwegian peasantry had strong bargaining power during the struggle between the mountain-dwelling populace and the hostile Swedish state. On the other hand, the Scottish peasants had no bargaining power, particularly after the end of the wars with England. Certainly the case can be made that because of Euro-American events in the nineteenth and twentieth centuries, the rights of minority groups, of lower economic classes, rose, relatively, in and immediately after the period of the wars.[35]

VI *Scandinavia*

I shall offer a composite wealth distribution for Scandinavia at the end of the eighteenth century that can be compared to the Scottish pattern. It consists of distributions for Norway and Denmark in 1789 and for Sweden and Finland in 1800, enabling us to note differences between the various countries and to test certain aspects of the hypotheses of Tocqueville and Malthus. The emphasis is placed on wealth, in general — personal as well as wealth in real estate — for rural and urban areas combined. I wish I could develop composite distributions for various decades and centuries on each side of these dates, but I am not able to do so.[36]

The data of Table 4 (overleaf) display the summary measures, as developed from samples I have drawn over the course of the last eight years. The aggregate sample size is 12,463. All distributions are subject to measurement error, and must be treated with caution. Particularly questionable are the data for those whose wealth is less than SPD 10. Wealth presumably includes personal and real estate, and, in the case of Denmark and Norway, some capitalized income of officials. Adjustments of the Danish and Norwegian distributions to prices and populations in 1800 do not alter relative distributions significantly; therefore, I have not corrected the data in the table for these changes.

The most prominent feature of the data set is the proportion reporting or holding wealth, PHP, the last row of the table. Norway truly was an exception, with propertyholder participation being much greater than in the other three countries. Especially noticeable is the low participation rate in Finland. The 1805 census of farmers and peasants revealed 27 per cent in Sweden and 23 per cent in Finland who were farmers on their own land. There were large numbers of males in Finland who were classified as farm hands.

Turning to the inequality of wealth among wealthholders ($G_W > 0$), we see that Denmark had the greatest inequality. There were 83 persons, largely nobles and often living in Copenhagen, who had an overwhelming proportion of aggregate

Table 4. The Distribution of Wealth Among Adult Males 20 and Older in Denmark and Norway in 1789 and in Sweden and Finland in 1800 as well as a Composite for all Four Scandinavian Countries.

Wealth (W) in specie daler or rigsdaler	Number of persons with wealth $\geq W$				
	All four	Denmark	Norway	Sweden	Finland
2,000,000	1	1			
800,000	3	3			
500,000	15	6		9	
200,000	45	29	3	12	1
100,000	133	83	11	36	3
50,000	373	202	40	125	6
20,000	1,692	558	160	924	50
10,000	4,069	1,428	368	2,122	151
5,000	8,781	2,743	852	4,807	379
2,000	23,005	5,745	2,968	12,873	1,419
1,000	49,704	8,915	7,859	28,254	5,116
500	102,566	11,882	13,113	60,396	17,174
200	208,520	26,226	36,719	113,920	31,655
100	264,429	34,526	42,572	146,357	40,974
50	317,595	46,306	57,727	166,367	47,195
20	361,425	55,486	75,287	180,082	50,569
10	367,592	57,426	77,403	181,891	50,871
5	369,481	57,786	77,403	183,281	51,011
2	371,070	58,746	77,403	183,911	51,011
1	373,095	60,706	77,403	183,975	51,011
0.2	385,755	73,366	77,403	183,975	51,011
0.0	1,352,590	276,874	215,934	642,909	216,873
W $>$ 0					
Number	385,755	73,366	77,403	183,975	51,011
Mean	807	1,095	487	900	541
Inequality, G	0.774	0.899	0.738	0.734	0.588
Sample size	12,463	2,536	3,616	4,627	1,684
W $\geqslant$ 0					
Number	1,352,590	276,874	215,934	642,909	216,873
Mean	230	290	175	258	127
Inequality, G	0.936	0.973	0.906	0.924	0.903
Propertyholder proportion, PHP	0.285	0.265	0.385	0.286	0.236

Sources: Lee Soltow, 'The Swedish Census of Wealth at the beginning of the 19th century', *Scandinavian Economic History Review* (hereafter *SEHR*), 33 (1985); idem., 'Wealth distribution in Finland in 1800', *SEHR*, 29 (1981); idem., 'Wealth distribution in Norway and Denmark in 1789', *Historisk Tidsskrift* (1981); idem., 'Wealth distribution in Denmark in 1789', *SEHR*, 27 (1979). The distributions include the wealth of men and a small number of women. The population total of 1,352,590 is derived from estimates of the number of males 20 and older in Denmark and Norway in 1789 and Sweden and Finland in 1800. Relative inequality changes very little for the compositive distribution if adjustments are made for Danish and Norwegian population and price increases from 1789 to 1800 (grain prices increased about 50% in the 11 years).

wealth. This small number had almost one-fourth (23.5%) of Denmark's total. Most surprisingly, the Gini coefficient for Norway (.738) was as high as that for Sweden. In a certain sense, Norway had its own plutocratic group, led by Fru Holter and Bernt Anker of Christiania, Danckert Krohn of Bergen, and Grosserer Henrich Meinche of Trondheim. The inequality ($G_{W>0}$) in Sweden and Finland may be somewhat understated in the table at top levels. I was unable precisely to collate holdings of the very rich holding properties in several counties. Yet urban wealth was prominent, including that of the very rich Scottish merchant of Gothenburg, John Hall.

The overall inequality coefficient ($G_{W \geq 0}$), the measure incorporating both $G_{W>0}$ and PHP, shows Norway and Finland at the lowest levels (.906 and .903) and Denmark at the very top. Sweden occupies the intermediate position. Average wealth per adult male ($Mean_{W \geq 0}$) in the four countries is arrayed as we might expect. It varied from daler 290 to 127, with Denmark at the top, followed by Sweden, Norway, and Finland. If adjustment were made for price increases from 1789 to 1800, Denmark's wealth reaches an average over three times that in Finland; Norway's wealth conceivably was not much different from that in Sweden. (The definition of wealth was a little broader in the case of Denmark and Norway.) Of interest is the fact that the two dependent nations were in the same positions relative to their controlling countries. Norway's average was 60% of Denmark's, while Finland's average was 50% of Sweden's level.

It is very difficult to use Table 4 as a basis for accepting or rejecting the U-shaped Tocqueville model. What we need is a similar table for the years 1650 and 1900, and preferably for income rather than wealth. These goals someday will be achieved, at least for wealth, but in the meantime we must draw conclusions from resources we now have in hand. As the richest country, Denmark had the greatest inequality. Norway and Finland were the poorest and had the least inequality. This is contrary to the Tocqueville scheme at the end of the eighteenth century, as we view it. Tocqueville felt that countries and regions that were the most advanced experienced greater equality among upper groups. The middle classes were gaining relative to the noble or top class. Perhaps this was the case within countries but it is certainly not revealed in the cross-sectional pattern of Table 4.[37]

The data of the table do seem to corroborate Malthus's observations concerning comparisons between Sweden and Norway. He seemed to feel, as did Mary Godwin, that Norwegians performed well relative to their neighbour to the east. The means, but even more, the PHP ratios of the table display these characteristics. Smout's analysis concerning the transformation of Denmark's structure after 1792 certainly is consistent with the results of the table. Denmark's movement began from an extreme position of inequality, the greatest in Scandinavia.

VII *Scotland Revisited*

Timperley's 1770 data measure only wealth in land and probably should not be displayed in the same table as those for Scandinavia. Yet I shall do just that since the temptation to examine the relative positions of groups in the different countries is more than I can resist. Table 5 forcibly juxtaposes the Scottish and Scandinavian land patterns. The comparison is unfair to the extent that Scotland's data include neither personal estate nor farm animals. Nevertheless, there is a decided difference

Table 5. Distribution of Wealth in Scandinavia in 1789-1800 and Scotland in 1770

Wealth (W) in specie daler or rigsdaler	Number of persons with wealth $\geqslant$ 0	
	Scandinavia	Scotland
500,000	15	2
200,000	45	16
100,000	133	37
50,000	373	92
20,000	1,692	317
10,000	4,069	711
5,000	8,781	1,348
2,000	23,005	2,770
1,000	49,704	4,088
500	102,566	5,365
200	208,520	6,615
100	264,429	7,231
10	367,592	7,824
0.2	385,755	7,838
0.0	1,352,590	370,000
W $\geqslant$ 0		
Number	1,352,590	370,000
Mean	230	100
Inequality, G	0.936	0.995
Propertyholder proportion, PHP	0.285	0.021

Source: See Tables 3 and 4. I have assumed that 1 pound Scots rent = 10 daler, considering that rent was 5 per cent of value, that 12 pounds was the equivalent of 1 pound sterling, and that 1 pound sterling was 4.5 daler. 1770 data for Scotland are wealth in land only.

in the Scottish figures relative to the composite below SPD (RDL) 1,000, a fact demonstrating a relative absence of a Scottish middle class. In fact, there is a relative deterioration in the frequency ratio, beginning from the top class or row of the table. The Duke of Buccleuch had the economic resources of Count H C Schimmelmann whose estate, reported in 1789, was the largest in Denmark — and in Scandinavia. It was entailed upon his heirs just as would be the Duke of Buccleuch's estate.

An egalitarian can be deeply troubled by the inequality on both sides of the North Sea. A better distribution of land might have produced an earlier development of agriculture and certainly would have increased the incomes of the majority. It also could have stimulated higher rates of literacy, with higher proportions of yeomen. Greater equality certainly would have curtailed the innovative procedures established by some of the greater landlords.

Would there have been a 'hotbed of genius' in Edinburgh had there been less inequality? Professor Smout states that it is scarcely conceivable that the cultural golden age could have taken place if the gentry and nobility had been unwilling to become its patrons.[38] In the age of Linnaeus, Sweden, too, had its period of flowering. Support from crown lands played a more prominent role in this case, and it is conceivable that this avenue of approach could have been important in a country that otherwise was rather egalitarian.

As a minimum, we should examine the counterfactual proposition that significantly more equality in the eighteenth century in Denmark, Sweden, and even more so in Scotland, would not have deterred cultural activity or economic growth. Adam Smith very well might have written *The Wealth of Nations* without the support of the Duke of Buccleuch. Agricultural output from a nation of yeomen-farmers might have been greater than was the output of a small number of great landowners.

NOTES

1. Adam Smith, *An Inquiry into the Nature and Causes of the Wealth of Nations*, R H Campbell, A S Skinner, and W B Todd, eds, (2 vols, Indianapolis, 1979), 715. This passage appears in Michael Ignatieff, 'Smith, Rousseau and the republic of needs,' in T C Smout, ed., *Scotland and Europe, 1200-1850* (Edinburgh, 1986), 190.

2. Smith, *Wealth of Nations*, 712-13.

3. *Lecture Notes on Types of Economic Theory*, as delivered by Prof. Wesley C Mitchell (New York, 1949), i, 120; Thomas Malthus, *Population: the First Essay* (Ann Arbor, 1971), 53; T R Malthus, *An Essay on the Principle of Population* (2nd edn, London, 1803), book III, chap. i, 357.

4. Patricia James, *The Travel Diaries of Thomas Robert Malthus* (Cambridge, 1966), 160, 164, 202.

5. Ibid., 129, 155.

6. T R Malthus, *Principles of Political Economy* (London, 1820), 429, 433.

7. Ibid., 427-39.

8. This statement is based on the writings of Malthus in both 1803 and 1820. That his views underwent change between these two dates is undeniable. In 1803 he viewed Arthur Young's plan to give an acre or two of waste land to the poor as the means of stimulating births, which, in a few years, would lead to as many poor as there were before land redistribution. See Malthus, *Essay* (1803), 580.

9. Ibid., 194. This must have been self-evident to Norwegians because the population was small and because emigration was at a minimum; the plight of the poor could readily be observed.

10. Ibid., 187.

11. Ibid., 323, 327, 334.

12. One could be more comfortable with his personal observations if Malthus had reported on living conditions of *husmaend*, crofters, and cotters, as did Boswell and Johnson on a visit to the first cottage they saw on entering the highlands.

13. *Essay* (1803), 196-209.

14. Ibid., 206-8.

15. Ibid., 208.

16. Mary Wollstonecraft Godwin, *Letters Written During a Short Residence in Sweden, Norway and Denmark* (Fontwell, Sussex, 1970), 27, 74-5, 147, 169-76, 192, 244.

146   *Scotland and Scandinavia*

17. T C Smout, 'Landowners in Scotland, Ireland, and Denmark in the Age of Improvement,' *Scandinavian Journal of History*, forthcoming.

18. See Tables 1 and 2 as well as table 2 of Soltow and Hosar, 'Norway, 1647-1789,' for data and sources. For data for 1979 and 1980, see *Annual Abstract of Statistics* (London, 1982 and 1985), 368 and Table 15.2, respectively.

19. See tables 1 and 2 for sources for 1647, 1789, and 1913. Departementet for det Indre, *Folketaellingerne i aarene 1801 og 1825* (Christiania, 1874), 68-9 for 1825 data; ibid., *Statistiske Tabeller for Kongeriget Norge, 1855* (Christiania, 1857), ix, 2.

20. Lee Soltow, 'Wealth distribution in Norway and Denmark in 1789,' *Historisk Tidsskrift* (1981), 222.

21. Lee Soltow, 'The Land Tax Redemption Records, 1798-1963', *Economic History Review*, 2nd ser., 35 (1982), 433.

22. Loretta R Timperley, 'Landownership in Scotland in the Eighteenth Century', (Ph.D. thesis, University of Edinburgh, 1977), 127.

23. T C Smout, *A History of the Scottish People, 1560-1830* (London, 1969), 137-8; Ian Grant, 'Landlords and Land Management in North-Eastern Scotland, 1750-1850' (Ph.D. thesis, University of Edinburgh, 1978), vol. i, 19-30. Also see Robin Callander, 'The pattern of land ownership in Aberdeenshire in the seventeenth and eighteenth cnturies,' in David Stevenson, ed., *From Lairds to Louns: Country and Burgh Life in Aberdeen, 1600-1800* (Aberdeen, 1986), 3-5; Robin Callander, *A Pattern of Landownership in Scotland* (Finzean, Aberdeenshire, 1987). The number of heritors is given on page 145. Apparently a heritor is counted two or more times if he owned land in two or more parishes. For a contrary count see, for example, *The Valuation of the County of Aberdeen for the Year 1667* (Third Spalding Club, 1933), xxii. Ian Grant, of the Scottish Record Office, feels that the number of owners may be several times the number given in Table 3.

24. *Parliamentary Papers*, 1854-5, xlvii, 686-7; ibid., 1874, vol. 72, pt 3, 1-199; Lee Soltow, 'Wealth Inequality in Scotland in the eighteenth century', working paper, (June 1987).

25. Malthus, *Principles* (1820), 177. Adam Smith felt that rents constituted a one-third part of the price of most commodities; *Wealth of Nations*, Edwin Cannan, ed. (New York, 1937), 49; John Ramsay McCulloch, *A Descriptive and Statistical Account of the British Empire* (4th edn, London, 1854), 560-1.

26. Robert Wallace, *Various Prospects of Mankind, Nature and Providence* (1758; New York, 1969), 25, 32, 98, 116; Sir James Steuart, *An Inquiry into the Principles of Political Oeconomy*, Andrew S Skinner, ed. (2 vols, Edinburgh, 1966), i, 26-7; Adam Smith, *The Wealth of Nations* (1979), 384-6; W C Lehman, *Henry Home, Lord Kames, and the Scottish Enlightenment: A Study in National Character and in the History of Ideas* (The Hague, 1971), 328-9; Tracts by Sir John Sinclair, British Library, B. 293, No. 3, 'Observations on the Means of Enabling a Cottager to Keep a Cow by the Produce of a Small Portion of Arable Land' (London, 1801), 1-13; Thomas Chalmers, *On Political Economy, in Connexion with the Moral State and Moral Prospects of Society* (2nd American edn, Columbus, Ohio, 1830), 278-97.

27. William Ogilvie, 'The rights of property in land', in M Beer, ed. *The Pioneers of Land Reform* (London, 1920), 35-178; quotations, 58-9. James McCosh, *The Scottish Philosophy* (New York, 1880), 241, 470-2.

28. Earl of Selkirk, *Observations*, 122; Lord Cockburn, *An Examination of the Trials for Sedition in Scotland* (1888; New York, 1970), 99-100.

29. Øvind Østerud, *Agrarian Structure and Peasant Politics in Scandinavia* (Oslo, 1978), 227-38; H Arnold Barton, *Scandinavia in the Revolutionary Era, 1760-1815* (Minneapolis, 1986), 151-4, 245; B J Hovde, in *The Scandinavian Countries, 1720-1865: the Rise of the Middle Class* (Ithaca, 1948), 277, states that the Danish-Norwegian monarchy had established a degree of absolutism exceeded nowhere in Europe.

30. For Norway in 1647, I emphasize 12,663 owners, not the 46,840 farm operators or the other 70,000 adult males.

31. *Essay* (1803), 194-5. The argument that the urban poor are more visible than the rural

poor is given in 'Considerations on the Interest of the County of Lanark in Scotland', in *The Works, Political, Metaphysical, and Chronological of the Late Sir James Steuart of Coltness, Bart.*, Gen. Sir James Steuart, ed., vol. 5 (London, 1805), 314.

32. Wealth-literacy patterns are given in Lee Soltow and Edward Stevens, *The Rise of Mass Literacy and the Common School: A Socio-economic Study of the United States to 1870* (Chicago, 1981), chap. 5; Harvey J Graff, *The Legacies of Literacy: Continuities and Contradicitions in Western Culture and Society* (Bloomington, 1987), 149-50, 223-30, 301-11; R A Houston, *Scottish Literacy and the Scottish Identity: Illiteracy and Society in Scotland and Northern England, 1600-1800* (New York, 1985), 33, 72, 142, 256-7.

33. *Odels* law is well handled by Østerud, *Agrarian Structure*, 101-2.

34. Lee Soltow, 'The Swedish Census of Wealth at the beginning of the nineteenth century,' *Scandinavian Economic History Review*, 33 (1985).

35. Correspondence from T C Smout, 8 June, 1987.

36. I continue to work in these areas. See Lee Soltow, 'Inequalities on the eve of mass migration: agricultural holdings in Sweden and the United States in 1845-50,' *Scandinavian Economic History Review*, 34 (1987).

37. Tocqueville's model included an emphasis on the plight of the poor or destitute who were seen to suffer relative to other groups, as development took place. The data of Table 4 shed no light on this issue since they concern only those persons with wealth.

38. Smout, *History*, 506. Also see Edward W Stevens, *Literacy, Law, and Social Order* (Dekalb, Ill., 1987), 131-2.

INDEX

This index is selective rather than exhaustive. It concentrates almost entirely on persons and places, since main subjects can be followed by use of the Contents table. Places are usually located by country, but where no country is stated it is to be understood that the place is situated in Scotland.

Aalborg, Denmark, 79, 84
Aberdeen, 15, 43, 75, 78, 93, 100-2
Albany, dukes of, see Stewart
Alberoni, Cardinal, Spanish politician, 112
Alcuin, Anglo-Saxon scholar, 4
Alexander II, king of Scots, 18
Alexander III, king of Scots, 6-7, 19-20
Alströmer, Jonas, Swedish industrialist, 121
Alv Erlingsson, jarl of Tornberg, 74
Anckarhielm, Mårten, Swedish admiral, 108
Anglesey, Wales, 14
Angus, earls of, 64
    see also Douglas
Anker, Bernt, Norwegian landowner, 135, 143
Anse, L', aux Meadows, Newfoundland, 5
Argyll, earls of, 67
Avignon, France, 39-45 *passim*
Ayr, 79
Ayrshire, 7

Baglar, Norwegian faction, 17
Balfour, Gilbert, Scottish officer in Sweden, 90
Bannockburn, battle of, 62
Beaduheard, Anglo-Saxon official, 1
Bedford, dukes of, 138
Bergen, Norway, 6, 19, 28, 31, 45, 74, 76, 82, 84
Berwick, England, 16, 74
Bethlehem, Palestine, 39
Birkibeinar, Norwegian faction, 17
Bjelke, Jens, Norwegian landowner, 134-5, 138
Blackness, port of Linlithgow, 61-2
Blackwell, Alexander, scientist, 119-23
Blekinge, Denmark, 83
Bohemia, king of, see Frederick
Bolingbroke, see St-John, Henry
Bordeaux, France, 79
Bornholm, Denmark, 49

Boston, England, 76
Bothwell, earl of, see Hepburn
Bothwell, lordship of, 63-4
Boyd family, of Kilmarnock, 65
Boyd, Robert, Lord, 65
Boyne, Ireland, battle of the, 109
Braemar, 111
Brechin, 40
Breitenfield, Germany, battle of, 94
Bremen, Germany, 31, 111
Brentford, earl of, see Ruthven, Patrick
Brest, France, 115
Bristol, England, 20
Britain, kings of, see Charles, James, William
Bruce, Andrew, of Muness, Shetland, 33-4
    Isabella, sister of Robert I, 75
    Laurence, of Cultmalindie, foud in Shetland, 29-31
Bruges, Belgium, 39, 79
Buccleuch, dukes of, 138, 144-5
Buchanan, George, historian, 7
Burnett, James, Lord Monboddo, Scottish judge, 123

Cahun, Hugh, Scottish officer in Sweden, 90
    Willem, Scottish officer in Sweden, 90
Caithness, 15, 18, 43
Campbell, Colin, director of Swedish East India Company, 114, 122
Canna, 22
Canute, see Knut Sveinsson
Carlingford, Ireland, 18
Carlisle, earl of, see Harcla
Castles, etc.
    Aalholm, 52
    Abercorn, 66
    Aggersborg, 51
    Avondale, 66
    Berwick, 62
    Bjørnholm, 50
    Blackness, 62

Castles, etc. (cont'd)
  Borthwick, 69
  Bothwell, 64
  Cawdor, 68
  Dean, 65
  Douglas, 66
  Doune, 63
  Dragsholm, 56
  Duborg, 57
  Dumbarton, 62
  Dunbar, 62
  Dundonald, 60-1
  Edinburgh, 61, 63
  Falkland palace, 61
  Gjorslev, 56
  Glimmingehus, 56
  Hald, 53, 55-6
  Helsingborg, 77
  Hermitage, 64
  Holyrood palace, 61, 82
  Horsholm, 55
  Inveravon, 66
  Kalø, 52
  Kindrochit, 60
  Linlithgow palace, 61, 64
  Newark, 70n
  Nørholm, 55
  Nyborg, 51
  Ørum, 51
  Ravenscraig, 67
  Rothesay, 60
  Spøttrup, 56
  Stalker, 67
  Stirling, 61-2
  Tantallon, 64
  Tarbert, 71
  Threave, 63-4, 66, 70n
  Tibrantsholm, 53
  Tranekær, 52
  Urquhart, 67
  Visborg, 56-7
Chandos, duke of, 120
Charles I, king of Britain, 94-5, 98, 107
Charles II, king of Britain, 107-8
Charles IX, king of Sweden, 91
Charles XII, king of Sweden, 98, 110-13
Chester, England, 20
Cheyne, Robert, of Ure, 30-1
  Thomas, of Vaila, 34
Choiseul, duc de, French politician, 114, 115
Christian I, king of Denmark, 83
Christian II, king of Denmark, 48-9, 55, 83

Christian III, king of Denmark, 49
Christian IV, king of Denmark, 34, 93
Christina, queen of Sweden, 95, 98, 107-8
Chydenius, Anders, Swedish economist, 126-7
Cockburn, Samuel, Scottish officer in Sweden, 91, 98
Cologne, Germany, 38
Colquhoun, Clan, 90
Columba, Saint, 19
Copenhagen, Denmark, 79-80, 124, 141
Crichton family, 62. 64
Crichton, Sir William, later Lord Crichton, 64
Crichton, Midlothian, 64
Cromarty, 67, 93, 139
Cromwell, Oliver, English statesman, 95, 108
Cumbraes, 7

Danzig (Gdansk), Poland, 79-80, 84
David I, king of Scots, 16
David II, king of Scots, 61, 63, 67
Denmark, 39, 43-5, 48-55 passim, 65, 73-89 passim, 92, 112, 126, 133, 143-5
  kings of, see Christian, Eric, Frederick, Hans, Knut, Valdemar
Denmilne, 68
Derwentwater, earl of, see Radcliffe, Charles
Dishington, James, Shetlander, 35
Dorestad, Netherlands, 4
Douglas family, 96, 98
Douglas, earls of, 63-5, 68
  Alexander, of Spynie, 34
  Archibald, 6th earl of Angus, 64
  Archibald, 3rd earl of Douglas, 63
  Archibald, 4th earl of Douglas, duke of Touraine, 64
  James, 4th earl of Morton, Regent, 29
  William, 1st earl of Douglas, 63
Draebye, Frants, Danish translator, 126
Dromore, Ireland, bishop of, 40
Drummond family, 96
Dublin, Ireland, 17, 21, 91
Duggáll Mac Ruairidh, Hebridean king, 19-20
Duncan, Andrew, Scottish scientist, 123-4
Dundas family, 68
Dundee, 81, 84
Dunkeld, 40, 42

Edinburgh, 16, 108, 111, 123-4, 144
Edward I, king of England, 75

Edward III, king of England, 75
Elbe river, Germany etc., 93
Elsinore, Denmark, 79
England, 39, 41-2, 64, 66, 76, 82, 109
    kings of, *see* Edward, Henry, John,
    Knut
Eoghan of Argyll, 18
Ephesus, Turkey, 39
Eric VII, king of Denmark, Norway and
    Sweden (of Pomerania), 41, 45-8, 52,
    58n, 78
Eric II, king of Norway, 75
Eric XIV, king of Sweden, 90
Eric, son of Duggáll mac Ruairidh, 20
Eric the Red (Viking), 5
Erskine, John, 11th earl of Mar, 111
Ethelred, king of Northumbria, 4
Eysteinn, son of Harald Gilli, 15
Eythin, Lord, *see* King

Faeroes, in N. Atlantic, 4, 21, 40, 42
Falsterbo, Norway, 77
Finland, 92, 141
Flanders, 77, 85
Fleury, battle of, 109
Forbes, Clan, 96
Forbes, William, head of clan and officer
    in Sweden, 98
Forth, earl of, *see* Ruthven, Patrick
Forth (river), 77
France, 39, 52, 79, 109-11, 113-15, 132
    king of, *see* Louis
Frederick, king of Bohemia and Elector
    Palatine, 92-3
Frederick I, king of Denmark, 83
Frederick I, king of Sweden, 121
Funen, Denmark, 58

Galloway, 43, 63
Gardar (Greenland), bishops of, *see* John,
    Henry
Gardie, Jacob de la, commander of
    Swedish army, 91
George I, king of Britain, Elector of
    Hanover, 109-12
Gifford, Thomas, Shetlander, 28
Giraldus Cambrensis, chronicler, 17
Gizurr Thorðarson, Icelander, 22
Glasgow, 40, 115
Glenesk, Robert of, Scottish notary, 76
Gluckstadt, Germany, 93
Godwin, Mary, writer, 133, 138
Gordon family, 96

Görtz, Freiherr Georg Heinrich von,
    adviser of Charles XII of Sweden,
    111-12
Gothenburg, Sweden, 107-15 *passim*, 119
Graham, James, Marquis of Montrose,
    107-8
Greenland, 5, 20, 43, 46
    see also Gardar
Grimsby, England, 21
Grubbe family, of Gunderslevholm,
    Norway, 54
Guðröð Ólafsson, king of the Isles, 17
Guðmund Árason, bishop of Hólar,
    Iceland, 21-2
Guelders, 75
Gulbrand, Hans Wilhelm, Danish
    physician, 124-5
Gunni, brother of Sveinn Ásleifarson, 16
Gustavus Adolphus, king of Sweden,
    91-6 *passim*
Gyllenborg, Count Carl, Swedish envoy
    in London, 110-11, 113, 122

Haakon IV (the old), king of Norway,
    6-10 *passim* 17-19, 22
Haakon VI, king of Norway, 45, 52, 77
Haakon Magnusson, duke, 26
Hafrsfjörd, battle of, 3
Hague, The, Holland, 107
Halland, Denmark, 83
Hamburg, Germany, 4, 31
Hanover, Elector of, *see* George I
Hans, king of Denmark, 48-9, 57
Hans Sigurdssøn, landowner in Shetland,
    30
Harald Finehair, king of Norway, 3, 6, 14
Harald Gilli, son of Magnus Barelegs,
    15, 21-2
Harald Harðraða, king of Norway, 3, 15
Harald Haddaðarson, earl of Orkney, 15-18
Harald Ólafsson, king of Man, 18
Harcla, Andrew, earl of Carlisle, 75
Harlaw, battle of, 42
Hauk, lawman of Shetland, 26
Havre, Le, France, 115
Hawick, Andrew, of Scatsa, Shetland, 30
Hebrides, 6, 15-17
    see also Western Isles
Heguerty, Daniel de, Jacobite, 113-15
Helsingborg, Sweden, 42
Henderson, Thorvald, of Brough,
    Shetland, 31
Henry III, king of England, 19
Henry, bishop of Gardar, 43-5

Henry, archbishop of Uppsala, 53
Hepburn, John, Scottish officer in Sweden, 94, 96
    Patrick, 1st earl of Bothwell, 64
    Patrick, 3rd earl of Bothwell, 64
Herdis Thorvaldsatter, in Shetland, 27
Hólar, bishop of, *see* Guðmund Árason
Holdbóði, chieftain in Tiree, 16, 23
Holstein, counts of, 49
Hooke, Nathaniel, French agent, 110
Hope, John, Scottish scientist, 122-3
Huntly, earls of, 66-7

Iceland, 4-5, 8-9, 21, 40, 42, 46
Ingi Haraldson, king of Norway, 17
Inverleith, 123
Inverness, Treaty of, 74
Iona, 14, 17
Ireland, 15-16, 18-19, 23, 52, 91-2
Islay, 14
Isles, Lords of the, 42
Ivar, lawman of Shetland, 26

Jacobites, 107, 109-13, 115, 122
James I, king of Britain, *see* James VI, king of Scots
James II, king of Britain, *see* James VII, king of Scots
James III, king of Britain, *see* James VIII, king of Scots
James I, king of Scots, 41, 45, 61, 64, 66, 92
James II, king of Scots, 63-6, 68
James III, king of Scots, 62, 65, 78, 80
James IV, king of Scots, 60-2, 64-8, 71n, 79, 82
James V, king of Scots, 60-1, 64-5, 83
James VI, king of Scots, I of Britain, 30
James VII, king of Scots, II of Britain, 109
James VIII, king of Scots, III of Britain, 110-11
James the Steward, Scottish Guardian, 74
Jerusalem, Palestine, 17
Joan, queen of Scots, 19
John, king of England, 18
John III, king of Sweden, 90-1.
John XXIII, pope, 44
John, bishop of Orkney and Gardar, 43-4, 46
John of Windhouse, trader in Shetland, 32
John Haftorssøn, Norwegian noble, 27
Jutland, Denmark, 51, 55

Kali, Norwegian, 21
Kalmar, Sweden, 46, 83, 92
    Union of, 48
Kames, Lord, 139-40
Kattegat, Denmark, 83
Keith, Andrew, baron in Sweden, 91
    James Francis Edward, Jacobite, 113-14
Kerrera, 18
King, James, Lord Eythin, 107-8
Kintyre, 14, 18
Kirkwall, Orkney, 7, 108
Knut Sveinsson (Canute), king of Denmark and England, 2, 52
Kringelen, Pass of, Norway, 92
Kormákr Ögmundarson, Icelandic saga hero, 1

Lacy, Hugh de, 19
Lambkar, saga writer, 21
Laodicea, Syria, 39
Largs, battle of, 2, 6 7, 9, 19
Law, James, bishop of Orkney, 32-3
Leif the Lucky, 5
Leith, 79
Lennox, earl of, 62
Lermont, Captain David, Scottish emissary of Frederick, Elector Palatine, 92-3
Lerwick, Shetland, 35
Leslie family, 96
Leslie, Alexander, Scottish officer in Sweden, 94-5
    see also Stuart, William
Lewis, 14, 16, 43
Leyell, Henrik, Scottish officer in Sweden, 91
Lindisfarne, England, 1, 2, 4
Lindsay, Clan, 96
    James, 40
Linné, Carl von (Linnaeus), 121-3, 145
Lodehat, Jens, bishop of Roskilde, Denmark, 53, 56
Lödöse, Sweden, 81, 83
London, England, 92, 111
Louis XIV, king of France, 107, 111
Louis XV, king of France, 113
Lübeck, Germany, 77
Lüneburg, Germany, 77
Lutter am Baremberge, Germany, 93
Lützen, battle of, 94

MacFarlane, Clan, 96
Mackay, Clan, 92
    Donald, head of clan and 1st lord Reay, 92-4

MacLean, Clan, 96
  James, Scottish merchant in Sweden,
    108-9
MacLeod, Clan, 96
Magnus Barelegs, 6, 14-15
Magnus the Lawmender, king of Norway,
  7, 10, 19-20
Magnus, king of Man, 19
Magnus, Saint, earl of Orkney, 15, 19, 20
Malmö, Sweden, 93
Malthus, Thomas R., economist, 131-6,
  138, 140-1, 143
Man, Isle of, 13-21, *passim*, 40
  Chronicle of, 19
Mar, earl of, *see* Erskine
Margaret of Denmark, regent of Norway,
  44-6, 48, 50, 52-6 *passim*
Margaret of Denmark, wife of James III,
  61, 70n, 78, 80
Martin V, pope, 43, 45
Mary, queen of Scots, 30
Maule, James, captain in Swedish East
  India Company, 114
Maxwell, Robert, of Arkland, Scottish
  scientist, 121
Menteith, earldom of, 63
Menzies, David, of Weem, 78
Middleburg, Holland, 79
Moncrieff, William, Scottish officer in
  Sweden, 90
Monro, Clan, 96
  Robert, Scottish officer in Sweden,
    93-4, 96-7
Montrose, marquis of, *see* Graham
Moray, bishop of, *see* Stewart, David
Moray Firth, 114
Morton, regent, *see* Douglas, James
Moscow, Russia, 91

Narva, Russia, siege of, 98
Nazareth, Palestine, 39
Nedstrand, Norway, 100-1, 104-5
Nef, Jacob, governor, in Sweden, 91
Neven, John, of Luning, 34
Newcastle, England, 110
Nidaros, *see* Trondheim
Nisbet, family of Kirkabister, Shetland,
  32
Nördlingen, Germany, battle of, 94
Norfolk, England, 78
Norrköping, Sweden, 83
Northern Isles, 4, 7, 10, 13-14, 16-21
  passim
  see also Orkney, Shetland

Norway, 1, 3, 6, 45-6, 73-89 *passim*, 92,
  132-43 *passim*
  kings of, *see* Eric, Haakan, Harald, Ingi,
    Magnus, Olaf, Sigurd, Sverrir
Noss Goods, Shetland, 30, 34
Nylöse, Sweden, 81, 83

O'Brien, Colonel David, Irish officer, 113
Odense, Denmark, 38-9
Olaf, king of the Isles, 22
Olaf, king of Norway, son of Haakon and
  Margaret, 45, 48
Olaf Tryggvason, king of Norway, 3
Olaf, Saint, of Norway, 19
Ordericus Vitalis, chronicler, 21
Orkney/Orkneys, 4, 6-7, 13, 16-21 *passim*,
  32, 34, 40, 42-6 *passim*, 52, 75-6,
  78, 82, 108 *see also* Northern Isles;
  bishops of, *see* John, Law, Pak,
    Sinclair, Stephenson, Tulloch, Vaus,
    William
  earls of, 14, 26
    see also Harald, Magnus, Rögnvald,
      Sinclair, Stewart
Oslo (Christiania), Norway, 82, 112
Óspakr, king of the Isles, 17-18

Pak, John, of Colchester, bishop of
  Orkney, 44-6
Palestine (Holy Land), 11, 39
Papa Goods, Shetland, 30, 34
Papa Stour, Shetland, 26-7, 31
Paris, France, 4
Peenemünde, Germany, 94
Perth, treaty of, 19-20, 74
Philippa, English princess, 41
Pisa, Italy, 39
Poland, 98
Pomerania, dukes of, *see* Eric VII,
  Wratislas VII
Portland harbour, England, 1
Portsmouth, England, 115
Preston, battle of, 95
Prussia, 83

Quiberon Bay, battle of, 115

Radcliffe, Charles, earl of Derwentwater,
  113
Ramsay, Alexander, Scottish officer in
  Sweden, 92
Renfrew, 17
Robert I, king of Scots, 74-5
Robert II, king of Scots, 60

Rochelle, La, France, 79
Rögnvald, earl of Orkney, 11, 15-16
Rögnvald, king of Man, 18
Rome, Italy, 39-40, 44, 112
Roskilde, bishop of, *see* Lodehat
Ross, Clan, 96
Ross, 43, 139
Russia, 90-1, 115
Ruthven, Archibald, Scottish officer in
   Sweden, 90-1
   Patrick, earl of Forth and Brentford,
   95, 97, 107
William, Scottish officer in Sweden, 90-1
Ryfylke, Norway, 100-103, 105

Sagas
   Edda, Prose, 9
   Egils saga, 8, 9
   Eyrbyggia saga, 8
   Grettis saga, 8
   Hákonarsaga, 8, 17, 18
   Heimskringla, 3, 9, 10
   Laxdæla saga, 8
   Njáls saga, 8
   Ólafs saga helga, 10
   Orkneyinga saga, 17, 21
   Sturlunga saga, 21
   Sverris saga, 21
Sahlgren, Niklas, director of Swedish East
   India Company, 114
Saint Kilda, 22
St-John, Henry, Viscount Bolingbroke, 110
Sandey, 14-15, 22
Sardinia, Italy, 11
Saxkøbing, Sweden, 49
Saxo Grammaticus, Danish historian, 11
Scania, *see* Skåne
Scanör, Denmark, 77
Scheffer, Carl Frederick, Swedish
   minister, 113
Schimmelmann, Count H.C., landowner
   in Denmark, 144
Scots, kings and queens of, *see* Alexander,
   David, James, Mary, Robert, William
Scott, David Sanderson, of Reafirth,
   Shetland, 32, 34
Sealand, Denmark, 51, 55
   Chronicle of, 51
Selkirk, Lord, 139-40
Shetland, 5-6, 13, 20-1, 25-36 *passim*, 43
   see also Northern Isles
Sigismund, king of Sweden, 91
Sigurd, king of Norway, son of Magnus
   Barelegs, 15

Sinclair, Clan, 96, 98
   Arthur in Shetland, 29, 33
   David, of Sumburgh, foud in Shetland,
   31
   Edward, of Strom, foud in Shetland, 31
   Henry, earl of Orkney, 42, 52
   James, of Scalloway, 33-4
   Olla, of Broo, foud in Shetland, 31
   Robert, bishop of Orkney, 42
Skåne (Scania), Denmark/Sweden, 55-7,
   77, 83-4
Skye, Isle of, 14
Slesvig, Germany, 52
Smith, Adam, Scottish economist, 125-6,
   130-2, 139-40, 145
Snorri Sturluson, saga writer, 3, 8-11, 15,
   22
Söderköping, Sweden, 83
Sparre, Eric, Swedish ambassador to Paris,
   110-11, 113
Sperra, Malise, 42
Spynie, 65
Stamford Bridge, England, battle of, 15
Stavanger, Norway, 2, 3, 100, 102, 104-5
Stephenson, William, bishop of Orkney, 43
Stewart dynasty, 60-1, 63, 66, 96, 98, 107,
   109, 122
Stewart, Prince Charles Edward, 113-15
   David, bishop of Moray, 65
   Murdoch, duke of Albany, 63
   Patrick, earl of Orkney, 30-2
   Robert, duke of Albany, 63
   Robert, earl of Orkney, 30
   see also Stuart
Stockholm, Sweden, 83-4, 90, 113, 121
Stralsund, Denmark, 77
   peace of, 77
Strathclyde (British kingdom), 62
Strath Naver, 93-4
Stuart dynasty, *see* Stewart
Stuart, Hans, Scottish officer in Sweden,
   91
   William, Lord Blantyre, (*also called*
   Leslie), 113-15
Sturla Thórðarson, saga writer, 8, 10,
   17, 20-1
Sullom Voe, Shetland, 5
Sumarliði, Hebridean chief, 16-17
Sumburgh Roost, near Shetland, 18
Sutherland, 1
Sveinn Ásleifarson, 15-18, 21
   brjóstreip, 16
Sverrir Sigurdsson, king of Norway, 8, 17,
   21-2, 26

Svold, battle of, 3
Sweden, 45, 73, 77, 79, 81, 83-4, 90-99 *passim*, 107-15 *passim*, 121-2, 126, 133, 141, 143, 145
    kings and queens of, *see* Charles, Christina, Eric, Frederick, Gustavus, John, Sigismund

Tait, Jacob, of Laxfirth, Shetland, 35
Telford, Thomas, engineer, 127
Tessin, Carl Gustav, Swedish chancellor, 122
Thjóðólfur Árnarson, Icelandic court poet, 3-4
Thorvald Thoressøn, governor of Shetland, 26-7, 30, 32
Tilly, Johann, count of, general, 93-4
Tiree, 14, 16
Tocqueville, Alexis de, philosopher, 131, 135-6, 141, 143
Tode, Johann Clemens, Danish scientist, 124
Tönsberg, Norway, 82
Torstensson, Count Lennart, Swedish commander, 108
Trondheim (Nidaros), Norway, 19-21, 76, 112, 132, 134
Tulloch, Thomas, bishop of Orkney, 41, 43-5, 47n
    William, 31

Uists, 14, 22
Ulster, Annals of, 19
Unst, Shetland, 34
Uppsala, Sweden, 127
    archbishop of, *see* Henry

Vaila Goods, Shetland, 30, 34
Valdemar IV (Atterdag), king of Denmark, 45, 48, 50-5, 77
Vaus, Alexander, bishop of Orkney, 43
Vikings, 2-6 *passim*

Wales, 16
Walker, William, merchant, 100-2
Wesenberg, Livonia, 90
Western Isles, 6-7, 13-23 *passim*, 73
    see also Hebrides
Widahel, Norway, 75
William I, king of Scots, 18
William of Orange, king of Britain, 109
William (the Old), bishop of Orkney, 16
William (*another*), bishop of Orkney, 42
William of Malmesbury, chronicler, 21
Wratislas VII, duke of Pomerania, 45-6

Yell, Shetland, 26

Zeland Pursuivant, herald, 79